Presented To

St. Mary's
College of Maryland
Library

By Dr.& Mrs. Robert E.L. Knight

Date   Processed
         January 1977

U. S. POLICY
TOWARD CHINA

TESTIMONY OF THE TIMES:
SELECTIONS FROM CONGRESSIONAL HEARINGS

John A. Garraty, General Editor

U. S. POLICY TOWARD CHINA

*Testimony taken from the Senate Foreign
Relations Committee Hearings — 1966*

Edited by
AKIRA IRIYE
University of California, Santa Cruz

 LITTLE, BROWN AND COMPANY   *Boston*

Contents

INTRODUCTION

As Professor John K. Fairbank of Harvard remarked at a recent Senate hearing, "The fact is that we have been in East Asia just as much as we have been in Europe." The same cannot be said of Africa, the Middle East, or South Asia. American involvement in these areas has been of relatively recent origin, a concomitant to the nation's emergence as the most powerful country in the world. In East Asia, however, Americans developed a special interest long before their country attained big-power status at the turn of the century. It was not simply that thousands of traders and missionaries went to Asia to make money or to save souls. Throughout the nineteenth century the United States behaved as though it were one of the major Western countries in East Asia. As early as the 1840's and the 1850's, it was one of the big four — together with Britain, France, and Russia — that acted, often in concert, to break down the walls of isolation of China and Japan. The United States was willing to use force. Some Americans even dreamed of the nation's becoming the greatest power in the Pacific and East Asia.

It is a matter of considerable historical interest that in the nineteenth century the United States was much more willing to involve itself in the power politics and domestic convulsions of East Asia than it ever was in Europe. American policy toward European affairs was on the whole cautious and nonidealistic, and there was no pretense that the United States should or could count much. The Washingtonian dictum of nonentanglement was applied with almost single-minded devotion. In the Western Hemisphere, on the other hand, the United States was at times ready to act unilaterally to prevent a joint intervention by European powers or to assert its own territorial claims. In Asia, the United States rarely acted unilaterally (Commodore Perry's expedition to Japan was a significant exception), but as one of the major "treaty powers." There was a kind of geographical particularism about United States policy; different principles and means were employed in different geographical areas.

Such geographical particularism reflected the realities of world politics in the nineteenth century. In East Asia there were objective conditions which enabled America to play a role as a power. The Chinese empire, for two millennia the definer of Asian world order, was in a stage of dynastic decline, ruled by the "alien dynasty" of the Manchus. Instead of holding together the states on the periphery of China as tributaries, the empire was disunited. Regional power centers were developing. There was no indigenous move toward economic modernization. For centuries an imperial country, China now became an object of Western, and later Japanese, imperialism. But European powers were newcomers to China; they had not made much headway toward "opening" the country when America became independent. Thus the United States could participate on an equal footing with the European nations in establishing an influence in East Asia. The Chinese, Japanese, and Koreans regarded the United States as a major power, long before the British, French, Russians, and Germans did.

Asia's peculiarities have persisted to this day, but American policy has not always taken account of peculiarities. Herein lie some of the difficulties encountered by U.S. policymakers in China in the twentieth century, in particular since 1945. East Asia today, of course, is vastly different from what it was a century ago. China is no longer a "semi-colony." It is a nation with many of the attributes of the modern nation-state — centralized administrative organization, modern military power, mass participation in politics, nationalistic ethos. Western colonialism has produced its antithesis, Asian nationalism. But nationalism in Asia, because of its anti-colonial origin, cannot be equated with Western nationalism. Nor are nation-states in Asia quite the same as those in Europe. China, Korea, and Vietnam are divided politically despite their respective overall cultural and ethnic unity. The Asian world order that had been maintained by the Chinese empire and later by the imperialist powers is gone; there has been no clearly definable status quo since 1945. For all these reasons, East Asia has never been absorbed into a larger world order. It has lost neither its political nor its cultural uniqueness.

Nevertheless, the United States has often applied the same principles and policies to Asia as it has to Europe. President Wilson talked about self-determination for all peoples, not just for Europeans, and called for a new diplomacy for the entire world to replace a diplomacy dictated by the interests of the Old World. In the early 1930's Secretary of State Henry L. Stimson's "nonrecognition doctrine" was an application of Western principles to Asia, presented as a body of universal moral precepts. The Atlantic Charter also enunciated allegedly universal principles, and the wartime alliance of the United Nations envisioned a postwar order in which the ideas of peace, territorial integrity, and self-determination would reign in the whole world. After the war, there emerged the dualism of communism versus anti-communism. The world, as Americans saw it, was divided into two camps, again irrespective of particular localities. At the same time, in practice, priorities have tended to be given to Europe; American manpower and resources have on the whole been focused on the defense of national interests in the West rather than in the East. The war in Vietnam has been a strain on American policy at least in part because of the risk that it might cause a shift in the primacy traditionally given to Europe.

Difficulties and problems faced by U.S. policy toward China are thus part of the overall development of the international system and America's definition of it. At one level, China is considered a nation, whose military capabilities and policy orientations are weighed and assessed just like those of any other country, friendly or hostile. At another level, Communist China is viewed as a communist tyranny, suppressing freedoms within and dreaming of subjugating peoples without — China is always in the other camp, the anti-American side. Finally, there is the Asian level; the United States has viewed Chinese-American relations in the larger context of its desire for stability in Asia. Policies must be pursued at these three levels, and it is little wonder that there should exist ambiguities and uncertainties in America's attitude toward the China mainland.

It is evident that there is little abnormal about these various aspects of Chinese-American relations. Compared with the situation in the nineteenth century, when China was a semi-colony and Asia was 60 percent colonized, today's conditions may seem far more "normal." What has been unusual is the perpetuation in the 1960's of a policy adopted at the time of the Korean war: that policy was to refuse to deal with Communist China in any frontal fashion. Not only in official pronouncements but in public opinion as well, there has been a reluctance to give up the stance of nonrecognition. Although, as A. T. Steele reported in 1966, "Nowadays, when Americans speak of China they usually mean Communist China,"[1] public ignorance about China is enormous. With a few exceptions, the mass media have failed to cover China adequately; they have tended to give sensational, and mostly secondhand accounts of happenings on the mainland. Since about 1960, Communist China has replaced the Soviet Union in public opinion polls as the greatest threat to world peace and American security. Nevertheless, the United States government and scholarly specialists today probably know more about China than they did about Japan before Pearl Harbor. Communist China's political, economic, and military affairs are scrutinized with care and precision, and public funds are being used to enable hundreds of students to study Chinese language, history, and institutions.

The gap between the knowledge possessed by the specialists and the simplified images of China shared by the majority of Americans has provided fertile ground for public lectures, gatherings, and conferences on China. These have taken place in ever-increasing number in the last few years. There has been a growing desire to know more about China, especially among the younger generation. The Senate hearings on China that took place in March 1966 were perhaps the most notable of the attempts at expanding the public's knowledge of China.

Senator J. William Fulbright, Chairman of the Committee on Foreign

[1] A. T. Steele, *The American People and China* (New York: McGraw-Hill, 1966), p. 106.

Relations, characterized the hearings as primarily "educational," although "the ultimate objective must be political, to prevent a war."[2] The Foreign Relations Committee had, in January and February 1966, conducted hearings on Vietnam, and the key witnesses — Secretary of State Dean Rusk, diplomat-historian George F. Kennan, Generals James Gavin and Maxwell Taylor — had discussed the implications of the Vietnam war for American relations with Communist China. These hearings, as well as statements by government officials on Chinese-American relations, convinced Senator Fulbright that the time was ripe for a full public debate on the question of China. As he said, China experts, in and out of government, seemed to have little or no influence on American policy, and the public's lack of knowledge about China could precipitate a serious crisis between the two countries. What was of the greatest significance was Senator Fulbright's judgment, undoubtedly shared by most of his colleagues, that the subject of China which had been "taboo for so long" had at last become "respectable" to discuss.[3] The gap between the reality of Chinese power and the perception of it, a legacy of the late 1940's and the early 1950's, had grown so wide as to make a meaningful American response difficult. Now that the two countries had emerged as the powerful antagonists in Asia, the time was long overdue to develop a language of mutual confrontation, in which China would be viewed not only as an ideological opponent but also as a nationalistic Asian nation, and in which American policy would take account of Asian peculiarities as well as worldwide problems. The Senate hearings on China were a first chapter in the acquisition of the new vocabulary.

The hearings took place on nine different occasions and were attended by fourteen witnesses. Their names and dates of appearance before the committee were:

March 8, all day	*A. Doak Barnett* (Professor of Government, Columbia University)
March 10, all day	*John K. Fairbank* (Director, East Asian Research Center, Harvard University)
March 16, all day	*Benjamin I. Schwartz* (Professor of History and Government, Harvard University); *John M. H. Lindbeck* (Associate Director, East Asian Research Center, Harvard University)
March 18, morning	*Samuel B. Griffith* (Brigadier General USMC, retired); *Morton H. Halperin* (Assistant Professor of Government, Harvard University)
March 18, afternoon	*Alexander Eckstein* (Professor of Economics, University of Michigan)

[2] *New York Times*, March 7, 1966.
[3] *U.S. Policy with Respect to Mainland China* (Washington, D.C.: U.S. Government Printing Office, 1966), p. 178.

March 21, morning	*Harold C. Hinton* (Associate Professor of International Affairs, George Washington University); *Donald S. Zagoria* (Associate Professor of Government, Columbia University)
March 28, morning	*Walter H. Judd* (former member of the House of Representatives); *George E. Taylor* (Director, Far Eastern and Russian Institute, University of Washington)
March 28, afternoon	*David N. Rowe* (Professor of Political Science, Yale University)
March 30, morning	*Hans J. Morgenthau* (Professor of Political Science and History, University of Chicago); *Robert A. Scalapino* (Professor of Political Science, University of California, Berkeley)

Of the nineteen members of the Foreign Relations Committee, Senators Mike Mansfield and Thomas J. Dodd do not seem to have attended any of the sessions. The remaining seventeen who attended all or some, were Senators Fulbright (Arkansas), John Sparkman (Alabama), Wayne Morse (Oregon), Albert Gore (Tennessee), Frank J. Lausche (Ohio), Frank Church (Idaho), Stuart Symington (Missouri), Joseph S. Clark (Pennsylvania), Claiborne Pell (Rhode Island), Eugene McCarthy (Minnesota), Gale W. McGee (Wyoming), Bourke B. Hickenlooper (Iowa), George D. Aiken (Vermont), Frank Carlson (Kansas), John J. Williams (Delaware), Karl E. Mundt (South Dakota), and Clifford P. Case (New Jersey).

This book provides excerpts from the hearings, both from the formal statements and from the exchanges between witnesses and Senators. These excerpts are arranged topically to give unity to what was said. The volume from which I have compiled this collection is *U.S. Policy with Respect to Mainland China* (Hearings before the Committee on Foreign Relations, United States Senate, 89th Congress, Second Session). Because the hearings on Vietnam (which preceded the China hearings) contained important testimony on China, I have also taken extracts from *Supplemental Foreign Assistance, Fiscal Year 1966 — Vietnam* and have grouped them at the beginning of this text. These two sets of hearings reveal the interrelatedness of the questions on Vietnam and on China. I have, however, omitted material dealing exclusively with the war in Vietnam.

I would like to express my thanks to Professor John Garraty, who gave me this interesting assignment, and to my research assistant William Steele, who cooperated with me loyally and efficiently.

U. S. POLICY
TOWARD CHINA

PROLOGUE:
FROM THE VIETNAM
HEARINGS

Testimony of Dean Rusk

January 28, 1966

Sen. Pell: In conclusion then, Mr. Secretary, would you not think that the course we have followed so far and the expansion so far has resulted in little expense and no real loss to China and that this has really coincided with China's national interests?

Sec. Rusk: Well, I think what China considers to be a national interest of theirs is very much engaged here; that is, the application of the technique of a militant "war of liberation," as they call it. I don't believe myself that Peiping welcomes us in southeast Asia. I don't subscribe to the view I have heard expressed by some, that the Soviet Union is very glad that we are all mixed up in this problem, and that China is very glad to see us all mixed up in this problem. I think that they would prefer that we not come there at all. They would prefer to have seen their world revolution move ahead. I don't think that they are getting what they want in this present situation — nor are we, yet. [p. 132]

Testimony of James Gavin

February 8, 1966

Sen. Sparkman: General Gavin, I remember that in the MacArthur hearings, General Bradley at one time used the expression — with reference to a land war in Asia, particularly in China — that it would be the wrong war in the wrong place at the wrong time. You hold somewhat to that view, I take it?

Gen. Gavin: Well, I — may I speak for myself, sir? I think he was referring to combat in Korea and Manchuria. Unfortunately we are in, we are involved in southeast Asia, our young men are doing a splendid job there. I don't think the Armed Forces have done a better job right from the outside of the word "go" in combat. They have done a fine job

1

and we must give them the best support we can, keeping in mind the Nation's total commitments. So I couldn't quite agree with that as General Bradley once expressed it.

Sen. Sparkman: You do point out in your article [in *Harper's,* February 1966] though, if we are going to have a war with Red China it ought to be in the Manchurian area rather than in the southern area.

Gen. Gavin: To be very objective in a military sense about this as an adviser, if I were called upon in advice to my people, I would say if China brings upon herself a global war, the place to fight her is not in southeast Asia. The place to fight her is where you can take away the real heart of her war-making capacity, the Ruhr of China, and this is the Manchurian area.

Sen. Sparkman: There is one statement in your article that seems to me to be of considerable importance and concern and it is this:

If the Chinese Communists continue on their present course of aggression and, at the same time, continue to develop more devastating weapons — and I refer to nuclear weapons — the time may come when China will bring upon herself a nuclear war.

Gen. Gavin: Yes, sir.

Sen. Sparkman: Do you believe that is——

Gen. Gavin: Of course, I write it for that reason.

Sen. Sparkman: Do you think it is likely?

Gen. Gavin: I don't know.

Sen. Sparkman: Of course you have some "if's" in there.

Gen. Gavin: I have hoped as we do — I know nuclear weapons well. In 1947 I attended our nuclear weapons school, went to Operation Greenhouse in the Pacific where the first nuclear trigger as well as a 50-kiloton weapon was exploded. I was later responsible for the small yield weapons and one gained tremendous respect for these weapons once you know their real capability. I think the Soviets understand it. I would hope that the Chinese would begin to understand it.

For example, they have said, and I have here in my papers the source of the quote and it wasn't from Mr. Mao, it was from one of his staff, that what does it matter if they lose a couple of hundred million people, there are still 300, 400 million more. This is very primitive thinking that is quite unreal. His problems would be catastrophic beyond belief and people would be a real liability to him. He wouldn't be better off. I hope he will learn this and Mao will learn this in time.

In the meantime judging by what they say and how they behave, they are quite aggressive in what they are doing. This may relate to their position in nonadmission to the United Nations and the way they are treated in global affairs, I don't know, but there is no doubt they are very aggressive right now. . . . [pp. 239–240]

Sen. Morse: My first question will deal with a concern that you have expressed throughout your testimony at various times this morning and I would put it this way. It seems to me you are concerned about where may we end up——

Gen. Gavin: That is right.

Sen. Morse (continuing): In this war in southeast Asia vis-à-vis China. We have to face that general question of policy. We can't stick our heads in the sand and say there is no danger of a war with China. I hope they will have sense enough not to involve themselves in a nuclear war but who knows.

So my first question is, suppose they do, suppose they decide to move on the ground. Suppose we get into a war with them and we do the bombing and we knock out their cities and their nuclear installations and their industrial complex but they still carry on on the ground, what is your estimate of how many American troops we will have to send over in the early stages of that war.

Gen. Gavin: That is quite a complex question, Mr. Senator, and I would like to be fully responsive to it. Much would depend on the theater, much would depend on where they would have to go. I sometimes wonder what the theater slice is for Vietnam because to maintain a division must take four to five times that many people really behind the slice to keep them there. If the major confrontation were to occur as I would hope it would in northern China, in the Manchurian area, operating out of Korea we could probably do quite well with perhaps double the forces we had in Korea and when we were involved there, when General Ridgway was in command. I would like to be specific but the question does not lend itself to specific answers.

Sen. Morse: I understand. I don't see how you can be specific but I think it is important, however, in this public hearing that the question be raised.

Gen. Gavin: Yes; I think so.

Sen. Morse: To elicit from you——

Gen. Gavin: Yes.

Sen. Morse (continuing): A response as to whether or not you could do it with the number of men that we now have in southeast Asia or double that or triple that.

Is it not true, judging from what other military leaders have said in the past, that it would take a good many hundreds of thousands of men to fight Red China on the ground whether you do it in Manchuria or whether you move up from South Korea to the border of China?

Gen. Gavin: Yes. If the commitment began with Chinese volunteers followed by some semblance of semiregular forces, I would say our commitment would escalate very rapidly to double and double again the force we have in southeast Asia just to save themselves and save their own resources and bases.

Sen. Morse: And when we got through forcing her to her knees, and I am satisfied we could, at a horrible cost but that we could, final surrender, does that end our occupation in China?

Gen. Gavin: No. I have a feeling that at this point, if you got that far down the road in total conflict you would involve the U.S.S.R. in some role or another, and whether they would seek to enter the vacuum in Mongolia and China I don't know but I suspect they would and there would be real problems in further confrontations in the successive stages — following the defeat of China.

Sen. Morse: I would expect one with your brilliant mind to be way ahead of me, I was coming to the Russian question in a moment but I tarry a moment on my last question. Assuming Russia doesn't come in and it is the United States versus China, after we force her to surrender, there is still going to be a China, devastated as she is, would it be possible for us to just automatically withdraw our troops and go home or would we have a policing job to do for a long time thereafter?

Gen. Gavin: Well, there is no doubt that there would be hundreds of millions of Chinese left who would be in dire, dire straits, many of them very ill from the effects of the use of nuclear weapons, the whole base of food production, food availability, the economy, the agriculture would be laid flat, and I would assume we would take some responsibility for trying to get the situation straightened out. It would be a very, it would be an appalling problem to deal with, I would think.

Sen. Morse: Would that not be also an appalling drain on the economic resources as well as the manpower of our country?

Gen. Gavin: Yes; it would, no question about it. . . . [pp. 246–248]

I rather suspect that basic to the Chinese problem is the problem of isolation in the affairs of the world. It seems to me sooner or later we are going to have to find a way to bring China into the councils, and I speak of the United Nations, the councils of the world. We have got to get these people into the society of people to talk about these problems.

Now, I think they will go ahead on an aggressive course, that is the course they are now on, and will develop nuclear weapons, fission weapons and fusion weapons; hopefully they will learn the appalling and shocking casualties that these weapons can inflict both directly and indirectly, and hopefully their adjustment to the problems of the world, their acceptance into the family of nations, their education as a result of their own technical developments may bring about a point of view on their part such as we can live together and coexist together and trade together. But this is not in prospect now.

The way things are now going I think they will continue on an aggressive course, they will continue to be aggressive in southeast Asia, they will continue to export their brand of totalitarian communism in Africa, in South America, and wherever they can find a foothold, pleading the cause they peculiarly plead: "that it is us, the colored people against the other people, we understand your problem, and these other people do not, the Soviets or the United States or the Europeans."

I think they will continue on this course for some time, and I can foresee the possibility of them initiating a war that will end up in a nuclear holocaust, I can see this possibility happening. I hope it could be avoided.

Sen. Mundt: On the basis of your vast military background and knowledge and training, would you care to give us a "guesstimate" as to when you think China will have the delivery system with which to take their nuclear weapons out of their country and use them someplace else?

Gen. Gavin: Sir, I really do not know. This I do not have the knowledge of. It would be the worst sort of a guess.

Sen. Mundt: Can you estimate it from five to ten years? I am a little concerned because the Pentagon underestimated by quite a number of years the time when they could come up with their nuclear devices. But even taking the most optimistic figure of ten years, that is not a very long time.

Gen. Gavin: We underestimated the Soviets by five years. And I know, I have talked to a number of nuclear physicists who trained the Chinese before World War II, and they were always of the opinion that the Chinese, it was just a case of time when they would come up with weapons. I think they have some brilliant nuclear physicists, and they will come up with weapons.

Then you talk about a nuclear delivery capability, can they get delivery of vehicles from the Soviet, can they make their own, do they have missiles — these questions, I am sorry, I do not have an answer for. I would be guessing.

Sen. Mundt: Have you any suggestions to make as to specific steps in American military or diplomatic policies we might take to avert this awful calamity that you allude to?

Gen. Gavin: Yes, sir; I sure have, I sure have.

Sen. Mundt: I would like to hear them.

Gen. Gavin: I think we ought to mind our business and get on to developing a strategy that we have in recent years that is totally successful. I left the service in 1958 honestly concerned about the strategy we were then embarking upon. It was one of massive retaliation, the time and place of our choosing, and we are just beginning to suspect that at that time we needed a change. I felt it was totally wrong. I felt the problems we were going to live with were not total war but limited war all around the periphery. I was then concerned with the success of the Soviet system as I saw it, from a scientific point of view they were doing extremely well. I am satisfied that in the last eight years we have definitely demonstrated to them that our system is far more productive, not only of material goods and comforts for our people, but of weapons as well, and they are now seeking to find some accommodations in the world of economic competition.

Sen. Mundt: I just have ten minutes. I wish you would get on to China for us.

Gen. Gavin: All right. Then I believe in dealing with the Chinese problem. If we keep in mind our total global strategic commitments and take care of those and conduct ourselves well, dealing with the confrontations the Chinese give us on this very abrasive interface with ourselves and China as best we can, discreetly and with some wisdom, to overcommit ourselves in southeast Asia or anyplace else, for that matter, Thailand, could be a very serious mistake in case of our total equipment.

Sen. Mundt: Do you think success or failure, either alternative, is going to have any impact on this problem of whether the Chinese develop a system of nuclear weapons?

Gen. Gavin: No, no. I think they will go on with that as fast as they can.

Sen. Mundt: Do you think it will make any difference in the overall picture, whether we lose or win in Vietnam?

Gen. Gavin: Oh, I think — I think regardless of the outcome of the Vietnamese confrontation, and I cannot conceive of us really losing there with the resources we have, I think that they will get on with their nuclear weapons program. It is a matter of the highest priority. . . . [pp. 262–264]

The Chairman: General, I understood you to say in the course of one of the questions — I forgot who asked you — that the Chinese are quite aggressive in what they are doing. I wish you would elaborate a bit. In what respect are they very aggressive, contrasting what they are saying to what they are doing?

Gen. Gavin: Yes. In the first place I have been exposed to, as many Americans, to the filmed reports coming out of China of their militancy, of their training of their youth and their industrial workers and their people in the use of arms, in the military tactics and so on. There is a widespread national program I am led to believe to train their people for military operations.

The Chairman: Do you consider that aggressive necessarily?

Gen. Gavin: Not necessarily.

The Chairman: Per se?

Gen. Gavin: No. I would like to go beyond that. But this basic militancy I think exists in their society. I am well aware of the penetrations they have made into North Korea and how costly they were to us. They were certainly aggressive then.

I think that they are supplying the Vietcong with ammunition and medical aid and other logistical support, and certainly they are not passive in that tactical area.

Beyond this I don't know that there is much I can say about them, except their published statements about their lack of apprehension about a nuclear war, because of the vast manpower they have, and their charges against the Soviets really of tending to go along with us in our endeavors in Vietnam, rather than being more militant in opposing us.

The Chairman: I was trying to draw the distinction between what they actually do and what they say. I know they speak very offensively and aggressively, but do you consider their reaction to our approach to the Yalu River as an act of aggression on their part?

Gen. Gavin: Well, I would say their penetration all the way down to the 30th parallel was, yes.

The Chairman: Do you mean that training of their troops internally is an act of aggression?

Gen. Gavin: Their movement of troops deep into Korea was.

The Chairman: No; now I was passing on to their internal training — that is, the training of troops within China. Is that an act of aggression?

Gen. Gavin: No, no. No, no.

The Chairman: Well, is there any evidence that they moved troops into South Vietnam or North Vietnam?

Gen. Gavin: There is not at this time, although some people have been there, who have been to Vietnam, told me that there are Chinese trainers and technical people there, and the Chinese I believe themselves have alleged that volunteers would participate if necessary, and they have also been reported in the press as stating flatly that if we think that we can get away with our efforts in Vietnam without Korea being reopened, we are badly mistaken.

The Chairman: I understand they have made many threats.

Gen. Gavin: Yes.

The Chairman: Of much graver import than that as far as threats go. I was trying to elucidate just how far they have aggressed in recent years actively and by force. Normally we used the word "aggression," I will admit, very loosely.

Gen. Gavin: Yes.

The Chairman: But normally it means some action.

Gen. Gavin: Yes.

The Chairman: As distinguished from a word or a statement or a threat, doesn't it?

Gen. Gavin: Yes. Mr. Chairman, if I understand what you are getting at, they haven't made any major forays out of China itself, going after other peoples.

The Chairman: Do they have any troops outside of their own borders that you know of at the present time?

Gen. Gavin: Except perhaps those on the northeast Indian frontier. I am not sure of the state of affairs there now, but of course they were into India at one time.

The Chairman: That was the border incident you are speaking of in 1962?

Gen. Gavin: Yes, that is correct.

The Chairman: You will recall — I believe I have the statement of General Taylor — he made a statement before the Appropriations Committee that the Indians precipitated that particular incident, did he not? Do you recall that?

Gen. Gavin: I don't recall that, Mr. Chairman.

The Chairman: I will ask the staff to get that statement and put it in the record with regard to that specific incident.

Gen. Gavin: Yes.

(The information referred to follows:)

(Source: Department of Defense appropriations for 1964 hearings before a subcommittee of the Committee on Appropriations, House of Representatives, 88th Cong., 1st sess., part 2, Thursday, Feb. 14, 1963 [pp. 9–10].)

Mr. Sikes: Let me talk about Red China and the Indian operation. Did the Indians actually start this military operation?

Gen. Taylor: They were edging forward in the disputed area; yes, sir.

(Discussion off the record.)

Mr. Sikes: Is the area of the neutral zone on territory that was formally claimed by India or claimed by China?

Gen. Taylor: In most cases claimed by both.

Mr. Sikes: Where is it with relation to the generally accepted international boundary?

Gen. Taylor: That is hard to say because there is no generally accepted international boundary. I am sorry to be vague about this, but I can assure you that I spent several hours trying to find out where the McMahon line is. Actually, you find the maps differ on this. The terrain is so terribly rugged, there has been no accurate mapping and no accurate boundary lines or markers placed.

(Statement off the record.)

Mr. Sikes: Is the proposed neutral zone generally within territory which was occupied prior to all of this activity by Indian or Chinese forces?

Gen. Taylor: Most of it was unoccupied by anybody. General Hall, are you an expert on this subject?

Gen. Hall: Yes, sir. I would say in general it was occupied by neither force, but that the NEFA was occupied predominantly by Indian forces. One thing I think it is very important to point out is that the Chinese Nationalists, when they were in control of China, did not recognize this line either. So it is not a question of the fact it is a Chinese Communist line vis-à-vis an Indian line. It is an Indian line that has never been recognized by either the Chinese Communists or the Nationalists.

Mr. Sikes: Generally the neutral zone is in territory which was claimed by both?

Gen. Hall: Claimed by both; yes sir.

The Chairman: I think I recall that in testimony before the Appropriations Committee General Taylor made such a statement. I could be wrong. I think I have it somewhere in my files.

There was a very interesting article in a small provincial paper, the *New York Times*, on last Sunday, February 5, by Seymour Topping. The whole purport of that — this is from Hong Kong — is that the Chinese are alleging that they are being encircled. In answer to Senator Hicken-looper, he advanced I believe the thesis that if we didn't stop the Chinese here, that we would be encircled. Now who is encircling whom at the present time?

Gen. Gavin: I would be inclined to believe that the Chinese think that they are being pretty well hemmed in.

The Chairman: Is it a fact, do you think, that relatively speaking they are more encircled today than we are?

Gen. Gavin: There is no question about that.

The Chairman: Do you think it is reasonable for them to feel that they are being encircled?

Gen. Gavin: I think in their position I would feel that way. . . . [pp. 284–286]

The Chairman: You know a great deal about both military and political history. Have the Chinese as a nation over the last one hundred or two hundred years been especially aggressive? I use that word to mean military, overt aggression on their neighbors.

Gen. Gavin: No.

The Chairman: Is that true?

Gen. Gavin: They haven't been, to my knowledge.

The Chairman: Who aggressed against whom during the last century in regard to Western nations? Was it China attacking the Western nations or vice versa?

Gen. Gavin: The other way around. The Western nations attacking China.

The Chairman: Was this to a very great extent?

Gen. Gavin: Yes. I remember quite well reading about the moving from Tientsin in the Boxer Rebellion, and I remember not so many years ago reviewing the life of Gordon and the British occupation of major segments of China as well as that of other European nations.

The Chairman: As a matter of fact, various Western nations practically occupied and humiliated and decimated China throughout almost a century, did they not?

Gen. Gavin: That is true absolutely.

The Chairman: That also ought to be in this perspective that you give us.

Gen. Gavin: I would say so.

The Chairman: Don't you think that might not be a significant element in our present situation?

Gen. Gavin: Indeed, surely. [pp. 288–289]

Testimony of George F. Kennan

February 10, 1966

Sen. Morse: I would like to ask if you think that part of the concern you express in respect to foreign attitudes toward us and misunderstandings toward us, irrespective of what the facts are, is based somewhat upon a fear in many places of the world that we may be headed in the direction of a war with China?

Mr. Kennan: Yes, I think this is true. I think this fear exists in many quarters.

Sen. Morse: Do you know any basis at the present time that would justify our escalating the war in South Vietnam thereby increasing the danger of a unilateral war between the United States and China?

Mr. Kennan: Senator, I am not absolutely sure that I understood the question.

Sen. Morse: Let me repeat it. Do you know of any justification for an American foreign policy that would cause us to follow a policy of escalation in southeast Asia that would really increase the danger of the United States unilaterally becoming involved in a war with China?

Mr. Kennan: Senator, I can see why reasons could be offered for such a policy but in my opinion these reasons are overweighed by other ones, and such a procedure, such a policy, is not warranted by the considerations that present themselves to me. . . . [p. 342]

Sen. Hickenlooper: But here sits China with 600, 700 million people. It is basically international Chinese [Communist?] in its orientation, I believe. Do you agree with that?

Mr. Kennan: Of course it is.

Sen. Hickenlooper: That is as differentiated from purely a nationalistic communism which doesn't intend to extend its influence beyond its borders.

Mr. Kennan: Well, the government is certainly Communist-oriented.

Sen. Hickenlooper: When I speak of China, I speak of the governing forces of China who set the policies.

Mr. Kennan: May I put in a caveat there? I believe that the Chinese Communists would certainly like to have influence, dominant influence, all over the mainland of Asia, and they would certainly like to have Taiwan. I am not sure that they are anxious to launch invasions against these other countries and to take them under the Chinese sovereignty, at this stage of the game anyway.

Sen. Hickenlooper: They extended their influence in the disputed area of Tibet, did they not?

Mr. Kennan: Yes.

Sen. Hickenlooper: They also invaded India.

Mr. Kennan: Yes.

Sen. Hickenlooper: With force of arms.

Mr. Kennan: But the areas to which they extended their power through these actions were ones for which they claimed the argument that the areas had been under Chinese sovereignty before. I don't excuse it by this. I merely say that it puts them somewhat in a different category.

Sen. Hickenlooper: Do you think that the withdrawal of the United States from South Vietnam, again realizing that you have entered the caveat about the way it was done, would have some influence?

Mr. Kennan: Yes. . . . [p. 344]

Sen. Gore: If the war in Vietnam should be escalated or, if by some unfortunate incident, God forbid, war comes between the United States and China, would it be within the purview of possibility that Russia would again, seeing us bogged down, press her point of view in Berlin, and seek to work her machinations in Latin America and elsewhere?

Mr. Kennan: It is certainly within the realm of possibility. One of the things that worries me most about an extension of our present commitment in Vietnam is that it might leave us very poorly prepared to face crises that might arise in other areas of the world.

I think it has already caused a diversion of our attention and our resources to a point that holds dangers for the balance of our world responsibilities elsewhere. And if we are now, as some people fear, to double the amount of the manpower and the resources we are putting into Vietnam, I am afraid that we would not be in a good position to defend our interests in other areas if they were suddenly challenged.

Sen. Gore: As unwisely as you think these commitments have been made, I remind you that through three administrations we have inched or been inched into this unfortunate situation.

Mr. Kennan: Yes.

Sen. Gore: Upon many occasions the Congress has been led to believe that a subsequent step would not follow a step presently being taken. This is behind us. We are now in Vietnam in the situation which you have so eloquently described. The real issue, it seems to me, is whether this conflict in Vietnam is to be held within bounds which we think we can reasonably master, maintaining control of events.

You referred this morning to the damage to America's prestige around the world, the pictures of great damage that is wrought. Of course all of us know that war is hell, but the pictures of a great power, with big bombers, big bombs, big money, wreaking havoc upon a small nation is one which we all regret.

Is this element, plus the encroaching threat of China, a benefit to the Chinese Communist apparatus in more effectively regimenting her people and engendering hate of the United States?

Mr. Kennan: Yes, sir, in my opinion it is.

Sen. Gore: Then, you conclude, and I conclude with you that it is in our national interests and in the interest of our national security if at all possible to prevent this conflict from further major escalation and most of all to prevent it from becoming a war between the United States and China.

Mr. Kennan: This is precisely my position, and I think you have stated it in a way that I couldn't possibly improve upon. . . . [pp.346–347]

Sen. Clark: Now, my understanding is that you feel the present situation in Communist China is somewhat different in that they are in the early stages of a revolution, a belligerent stage. I wonder if you would state for the benefit of the committee what you think the capabilities and intentions of the Chinese Communists are with respect to the possibility of — in due course — arriving at a detente or an adjustment with us.

Mr. Kennan: I think that at the moment the Chinese Communist leaders are in an extremely difficult and almost hysterical state of mind. They have had frustrations of one sort and another both internally and externally over the course of recent years.

I believe they are really weaker than they like to admit. They are very troubled by what does seem to them to be a sort of encirclement, and an exclusion for which admittedly they are themselves mainly to blame, from the counsels of the world. But this puts them into a highly excitable and irritated state of mind, and I think there is very little opportunity of talking with them or dealing effectively with them today.

On the other hand, I do not feel that they have the capability to create much mischief beyond the Asian land mass. I am not really too terribly worried about the island territories of the Pacific. I think the Chinese Communists have suffered an enormous reverse in Indonesia, one of great significance, and one that does rather confine any realistic hopes they may have for the expansion of their authority, confine them pretty much to the Asian land mass, most of which in East Asia they already occupy.

I think it will take a long time before we could deal with them effectively. But meanwhile, I think that we should leave them alone. I don't think that it is necessary for us to or desirable for us to try to solve this vast problem by military means. I don't think it is susceptible to solution by military means any more than the problem of Vietnam is.

I am quite prepared to recognize that we face a great and serious problem in the cultivation by the Chinese Communists of a nuclear striking capacity. I don't wish to minimize that for a moment. But I would prefer to see us tackle that problem, and approach it, by finding as soon as we can an acceptable ending to the conflict in Vietnam, and then pursuing with the Soviet government, and even with the French, agreements which would permit us to bring the pressure of world opinion to bear a little more effectively on the Chinese.

Sen. Clark: With the ultimate hope that we could get into a meaningful dialog with them, as well as with the Russians?

Mr. Kennan: Yes, with an ultimate hope that we could at least bring this terrible problem of nuclear weaponry under some measure of control. And then I think things will change in China, as they changed in Russia. They always do. A new generation of Chinese leaders will come. They could scarcely be worse in their attitude toward us than the present ones. And as I look back over the history of international affairs, it seems to me that the counsels of patience and restraint have been more effective as a general rule, than the counsels of violence and particularly the unleashing of unlimited violence.

Now, there has been great confusion sowed precisely in this respect by Hitler and the National Socialists; and no statement of this sort that you make can be without its exceptions. There are no universally valid generalizations here. There are, there can be, threats to the peace that have to be faced in the way that Hitler should have been faced. But, by and large, especially when one is dealing with conflicts which threaten to develop into great world conflicts on a scale that has never been known before in history, surely it is better to exhaust the counsels of patience and restraint before one plunges into the others.

Sen. Clark: Thank you, Mr. Chairman.

The Chairman: The Senator from Rhode Island.

Sen. Pell: Thank you very much, Mr. Chairman.

Mr. Kennan, I have long admired your thinking. I guess more than twenty years ago, as a junior departmental officer, I used to read your lucid reports — the most lucid and interesting we used to get — and afterward I followed you in middle Europe, and in a much more modest way was castigated by the Soviets, too, for my activities. I have followed your thinking all these years and I have spent most of my time in the Eastern European area when I was in the State Department, which is also the area of your specialization.

Do you believe that the course of events we are following now in Vietnam — which seems inevitably to lead to a commitment of many more troops, steady escalation, the capability of erasing of Hanoi and Haiphong, and the placement of North Vietnam with China — will lead to our fighting the Chinese on a man-to-man basis, or whether we will fight with nuclear weapons? Remembering the public response to the use of nuclear weapons at the time of Korea, do you believe the Soviet Union will feel compelled to retaliate, or will it stay out of that one?

Mr. Kennan: If we do not resort to nuclear weapons, and merely get into a conflict on land between our forces and the Chinese Communist forces in southeast Asia, I should not think that the Soviet Union would intervene in any formal sense.

But, if nuclear weapons come to be used, I simply cannot predict the effects of world opinion, the effects on our own opinion, the cumulative quality of such a conflict. It could lead to anything. I am afraid that I can only say to you that the consequences of such a development are unpredictable. They could be anything. They could be an entrance of the Soviet Union into the war. I am afraid if it went to the bitter end we probably would create a situation in which the Soviet Union would be almost forced to come out against us in a strong military way, and whether that, again, would develop into a nuclear exchange between the Soviet Union and ourselves, I do not know. But this represents, all of it, a fringe of apocalyptic danger on which I should never like to see this country play, if you see what I mean. This is the edge of a precipice, of an abyss, and we ought never to get near this edge.

Sen. Pell: To use another phrase, it is almost a brink.

Mr. Kennan: It is indeed a brink, but in a terribly serious sense. . . . [pp. 370–372]

The Chairman: Something has been said on this matter of China. I want to clarify it just a step further. The nature of the commitment to South Vietnam — and you have already described it considerably — seems to me so out of proportion to what is involved there that surely some other consideration beyond Vietnam must be involved. I can't imagine a commitment such as has been described could have been just for this rather limited purpose. I think it does involve China and I think previous questions have indicated this. There was some passing reference made this morning to the aggressive nature of China.

Now, as a historian, is it your impression that China, when she was a strong country in the past, has been inclined to military aggressiveness such as was characteristic of Germany in two instances recently and other countries from time to time?

Mr. Kennan: No. It is my impression that the Chinese are tremendously preoccupied with what used to be called "face" — with prestige — with the outward aspects of authority and respect; and that sometimes, as in the present situation, their language can be very violent, and extreme, but that by and large they are very prudent people when it comes to military action.

The Chairman: Perhaps I didn't phrase my question as carefully as I should have. I was really trying to exclude the present, as you said this morning, hysterical state of the present Communist regime. I was trying to make this a historical question. We realize that they are under very different circumstances now from what they were fifty years ago or a hundred years ago or a thousand years ago. They are suffering from what you described very well this morning as a kind of a hysterical state. But traditionally they have not been noted as very aggressive people militarily. Is that true or not in your view?

Mr. Kennan: That is my impression, yes.

The Chairman: More recently, a statement was made the other day and was this morning referred to during discussion of the Indian matter and I thought I remembered a statement made by General Taylor, while he was Chairman of the Joint Chiefs. This was made on Thursday, February 14, 1963, before the Committee on Appropriations. I think it bears upon the question. This is page 9 of that hearing — Mr. Sikes of Flordia asked him:

Let me talk about Red China and the Indian operation. Did the Indians actually start this military operation?

Gen. Taylor: They were edging forward in the disputed area; yes, sir.

I would be perfectly willing to put it all in the record; I don't wish to burden the record and take the time. On page 10 Mr. Sikes says:

Where is it with relation to the generally accepted international boundary?

They were talking about the northeast boundary that this incident referred to.

Gen. Taylor: That is hard to say because there is no generally accepted international boundary. I am sorry to be vague about this, but I can assure you that I spent several hours trying to find out where the McMahon line is. Actually you find the maps differ on this. The terrain is so terribly rugged, there has been no accurate mapping and no accurate boundary lines or markers placed.

This is all available. I won't burden the record with it. But it strikes me to say or to use this as an example of an aggression is rather tenuous. And with regard to Tibet, has not the status of Tibet been a matter of considerable controversy for a long time?

Mr. Kennan: Yes, of course it has, and the Chinese did regard it as part of their area of sovereignty. I don't say this excuses what they did there. It puts it in a different category.

The Chairman: But I mean a long time ago, and not just by the Communist Chinese.

Mr. Kennan: Yes.

The Chairman: Is it not true that the Nationalist Chinese regarded Tibet as a part of China, not since Mao Tse-tung came in.

Mr. Kennan: Senator Fulbright, there have been very few of the troubles we have been having in the last few years which we would not have had with any other Chinese regime. A lot of this is national.

The Chairman: I don't wish to overplay this but I think when we look at specific cases and examine the circumstances surrounding them, their actions as distinguished from their words have not been unusually aggressive or even as aggressive as many of our Western countries. In view of the history of China during the last century beginning with the opium wars, running up to the Second World War, would you not say there was considerable reason for their having some dislike to Western nations?

Mr. Kennan: Yes. I think we have to remember that we deal with the Chinese today at the end of a century in which they had very, very unhappy experiences with Western powers generally. I don't think that the blame for this was entirely on the Western powers. There was usually a good deal of connivance on the Chinese side at these relationships of imperialism. But, by and large, these were very unhappy experiences. They were humiliating to the Chinese people, and there has accumulated a fund here of sensitivity and resentment which we are probably harvesting today. We have to bear that in mind.

The Chairman: My time is up but I would like to clarify that one point that their connivance that irritated us or provoked us. If I remember my history at all, take, for example, the opium war. Do you see any excuse for waging a war to force a country to accept opium for the use of their people?

Mr. Kennan: No, Senator, I don't. All I meant to convey by that was something which is also relevant to the opium war: it was that a number of highly placed Chinese also profited very well from the opium trade. This was not all so simple.

The Chairman: Yes, that is true. They were bribed. They had a number of their people who were bribed; there is no doubt about that. This is quite true. But for a country to take advantage of another country, that was so weak — and China was very weak in the dying days of the Manchu dynasty — and to subvert its local officials and to wage a war for this reason seems to me about as outrageous as any war I can think of.

Mr. Kennan: Yes.

The Chairman: And you know there was a succession of, in effect, occupations and invasions of a very weak and helpless country. Isn't that generally so?

Mr. Kennan: Yes, I think this is true.

The Chairman: Did they attack any other Western country during that period?

Mr. Kennan: No, I fully agree with you here. I think that the ferociousness of Chinese policy in the past and somewhat today is often a matter of words rather than of actions. I just would say this: it seems to me that the Chinese, if you look back historically, have not been an easy country to deal with. They have had ideas of being the center of the universe——

The Chairman: Oh, yes.

Mr. Kennan: And all that, which have presented problems for other people. My own feeling is that I think a long period in which we had perhaps as little as possible to do with them, kept our distance and tried to be reasonably restrained and polite, might be helpful in our relations with them.

The Chairman: Don't misunderstand me, I don't cite this as an excuse for their present conduct. I think it is as outrageous as you think it is, but the fact is there are these old reasons that I think affect their attitude. . . . [pp. 391–393]

Sen. Hickenlooper: Do you think that the Chinese abandoned the idea of international communism that force and force of arms is the ultimate weapon necessary to advance their international aims and ambitions?

Mr. Kennan: Not at all. On the contrary, I think they are quite committed to such means. I don't doubt that the Chinese Communist leaders would love to unleash the bloodiest sort of revolutions in every country that they can think of that is not Communist.

Sen. Hickenlooper: I will get down to the wars of liberation in just a moment. I am now trying to see what you think about the Chinese at the present time.

If they have that as their continuing basic philosophy, then isn't it reasonable to assume that the Chinese are, in effect, urging the North Vietnamese on — as a cat's-paw in this idea of advancing communism clear down the end of the peninsula?

Mr. Kennan: Oh, yes, it is.

Sen. Hickenlooper: A step.

Mr. Kennan: I think it is unquestionable they are urging the North Vietnamese on. But, of course, this situation suits the Chinese book very well. They have us, locked into a conflict there with somebody else, and they want these people to bleed us as long and as profusely as possible.

Sen. Hickenlooper: You mean they follow the philosophy of "let's you and him fight?"

Mr. Kennan: Senator, I think the Chinese are the passionate partisans of a war between anybody else and the United States, anybody else except China. . . . [p. 406]

Sen. Symington: Well, within ten years, it is estimated, maximum, the Red Chinese will be a nuclear power. In that speech the Deputy Prime Minister, head of their military, stated that the great enemy of Red China is the United States in the world today, the imperialists that they must defeat is the United States; that the test place was now, in South Vietnam. Therefore, wouldn't it be better to realize this possible danger now, and to try to defend ourselves in South Vietnam if we believe that there is any truth in what he says, than a time until they become a nuclear power? I am not talking about attacking anybody. Let me emphasize that. I am talking only about continuing to defend with conventional weapons in a conventional way, the efforts of the Red Chinese who are now, many thousands of them, in North Vietnam; and defending against the North Vietnamese in the efforts of the latter to help the Vietcong, and themselves against the South Vietnamese, the Americans, the Koreans, and the Australians, and New Zealanders.

Mr. Kennan: Senator, I would far prefer that it was we and not they, who decided what was the test place in this contest, first of all.

But beyond that, I think that there may be better ways of tackling the problem of the Chinese approach to a nuclear striking capacity than by fighting Vietnamese down there in southeast Asia.

Sen. Symington: I'm sorry, would you repeat that.

Mr. Kennan: I think there might be better ways of tackling on our part the problem created by the Chinese approach to the acquisition of a nuclear striking capacity than by trying to fight Vietnamese in southeast Asia.

Sen. Symington: Surely you do not mean we should attack their nuclear developments.

Mr. Kennan: No.

Sen. Symington: Then would you state what you do mean?

Mr. Kennan: I would like to see us get back to the cultivation of our world relationships and to the pursuit of this whole question of the proliferation of nuclear weapons in talks with the Russians and with others, because I think that if we could develop the general agreement elsewhere in the world on this subject we might begin to bring some pressure to bear on the Chinese.

Sen. Symington: I agree with you. But aren't we doing that? Isn't Mr. Foster in Geneva now trying very hard to reach some agreement with respect to proliferation?

Mr. Kennan: I think we could do a lot better if we did not have the complication in Vietnam, with the burden that that places on our relationships with other people.

Sen. Symington: In other words, if we would get out of South Vietnam you think that would improve our possibilities of making a proliferation treaty with the Soviet?

Mr. Kennan: If the conflict there could be terminated, I think we could address ourselves to other problems of world affairs in a much more hopeful way. This is indeed my view. [pp. 425–426]

Testimony of Maxwell Taylor

February 17, 1966

Sen. Carlson: Here I go back to Senator Aiken again. You don't quote to one general the views of another, but I was interested in the comment of General Gavin. He told us, in his opinion, if we become further involved to the extent of vastly increasing our troop strength, the Chinese would surely open up in Korea. Do you have any comment on that?

Gen. Taylor: I — it is purely a matter of opinion, neither one of us can prove our case. I would not agree with that. There are so many reasons why the Red Chinese would want to avoid a military confrontation with us, and, of course, on our side we are certainly not seeking one.

Since both parties would be against a military confrontation, I would be surprised if it arose. There is always some risk, as I conceded in my statement, but when you look at the problems of China, there are enormous population food problems, their extreme vulnerability to air attack, to the fact that they can't afford to have their own strength diminished in relation to the Soviet Union, with whom they are engaged in a bitter competition, and all these factors, when they are looked at, it seems to me that the likelihood of deliberate military involvement in confrontation of the United States on the part of Peiping is unlikely. . . . [p. 468]

The Chairman: I think, General, in all honesty, behind the concern of many of us, is not just Vietnam. There is the possibility, or even probability, of this situation escalating into a war with China. We always hesitate to talk about these things, but that is one of my concerns. I would regret to see us continue this war to the point where we became engaged in an all-out war with China. Many people who are wiser than I am believe that this [is] a possibility.

Gen. Taylor: As we discussed this morning, obviously one cannot rule it out. But I wonder whether our government, or whether the Congress, would suggest complete supineness on the part of our foreign policy in the Far East because of that relatively small possibility.

The Chairman: I don't think anyone suggests supineness. But there have been several news stories in which the Chinese have stated that they are being encircled, and they are exhibiting considerable nervousness about the possibility of a war with us. I believe you said that you did not feel nervous about a war with China, but there is a real question that the Chinese may feel very nervous about a war with us.

Gen. Taylor: They should feel nervous about it. If they ever got in a war with us, it would be disaster for them. And we know we are not seeking such a confrontation.

The Chairman: You have confirmed their fears, I think. My greatest trouble is a feeling of inadequate knowledge and understanding of China and of this whole area to make very sound judgments. I don't profess to have the kind of knowledge to make sound judgments about these issues. My judgment is more by instinct and feeling. It would be a great disaster if we became involved in an all-out war against the Chinese on the Asian continent. . . . [p. 501]

Sen. Sparkman: General, referring to this question of war with China — and I believe you have shown in your statement, and your answers to questions here, that you certainly do not want a war with China, and do not believe that this war will push into that. But General Gavin said that if we should get into war with China, it ought to be a place of our own choosing, and that southern China was not the place where it ought to be. If we were going to have a war with China, it ought to be in the Manchuria area. Do you agree with that reasoning?

Gen. Taylor: Well, first, I don't believe there is any good place to have a war with China. But if indeed we had one, certainly we would not be confined to South Vietnam. I assume this would be general war against

China. And if our strategists preferred Manchuria, they could take Manchuria.

Sen. Sparkman: Of course a war with China would probably — well, I think probably we ought not to speculate on that. I started to say it probably would involve nuclear weapons; would it not?

Gen. Taylor: It is possible, but not necessarily so. . . . [p. 503]

Sen. Morse: But one more question: Do you think if we should get into a war with China, God forbid, that we could beat her by bombing, either nuclear or conventional?

Gen. Taylor: I wouldn't know what "beat her" means.

Sen. Morse: Force her to surrender.

Gen. Taylor: I don't know whether we would want her to surrender or not. We could make her pay a tremendous price for aggression.

Sen. Morse: She doesn't have anything to fight back with except manpower. Wouldn't we have to meet her on the ground?

Gen. Taylor: No, sir.

Sen. Morse: Just meet her in the air?

Gen. Taylor: To a large extent. That is one way of doing it.

Sen. Morse: This is very interesting. You take the position that if we get into a war with Red China, we are not going to have to send hundreds of thousands of men on to the mainland of China?

Gen. Taylor: Not necessarily so.

Sen. Morse: Tell that to Mr. McNamara, so we can get you two together on the same advice. That is all.

The Chairman: Senator Aiken?

Sen. Aiken: As I indicated, what we are really fighting is to defeat communism in the world, and if we don't defeat it in one place, it will pop up in one or more other places. Do you want to give us a short definition of what you consider communism to be?

Gen. Taylor: Well, Senator, in a short period of time I am afraid I could not give you an ample answer. First I think we all know what communism is. And we also know what the aggressive emanations of communism can mean. Here is a dogma, apart from its social and political implications, that carries with it the spirit of Moslemism at the time of the great expansion; that it must grow by absorbing and imposing itself upon other countries who are not believers. We certainly see in Peiping today the same kind of messianic attitude which was in Moscow at the outset until Moscow matured to some degree.

I think that we have a special virulent form of Communist aggressive threat in the Chinese leadership. I think that can go away with time, and if we are firm, as we were in the case of the expansive efforts of Soviet communism, I am hopeful enough to believe in a decade or two that we may find a new attitude in China which removes it from the very threatening position which it now occupies. . . . [pp. 514–515]

Sen. Church: I understand that it is your present feeling that the danger of the war in Vietnam escalating into a general confrontation with China is not as great as some have felt it might be. Is that correct?

Gen. Taylor: I do not know how urgent the feeling of other people is, but I suspect that that would be an accurate statement. I would not rule it out, but I would not put it high on my list of concerns at this time.

Sen. Church: Well, I also would think that China would hesitate very long before entering the war, considering the kind of power that we have to bring to bear, should such an eventuality occur.

But I am, nonetheless, concerned about this. One of the reasons, I suppose, is because of the experience we had in Korea. In his book, *The United States in the Korean War*, Larson reviews an exchange between President Truman and General MacArthur, a passage of which I would like to read to you:

In your opinion —

President Truman asked General MacArthur —

is there any chance that the Chinese might enter the war on the side of North Korea?

MacArthur shook his head.

I would say there is very little chance of that happening. They have several hundred thousand men north of the Yalu, but they haven't any air force. If they tried to cross the river, our Air Force would slaughter them. At the most, perhaps 60,000 troops would make it. Our infantry could easily contain them. I expect the actual fighting in North Korea to end by Thanksgiving. We should have our men home or at least in Japan by Christmas.

Well, we have heard in the course of the last few years, some optimistic predictions about how soon we would have our men home from Vietnam. Is there anything in the strategic situation confronting the Chinese in Vietnam that would make it less likely for them to enter the war in that region of Asia than in Korea?

Gen. Taylor: Yes, I would think so very clearly. When our armies moved to the Yalu, there was no certainty in the Chinese mind that they were not about to invade China. We, so far as I know — I do not think the record indicates there was any dialog, any conversation going on at all as to what our intention was. So in retrospect, and it is always easy to be wise in retrospect, one can see reason for very grave concern on the part of the Chinese as we came rushing forward.

Sen. Church: If we were to duplicate or tend to duplicate in North Vietnam what we did in North Korea, that is to say extend the perimeter of the war northward toward the Chinese frontiers, then do you think that China might respond as she did in fact respond in Korea?

Gen. Taylor: Undoubtedly the danger would increase dramatically as our ground forces approached the frontier of China. Again, however, I would say that there are two or three factors in such a situation which did not exist in Korea. The first would be, I assume, we would be talking very vigorously as we are talking now and did during the pause, talk to everybody. I do not think any country ever opened its books as completely to the world as we did in the thirty-seven days, what our intentions were, what we hoped to come out of the situation as we are explaining to the world right at this table now, and finally, the fact that now we are the great military power we are, with a nuclear arsenal of great proportions is another factor which did not exist before.

Sen. Church: At the time of Korea, were we not the only nuclear power in Asia?

Gen. Taylor: Our arsenal was extremely limited, and we were very much worried about what Russia would do in Europe.

Finally, the Chinese are extremely vulnerable in other ways, internal because of the tremendous population-food problem. They are also vulnerable in the fact they have worked so mightily to get a limited nuclear capability which is highly vulnerable to elimination.

So all of these factors, I would think, would add up — furthermore, they have a great rivalry with the Soviet Union. They cannot afford to be weakened in their strengths in a confrontation with us and thereby fall well behind the Soviet Union when they hope to be the Number one Communist power.

So in combination these are all pretty potent reasons, it seems to me, to suggest that China will not come in, and then we add quickly we have no plan to put our ground forces near the front, the Chinese frontier. [pp. 534–535]

Testimony of Dean Rusk

February 18, 1966

Sen. Gore: Let us come to what I think is a more important and a more current problem. I notice with some concern that in no place in your prepared text did you refer to the possibility that has aroused such deep concern in this committee and the country, to wit, the possibility that this war may be escalated into a conflict or war with China.

Will you first indicate why you made no reference to this, and then will you please, sir, address your remarks to the subject as ably as I know you may.

Sec. Rusk: Well, Senator, this is a grave question for a person sitting in my particular chair to discuss completely in an open session. I will do my best.

Sen. Gore: I shall not press you.

Sec. Rusk: I understand, sir.

Sen. Gore: You need not make any comment whatsoever which you think might involve the security of the country.

You do recognize this possibility, as you describe it, as a grave matter. I wondered why you made no reference to it as being so grave in your testimony, in your prepared statement.

Sen. Morse: I think the Secretary ought to have assurance in the matters that he wants to talk to us about in regard to the China issue in executive session, that he will be given that opportunity at his leisure and convenience and as soon as he wants it.

The Chairman: Certainly.

Sec. Rusk: Thank you very much, Senator.

Sen. Gore: Indeed, Mr. Secretary, if you prefer, I will withdraw the question; I would be glad to do that.

Sec. Rusk: Senator, perhaps I might comment on it, at least briefly, because, as you know, we have spent considerable time in the committee on this problem. The question of how far a crisis can go is of course the final question at the end of the day in handling any crisis.

In all of these postwar crises a possibility of a larger war has always been present: whether it is the Greek guerrillas or the Berlin blockade or the Korean war or the Cuban missile crisis, now here in southeast Asia. This is also a problem for the other side. . . . [p. 607]

Sen. Church: Now, here it is 1966. As I recall your testimony two weeks ago, Communist China withdrew Chinese troops from North Korea about ten years ago, and there has not been a guerrilla war in South Korea. We have, in the meantime, built up a very modern and effective Korean defense force. Yet 55,000 American troops appear to be permanently stationed in South Korea. In the face of this, it seems to me we didn't follow General MacArthur's advice, is that not true?

Sec. Rusk: That is correct. But I will comment on that when you have finished your——

Sen. Church: Fine. It is not also true that China is now developing a nuclear capacity; that is, she has already detonated two atomic bombs?

Sec. Rusk: That is correct, sir.

Sen. Church: Is it your surmise that China is engaged upon a serious effort to develop a nuclear capability of her own?

Sec. Rusk: Yes; it is.

Sen. Church: And a modern delivery system of her own?

Sec. Rusk: That is correct, sir.

Sen. Church: Would you say, then, looking ahead perhaps ten years, that China may build a formidable nuclear arsenal and perhaps a modern delivery system, including intercontinental ballistic missiles?

Sec. Rusk: I think that is entirely possible.

Sen. Church: Then, isn't it also possible that, at such a time, China may turn to us, assuming that we still retain military bases in South Korea, and say, "Get out. We don't think you belong here on the mainland of Asia with military bases so close to China."

Remember that we said to Khrushchev, when he attempted to establish Russian military bases in Cuba, "Get out, you don't belong here so close to the boundaries of the United States and we will not permit it."

I am trying, Mr. Secretary, to look ahead. Vivid is the memory of that crisis in 1962 which took the world to the brink of nuclear war. I thought then that the American position was absolutely valid. But I am wondering how the Chinese may view American military bases so close to China once they have developed a nuclear capacity that would give them a semblance of power commensurate with that of the United States.

Sec. Rusk: Well, Senator, it is true that we have retained 55,000 men in the Republic of Korea. This is our principal ground force in northeast Asia, directly relevant not only to our interest in the security of Korea, but also in the security of Japan, and indeed, the total strategic situation in the northern Pacific. I do not believe that this is a guideline for southeast Asia. Indeed, we have already demonstrated in the case of Laos that, if there is a peaceful situation, we are prepared to withdraw our forces and would expect others to withdraw their forces.

At the time of the agreement on Laos in 1962, we had several hundred military men in Laos. We took them out; we took them out. So as far as southeast Asia is concerned, what I would say to the other side is: "If you don't believe us, come and test it, come to the conference table. Work out these agreements. We will tell you that if peace is assured, American military forces will depart from southeast Asia."

Sen. Church: I, Mr. Secretary, am in full accord with that.

Sec. Rusk: We will write that into it. In other words there is no need for the other side to say, "Well, they still have them in Korea, so they will have them in South Vietnam." Let them come and test us so far as southeast Asia is concerned.

Now, as to the other question, on what might happen ten years from now, a great deal depends upon Peiping's attitude toward peace and toward the right of smaller nations to live next door to them without being molested, and what use Peiping might expect to make of the power which they may at that time have.

Sen. Church: May I just interject at that point, Mr. Secretary?

Sec. Rusk: Yes, sir.

Sen. Church: Because, in that connection, it was stressed this morning that Peiping is presently regarded, even by some Communist governments, as the principal threat to world peace, since it has not embraced the doctrine of coexistence.

Sec. Rusk: Yes, sir; that is correct.

Sen. Church: I think you emphasized that.

Sec. Rusk: Yes, sir; that is correct.

Sen. Church: That raised in my mind some questions relative to Vietnam. I think there is a tendency in our discussion of Vietnam to inter-mingle China and North Vietnam, as though there were no real distinc-tion between them. Do you feel that what we face in Vietnam is a case of Chinese aggression or is it a case of North Vietnamese aggression? Is there a distinction between the two, and does it matter?

Sec. Rusk: The instrument of aggression, that is the active agency of the aggression, is Hanoi. The doctrine which is used to support this ag-gression is from Peiping, and there is indication that Peiping, even more than Hanoi, has blocked the path toward a conference table.

Sen. Church: Do you regard Ho Chi Minh, then, as the mere agent of Mao Tse-tung?

Sec. Rusk: Not entirely, not entirely. I think there are elements of freedom of action, and we would hope that a situation could be found in which he could exercise that freedom of action and come to the con-ference table even though Peiping might object.

Sen. Church: So you do feel, after all, that North Vietnam has suffi-cient independence to come to a conference table even though China might object?

Sec. Rusk: Well, the sufficiency of that independence is still under test. As I indicated this morning, some nine months ago there was a joint communique by Hanoi and Moscow, expressing approval of the idea of a conference on Cambodia and Laos. We were interested in such a con-ference and approved it. Our information is that Peiping then moved in on Hanoi and possibly on Cambodia to block the prospects for such a conference. So the question of where the decisive influence exists on that particular point cannot be stated categorically at this point.

Sen. Church: But from the military standpoint, even though the extent of the political independence of North Vietnam might be somewhat ambiguous, Chinese combat troops have not become involved in the fighting in Vietnam.

Sec. Rusk: That is correct, sir.

Sen. Church: So that we are not faced here, as we were in Korea, with an actual Chinese invasion of Vietnam.

Sec. Rusk: That is not the present position, that is correct, sir.

Sen. Church: Do you regard the much-talked-about treatise of Chinese Marshal Lin Piao as a kind of Asian *Mein Kampf*, describing a blue-print for the Chinese conquest of Asia, or do you regard it as a do-it-your-self kit, outlining the Chinese revolutionary experience and advocating similar methods for Communist revolutionaries in other Asian lands?

Sec. Rusk: In practical terms thus far it takes on the shape of a do-it-yourself kit. Indeed in the Communist world, the general rumor going around is that Peiping is prepared to fight to the last North Vietnamese. That does not necessarily provide a guarantee for the future.

Sen. Church: No, no; I am trying to diagnose the present because it is upon the diagnosis of the present that we must project the future.

Sec. Rusk: That is right.

Sen. Church: And the present situation in Asia, as I understand it, is quite different from the threat posed by Hitler in Europe before the Second World War.

Sec. Rusk: There are differences but there are also enormous similarities, Senator.

Sen. Church: Well, I was trying to get at the differences in this series of questions and answers.

Sec. Rusk: Yes, all right. . . . [pp. 615–617]

Sen. Symington: There has been a great deal of apprehension about China. I worry about China, like every American must. Perhaps, based on my background, I worry a little more about the Soviets, based on what they now have; but our relations with the latter are improved. Do you think that our country should be afraid of Red China to the point where that fear should be the primary consideration incident to decision in the matter of our foreign policy?

Sec. Rusk: Senator, I think that anyone in a responsible position must keep this element very much in mind and must take it fully into account. And I think this is also a matter which the other side must take very much into account.

I do not believe that we can organize a peace, or even maintain the security of our own nation, if in successive crises we turn aside from what has to be done on the basis that at the end of the day or the end of the road it could move into something else. I mean that would have been the case with the Berlin blockade. It would have been the case with the Cuban missiles or with any of these other matters.

Sen. Symington: Let me repeat. Do you believe that the fear of Red China reacting to some action we took in protecting our interests under treaties and agreements in South Vietnam should be decisive with respect to decisions made about our foreign policy around the world?

Sec. Rusk: No, sir, because if we do not meet those responsibilities, we shall find a Red China much more voracious and much more dangerous if they should discover that this technique of aggression is successful. [pp. 676–677]

Part One

THE HISTORICAL
BACKGROUND

1 THE TRADITION OF SINO-WESTERN CONTACT

Testimony of A. Doak Barnett

Mr. Barnett: [Prepared Statement] For roughly 2,000 years prior to the mid-nineteenth century, China was the center of one of the great world civilizations. It was relatively isolated from comparable centers in Europe and elsewhere; it considered itself superior to all its neighbors, and it played a role of unchallenged primacy in the world as Chinese leaders knew it.

Then, in the mid-nineteenth century, its isolation was shattered by the restless, expanding, technologically superior nations of the West, and it became an arena for, and pawn of, competing imperial and colonial powers. The "Chinese revolution," if one uses this term in a broad sense, started at that time, in response to the traumatic impact of the West as well as to mounting domestic problems. It has been underway, therefore, for over a hundred years. In this revolution the Chinese people have been groping, painfully and slowly, to find effective means to modernize and develop their country, to build a strong, modern nation-state, and to reassert China's role in the world.

It is worth noting that to date there has been no extended period of peaceful relations between China and the Western world on the basis of reasonable equality. Before the mid-nineteenth century, the Chinese held a superior position and attempted, unsuccessfully, to fit the Western powers into its traditional imperial system of relations with subordinate states. During the next hundred years, the Western powers held a superior position and attempted, also without great success, to fit China into the modern international system of relations. The still unresolved problem for the future is whether both China and the West can, in time, reach an acceptable peaceful accommodation within the modern nation-state system, on the basis of relationships in which the rights and obligations of both will be recognized.

Part of the legacy of the past hundred years is the intense nationalism and self-assertiveness that all Chinese — whatever their ideology — now feel. All Chinese, non-Communist as well as Communist, are now determined to end China's recent position of inferiority and see their country achieve recognized major power status. [p. 6]

29

The Chairman: [Do] you think the history of Western nations other than the United States, beginning about 1942 [1842?], for example, has any effect upon their attitude toward the West, and is it reasonable to believe that we simply have become the symbol of their resentment against all Western nations?

Mr. Barnett: I think that is very much true. I think that the history of the last hundred years has created in the minds of all Chinese a feeling that China has been the pawn of colonial imperial powers, and that China has to reassert its identity, reassert its role in the world, and although comparatively speaking the U.S. record, I think, was good compared to that of many other powers, as you say, I think we have become the symbol of this.

I say all Chinese because I think if you read some of Mao's books, but then also read Chiang Kai-shek's book called "China's Destiny," you will find that in both of these books there is a deep resentment of the history of colonialism against China in the nineteenth century. So this aspect of Chinese attitudes, I think, is not simply anti-United States. It is more deep rooted. . . .

The Chairman: The only point I am trying to make is there is some historical justification for the extreme hostility of the Chinese toward Western countries and we simply happen to be the symbol of those Western countries although we were not the major culprit, is that correct?

Mr. Barnett: There are important historical factors that help to explain the intensity of Chinese feeling toward the West.

The Chairman: Countries such as Great Britain, Germany, France, the Belgians, Americans, all participated in this carving up of China, didn't they?

Mr. Barnett: Yes. I think, as I say, that comparatively speaking, the American record in the ninteenth century and early twentieth was a good one compared to that of the major powers. The United States did not — was not generally the power that took the initiative in imposing its will on China or in obtaining rights from China.

The Chairman: The British took the initiative, didn't they?

Mr. Barnett: Well, a great many powers did. The Russians did in the north, the British did in many areas, the French did in certain areas, the Germans did in certain areas. But the U.S. record is not wholly clean, in the sense that by most-favored-nation treatment, which was written into most treaties, we were able to benefit from most of the rights that were pried out of the Chinese by others.

At the end of the century, however, I think that our "open door" policy did play a significant role in preventing the complete carving up of China. This was a policy that was really a collaborative British–United States policy, not solely an American policy, and it was aimed at what seemed to be a danger at the end of the last century — which was a total colonial carving up of China. . . .

The Chairman: What was the purpose of the "open door" policy from our point of view?

Mr. Barnett: It had multiple purposes. I suppose at the heart of it was our desire to keep open equality of commercial enterprise in China. But we did link to this the necessity of preserving China's territorial integrity, and this was a very important thing at the time.

The Chairman: Is it true that the main reason for that "open door" policy was so that the other policies [countries?] that had moved in earlier than we had, could not exclude us from areas under their domination?

Mr. Barnett: Well, this was the fear: That China would be carved up and that each power would have a certain sphere of influence or area of control and would exclude other powers from that area. . . .

Sen. Sparkman: Were we in on occupying any of the area or taking any of the area or asking for any exclusive rights?

Mr. Barnett: Well, we did have extraterritorial rights in China and did not give them up until 1943.

Sen. Sparkman: With reference to the treatment of our citizens?

Mr. Barnett: Yes; our citizens were not under Chinese law.

Sen. Sparkman: But that was about the only offense from the standpoint of China of which we were guilty?

Mr. Barnett: The Chinese in the pre-Communist takeover did not look upon the United States as the symbol, the prime symbol, of the "imperialist" colonial policies.

The United States has become a symbol since then for several reasons; because of the ideological predispositions of the Communists but also because of the fact we are the only Western power that has a significant presence in Asia any more, so that the hostile feelings have been transferred to us.

Sen. Sparkman: We became the victim of their development of a composite hate for Western powers?

Mr. Barnett: To a degree. But I don't think that we can — if you are implying that our skirts are entirely clean — then I don't think that this is a ——

Sen. Sparkman: I understand your point on that.

Mr. Barnett: Yes. . . . [pp. 17–21]

Sen. Pell: One point you mentioned in your testimony was the history of maltreatment on the part of China by the other European nations. But I wonder if there is not one exception to that, and that is the Boxer Rebellion in which we were the only nation not to use our indemnity, but to spend our money in educating young Chinese in the United States.

Mr. Barnett: I think our decision to use those funds for purposes of scholarship was a very wise one.

Sen. Pell: Hasn't that left a reservoir of goodwill that still exists in spite of the regime?

Mr. Barnett: One could present different aspects of the historical background from those I have emphasized. I think that in the pre-Communist period there were many, many sorts of people, and groups, in China among whom there was a lot of goodwill toward us, and with whom we had very good relations. There is no doubt about that. But the other side of the picture is often ignored.

Sen. Pell: I wondered if one of the benefits of this sort of reverse Fulbright program of the Boxer Rebellion indemnity is the fact that many of the leaders in Taiwan are young men or men who were originally educated under that program.

Mr. Barnett: Many are. [p. 47]

Testimony of John K. Fairbank

Dr. Fairbank: [Prepared Statement] I imagine we would all agree on a first point — China's remarkable feeling of superiority. Here was a very big, ancient, isolated, unified, and self-sufficient empire, stretching from the latitude of Hudson's Bay to Cuba or from the Baltic Sea to the Sahara Desert, with a great deal of domestic commerce to meet its needs, cut off from west Asia by the high mountains and deserts of central Asia and thus isolated throughout most of its history, preserving a continuity of development in the same area over some 3,000 or 4,000 years, during most of which time the Chinese state has been a unified entity.

As we might expect, this biggest, most isolated and distinctive, most long-continued culture and society developed a strong tendency to look inward, an attitude of ethnocentrism or Sinocentrism, China being the center of the known world and of civilization, the non-Chinese being peripheral and inferior, China being superior to all foreign regions. . . .

A second point is that the old Peking rulers were the custodians and propagators of a true teaching, the Confucian classical doctrines of social order, an orthodoxy which told every man how to behave in his proper place and kept the social pyramid intact with the Emperor on top. . . .

This system did not believe in the equality of all men, which was obviously untrue. It believed in selecting the talented, training them in the orthodoxy, and promoting them as officials to keep the populace under control and maintain the system. We need not labor the point that China today still has a ruling class selected for their abilities who propagate a true teaching under a sage ruler and strive to keep the various social classes in order. . . .

In their foreign relations the Chinese rulers down to 1912 extended their domestic doctrines across their frontiers and applied the national myth of rule-by-virtue to their foreign relations. Foreign rulers could have contact with the Peking monarch only by sending tribute to him and having their envoys perform the three kneelings and nine prostrations of the kowtow ritual. This elaborate and prolonged ceremony, kneeling and prostrating oneself at command in front of the emperor — quite a lot of exercise — was absolutely insisted upon by the court to preserve the image of China's superiority and show the foreigner his proper place in the world hierarchy. It became well established that all foreign relations must be tributary relations, reinforcing the myth of Chinese supremacy and particularly the myth that foreign rulers were attracted by the emperor's virtue and "turned toward him" to offer their submission to the center of civilization. This grandiose concept reminds one of other ancient kings. The interesting thing is that the Chinese state was able to preserve it intact down to this century. The last tribute mission came from Nepal in 1908. . . .

We can conclude, I think, that the ideological component of power in China has been proportionately greater than in the West. Calling everything by its orthodox name helped keep things in order. The emperors were constantly spelling out the true doctrines, having them read in the Confucian temples and studied by all scholars. Heterodoxy and deviation could not be permitted, or if they did exist, could not be acknowledged to exist.

Even when the foreigners were more powerful, the myth of China's superiority had to be solemnly recorded and preserved in ritual. This stress on orthodoxy strikes one today when Peking is continuing its nationwide indoctrination in Chairman Mao's true teachings.

Applying all this background to the present moment, I suggest we should not get too excited over Peking's vast blueprints for the onward course of the Maoist revolution. Some American commentators who really ought to know better have overreacted to the visionary blueprint of world revolution put out by Lin Piao last September in Peking (about the strangling of the world's advanced countries or "cities" from the underdeveloped countries or "countryside"). This was, I think, a reassertion of faith, that the Chinese Communists' own parochial example of rural-based revolution is the model for the rest of the underdeveloped world to emulate. It was put out mainly as compensation for China's recent defeats in many parts of the globe.

To compare it to Hitler's *Mein Kampf* would be quite misleading. Rule-by-virtue required that the rulers proclaim their true teaching, claiming that it will still win the world even if they themselves are too weak to support it in practice.

The disaster that hit China in the nineteenth century is one of the most comprehensive any people ever experienced. The ancient tradition of China's superiority, plus this modern disaster, has undoubtedly produced one first-class case of frustration. It cannot seem right that a civilization once at the top should have been brought so low.

The nineteenth century disaster began with a great population increase during the peaceful eighteenth century, a subsequent weakening of administrative efficiency and maybe some popular demoralization, evident in the beginning of opium smoking.

In the Opium War of 1840 the Chinese were fighting against the opium trade, conducted by both foreigners and Chinese, while the British were fighting in the broad sense against the tribute system, demanding that China drop her claim to superiority and join the modern international trading world, the same thing we are waiting for today more than a century later.

The Opium War and the unequal treaties in the 1840's gave our merchants and missionaries a privileged status as agents of "Westernization" in the Chinese treaty ports. Throughout the next century, Western influence gradually disintegrated the old Chinese civilization. As the disaster gained momentum, Western gunboats proved that China had to have scientific technology, and then had to have Western industries, for which it was necessary to have Western learning, and eventually Western institutions and even a Western type of government.

The prestige of the Confucian classics evaporated. The Confucian type of a family structure began to crack. China's superiority vanished, even culturally.

The generation of Chinese that lived through this long-continued disaster, which happened in our grandfathers' time, experienced a deepening crisis. The sacred values of proper conduct and social order proved useless. The ancient faith in China's superiority as a civilization was slowly strangled. The privileged foreigners came in everywhere and gradually stirred up a Chinese nationalism.

So complete was the disaster that a new order had to be built from the ground up. Western doctrines of all kinds were tried out. The thing that proved effective was the Leninist type of party dictatorship, an elite recruited under discipline according to a new orthodoxy, organized something like an old Chinese secret society, united in the effort to seize power and recreate a strong state. This nationalistic aim overrode any other consideration. The kind of Western individualism propagated by our missionaries had no chance.

The retrospective humiliation and sense of grievance over the enormous disaster of the nineteenth century has made modern Chinese feel that their country was victimized, so it was, by fate.

Circumstances made China the worst accident case in history. But Marxism-Leninism offers a devil-theory to explain it: how "capitalist imperialism" combined with "feudal reaction" to attack, betray, and exploit the Chinese people and distort their otherwise normal development toward "capitalism" and "socialism." Thus a great Communist myth of "imperialist" victimization becomes the new national myth. . . .

As Americans we can only begin to imagine how the Chinese have suffered from being on the receiving end of modernization rather than the giving end. It has been hard for them to take, because under their traditional code there should be reciprocity between people, one should not accept gifts without paying them back. For China to be always receiving from the West not only hurts national pride, being on the receiving end with no chance of repaying the favors of missionaries, for example, also hurts personal self-respect.

We Americans, being on the giving end of modernization, got a great deal more fun out of Sino-American relations. In the privileged status thrust upon them by the treaty system, most Americans enjoyed their contact with China, the chance to be an upper-class foreigner riding in a rickshaw while still remaining an egalitarian grass-roots democrat in one's own conscience. For an average American to go abroad and find himself a rich man by comparison with the local people is also quite enjoyable. The Chinese were very polite, and countless Americans made warm friends among them. The American people built up a genuine, though sometimes patronizing, fondness for China.

Unfortunately, this now turns out to have been an unrealistic and rather naive attitude for two reasons. In the first place, the Americans were conscious of their own good intentions and less conscious of the humiliation that their superior circumstances often inflicted upon their Chinese friends.

In the second place, the Americans were able in the nineteenth century to share all the special privileges of foreigners in China under the unequal treaties without fighting for them. The British and others fought the colonial wars and the Americans enjoyed the fruits of such aggression without the moral responsibility. By 1900 the British, the French, and the Japanese had all fought wars with China; the Russians had seized territory; and all of them, together with the Germans, had seized special privileges in spheres of influence.

The Americans had done none of these things and came up instead with the "open-door" doctrine, which soon expanded to include not only the open door for trade but also the idea of China's integrity as a nation. Thus we Americans prided ourselves on championing China's modernization and self-determination. We considered ourselves above the nasty imperialism and power politics of the Europeans. We developed a self-image of moral superiority. The "open door" and benevolence toward Chinese nationalism became the bases of our Far Eastern policy until war with Japan brought us up against the realities of power politics. Then we began to realize, for almost the first time, that the power structure of East Asian politics had been held together by the British Navy in the nineteenth century, and by the British and Japanese Navies under the Anglo-Japanese alliance from 1902 to 1922.

Today we find ourselves in an enormous situation trying to maintain the power balance in East Asia. It is reminiscent in some ways of the colonial wars of the nineteenth century, a type of situation that we generally succeeded in avoiding in that era. I do not contend that we today are simply nineteenth-century imperialists come back to life, any more than Chairman Mao is actually a resurrected Son of Heaven in a blue boiler suit. But I don't believe we can escape our historical heritage entirely, any more than he can. We have been part and parcel of the long-term Western approach to East Asia and ought to see ourselves in that perspective, just as any view of our China policy has to include a perspective on our program in Vietnam. [pp. 98–104]

The Chairman: [Concerning the tribute system] But the value of the tribute was of no particular importance?

Dr. Fairbank: No; the tribute was compensated usually by gifts. It was worth your while to go and present tribute because the gifts outweighed the tribute.

The Chairman: It paid them to go.

Dr. Fairbank: If you went to Peking and paid tribute the gifts would more than repay the kowtow.

The Chairman: It is a very curious system.

Dr. Fairbank: If we would go and kowtow that would solve that problem. And one of our problems is that we don't want to kowtow. The British in 1840 refused to kowtow.

The Chairman: Well, come to think of it we have been dispensing considerable gifts around the world since the last war, haven't we?

Dr. Fairbank: We get our missions coming here, too.

The Chairman: We get our kowtow.

Dr. Fairbank: But we are not out after the same thing, of course. We are on a different tack. . . . [p. 111]

The Chairman: You made reference this morning to the humiliations of China during the nineteenth century and I thought were very informative about that.

I wonder if some of the statements then, with particular reference to one of the British Prime Ministers, Lord Palmerston, would evoke any comment from you. . . . In the 1850's, the British Prime Minister, Lord Palmerston, said, and I quote:

The time is fast approaching when we shall be obliged to strike another blow in China.

These half-civilized governments, such as those of China, Portugal, Spanish America, require a dressing down every eight or ten years to keep them in order.

Would you say that is sort of the same sentiment, or more realistic than as the statements of, Lin Piao's?

Dr. Fairbank: In the days of Queen Victoria when Lord Palmerston was saying this, and he had gunboats, he could get away with it quite easily, and he did. Whether it was a good thing or not is impossible to judge in my view. It occurred. There was a lot of it. It is the Western aggression into the East, into Asia, particularly.

Now, today we are in another world, and I do not think it is feasible to take exactly that attitude. I imagine Lord Palmerston if he were here today would have a different approach, because that is not healthy any more.

The Chairman: Would he, if he had comparable power today to what he had at that time? Generally aren't people who have the power to enforce their will inclined to talk very much the same way?

Dr. Fairbank: Well, people, of course, have so much more power today, and yet the power can be turned against us.

We have the capacity to destroy ourselves quite easily, and we know that, I think. We certainly say we know it, and I hope we act that way.

The Chairman: You assume a degree of rationality that sort of forecloses the case. This is what really worries us, whether we are any more rational now than we have been in the past. Are you sure we are or do you hope so?

Dr. Fairbank: As an historian, of course, I am a pessimist about human nature.

The Chairman: As a politician I join you. (Laughter.) . . .

The Chairman: . . . I wonder if one of our troubles does not arise from the fact that if we Western countries had suffered the humiliation that the Chinese did, and that if we had a resurgence of power, that we would not react in the way in which we interpret that [Lin Piao's] speech.

Dr. Fairbank: Possibly so. I think that one of our great troubles is, however, that we are in a different culture, and when we try to impute motives to the other side, the one thing we can be sure of is it is slightly different. In other words, the Chinese of today are motivated from a long-term past as well as the nineteenth century. . . .

The Chairman: I wonder if this does not lead us astray to reason from what we might do under similar circumstances because they have such an entirely different history?

Dr. Fairbank: Yes.

The Chairman: I am trying to explore the validity of our interpretation of China which, I think, is very questionable, because of the lack of knowledge and understanding of China's history.

I think you said this morning that because of their very long and successful tradition in history, it is likely in the long run to express itself in nationalistic attitudes more strongly than a recently acquired ideology would have. Is that a fair statement?

Dr. Fairbank: Yes, I think so.

The Chairman: In other words, you feel, given reasonable time, that these old traditions, rather than the doctrinaire attitudes of Marxism will reassert themselves.

Dr. Fairbank: Yes. This is the problem in the Chinese tradition, that they have an all-or-none approach, and this is very disconcerting to us because it means, whether it is a Marxist in Peking or somebody else, they are going to be awfully difficult for a long time to come.

But the all-or-none approach they believe in is personal rule. This is a tradition. The Emperor rules personally. He does it by his personal example. He is a good man and does the right thing and, therefore, he rules. And Mao Tse-tung is this type. He is the example, and he has the right idea, you can follow it. Chiang Kai-shek is this type. It is the Confucian emperor type. It is personal rule, and this personal rule commands personal loyalty, and you cannot have a loyal opposition. . . .

Now this means it is going to be awfully hard to get these people to play ball with our system. And when they have this all-or-none approach, why, on the one hand, Chiang says he wants the mainland and nothing else, Mao says he wants Taiwan and nothing less. They both say China is a unit, including Taiwan, and we are left just over a barrel in between them, and nothing we can do about solving their Taiwan problem. We are helpless in the middle, and so this kind of — this is what General Marshall faced when he was mediating between them, and General Hurley before him.

The old American idea that both sides have an interest, that we can represent their interest, they can compromise, just did not work, and it is not in this tradition. . . .

The Chairman: Lastly . . . I have another question. Is there any similarity in the Chinese attitude toward their rulers and the former attitude of the Russians toward the czars in the days of Ivan the Terrible, and Peter the Great? Peter did not have a loyal opposition either, did he?

Dr. Fairbank: No, he did not go for it. But he did have Boyars and such fellows you read about in the books who were magnates who would give him support. He had to have that kind of group. He wasn't so much a high priest.

The Son of Heaven was performing the sacrifices at the right time of year to keep the calendar in balance and keep everything operating, and so the Son of Heaven was a much more heavenly person than the czar or anybody outside of China.

The Chairman: So you cannot think of a really good example of any other country having developed to this extent?

Dr. Fairbank: Only if you put together the American President and the Pope in Rome and a few other combinations. (Laughter.) [pp. 150–153]

Sen. McCarthy: If you were to pass a rather sweeping judgment on administration policy, would you make any suggestions as to how it should have been different with reference to China had there been more attention paid to the historical record?

Dr. Fairbank: I think that in 1922 we could have done something to keep a power structure in the Far Eastern scene, perhaps tied in with

Japan in some way, instead of getting into a nine-power treaty which said that China should be given her chance, but with no sanctions and no power structure, no agreement.

We got rid of the Anglo-Japanese alliance, but we did not put anything in its place. This has been held up, I think properly, as an example of being a little too idealistic and not enough power conscious.

I think in a case of the decline of the Nationalist government we were caught by history, the way they were. We were just torpedoed. They were the people closest in touch with us, they were the people we knew, they were only part way toward developing their own position. The Japanese hit them, the Communists then had a chance to move in, and I do not know anything we could have done about it because we were torpedoed by history.

Sen. McCarthy: What about current policies, so far as you can determine what the administration's policies are? Do you recommend a change on the basis of history other than what you have indicated thus far?

Dr. Fairbank: I think everything I have said has been on the basis of history because I work as a historian and spend most of my time thinking about that. [p. 166]

Testimony of Samuel B. Griffith

The Chairman: You are familiar, I am sure, General, with the history of China. Do you think that in view of her experiences beginning with the Opium War on up to the Second World War that she naturally would have a desire to develop an adequate defense force?

Gen. Griffith: Well, after all, Senator, China was kicked, was kicked around for one hundred years. China is an old and proud nation. The Western nations on several occasions were on the verge of cutting her into pieces. Sun Yat-sen, the father of the revolution, compared the nation to grains of sand. There was no Chinese nation, really. There was no sense of nation in China until Chiang Kai-shek first made his appeal to nationalism in 1926. I would say that the Chinese reaction now to the Western world, and particularly to us, flows directly from China's historical experience; yes, sir.

The Chairman: That is what I meant. She became so helpless militarily during that period of humiliation time after time by both large and small Western countries that it is quite within human nature for her to seek to develop an adequate defense force; isn't it?

Gen. Griffith: Mr. Chairman, when such a country as Portugal was able to exert pressure on a nation like China, I would think the reaction that we see today is to be expected.

The Chairman: That is what I meant. It is quite logical. There is nothing unusual about her trying to develop a capacity for preventing a recurrence of such humiliation in the future; is that right?

Gen. Griffith: I think Dr. Halperin would agree with me and most other people who followed Chinese history that any strong central government in Peking would in many ways be behaving precisely as the Communist government is behaving today. [pp. 289–290]

Testimony of Alexander Eckstein

The Chairman: Were the trade policies of this country and of Great Britain beneficial to the economy of China between 1840 and 1900? . . .

Dr. Eckstein: One could spend hours on this very complicated question, and it is an extremely controversial one. It gets into this whole question of the payoff of colonialism, and there is a great deal of controversy in economic literature as to whether colonialism really paid off or has not paid off at all.

But more specifically in the Chinese case, I think there were elements of benefit and there are definite elements of damage. That is, modern industry, large-scale industry, probably would not have been established in China until much later if it had not been for Western incursion. On the other hand, Western incursion itself greatly undermined some of the native industries, small-scale industries, small-scale textile industry, and what undoubtedly happened is that you had some economic development in some areas and some economic regression in other areas.

Also another factor that must be considered is that our incursions contributed to the political fragmentation and weakening of the Chinese polity and Chinese government, so that the ability of the Chinese government to respond creatively and positively to the economic problems was profoundly undermined. That is one of the hallmarks of this hundred-year period, which is the weakness of the Chinese government which, of course, also reflected itself in its weakness to cope with the economic problems and in its weakness to take any kind of positive economic development measures. [pp. 358–359]

Testimony of Hans J. Morgenthau

Dr. Morgenthau: [Summary of Prepared Statement] China is potentially and actually a great power, but she is also a great power of a peculiar character. For throughout her history, the enormous influence which China has exerted on the Asian mainland was not primarily and not only the result of her military prowess. It was chiefly the result of the fact that China is not only a great power but also a great civilization. It has been the weight and the attractiveness and the unchallengability of this civilization which has determined the position of China among the nations of Asia.

It is here, I think, that we must correct one misconception about China's foreign policy, which is very common among us. We tend to think in terms of historic analogies and we can't help thinking of China in terms of our experience with Nazi Germany. That is to say, we have in our minds the image of Chinese armies being poised at their borders and ready to march across Asia as the hordes of Genghis Khan did, if they are not contained locally on the spot.

However, traditionally, especially insofar as China's neighbors to the west and southwest are concerned, China has not primarily relied upon military expansion but rather upon the establishment of subtle and complex tributary relationships between herself and her neighbors.

This militancy and this almost mad ranting with regard to the outside world, together with this lack of understanding of the outside world, is again a continuation of an old Chinese tradition which looks at the outside world as being naturally inferior to China, which regards China as the only power worthy of consideration, the only sovereign power of the world, to which all other nations by nature are tributaries. Thus the Chinese for ages have refused to deal with the outside world on equal terms. They have had a great deal of contempt for it, and are quite ignorant of it, for the simple reason that they didn't think it was necessary for them to know anything about the outside world. I would say that the present attitude of the Chinese government toward the outside world is very much in this Chinese tradition, aggravated and, in a sense, concealed by the Marxist-Leninist ideology. [pp. 551–552]

2 THE COMMUNIST
TAKEOVER IN CHINA

Testimony of A. Doak Barnett

Mr. *Barnett:* [Prepared Statement] The explanations for Chinese Communist successes in the 1930's and 1940's are numerous, but I would say that the most important ones were the following.

One was the Sino-Japanese War, which had a shattering effect on China and helped to create a revolutionary situation.

Another was the failure of the non-Communist leaders in China to achieve unity in their own ranks, to define and pursue effective programs designed to cope with such basic problems as landlordism, inflation, and corruption, or to build a firm grass-roots base of support — a failure which in effect created a vacuum into which the Communists moved.

Still another was the Communists' own success in building an unprecedentedly disciplined and strong revolutionary organization, in appealing to nationalism and reformism especially during the war, in developing a shrewd revolutionary strategy, and in implementing their programs with determination and, whenever necessary, ruthlessness.

Peking's leaders now maintain that their experience provides a primary model for revolutions throughout the underdeveloped world. It is a model calling for the creation of Communist-led peasant armies, the establishment of so-called liberated areas as bases for revolutionary struggle, the creation of broad anti-imperialist united fronts, and the overthrow of existing non-Communist regimes by violence. There is little doubt that the Chinese model has had, and will continue to have, an impact far beyond China's borders. . . .

We should not, however, magnify its significance. Careful analysis indicates, I think, that the particular constellation of factors and forces which made it possible for Mao Tse-tung's strategy to succeed in China are not widely duplicated, and there are many reasons to believe that the Chinese model cannot be exported as easily as Mao and some of his colleagues have hoped. . . . [pp. 6–7]

Testimony of Benjamin I. Schwartz

Dr. Schwartz: [Prepared Statement] In 1911, China witnessed the collapse of one of the most imposing political systems the world has ever known. What collapsed was not merely a government but the whole cosmology on which that government was based. In the ensuing vacuum, political power gravitated into the hands of local militarists. We then have the immense anarchy and chaos of the so-called warlord period. It is, I believe, a warranted assumption that during this period of chaos and political decay, the social and economic situation of the vast masses of China — in the aggregate — continued to deteriorate.

In 1927, the Kuomintang government ostensibly carried out the political and military unification of China. This speedy unification was, however, based on a network of flimsy agreements with many of the local militarists themselves — agreements which proved highly evanescent. In fact, the government in Nanking controlled directly only certain provinces of central China. This situation had, of course, not been created by the Nationalist government and the tendency of this government to direct much of its energy during the next few years to the task of achieving the genuine military unification of China may seem entirely justifiable.

Unfortunately, the resources available to this government were limited and the concentration of major energies in this task meant that other vital tasks were neglected.

Furthermore, the Kuomintang itself, which was the supreme political body of the society, was not a highly integrated movement. It was riven by cliques among which there was little lateral cohesion. The reasons for this failure of the Kuomintang to achieve inner unity still remain to be studied but the fact that the party rested on what has been called a "balance of weakness" can hardly be denied. One aggravating factor was undoubtedly the fact that these political cliques were often able to establish links with the independent military groupings mentioned above. . . .

During its early years, the Kuomintang did carry out positive programs in the realm of communications, education, foreign affairs, et cetera, but these programs were also limited in conception. They were largely urban in orientation and paid little attention to the vast rural hinterland which was hardly affected by the Nationalist rise to power. Local power in these areas by default remained in the hands of the incumbent holders of power.

. . . Since the government was unable, during the whole period of its tenure on the mainland, to solve the problem of military unification

43

or to launch a substantial industrialization program, it never did turn its attention seriously to the problem of the rural areas. There are those who contend that it could probably not have carried out substantial programs of reform in the countryside even if it had desired to do so because it had become indissolubly linked to the local holders of power and privilege. Whether this is so or not, the fact remains that even in terms of policy, rural reform was not high on the list of priorities.

It should also be pointed out that in spite of its orientation to military tasks, the Nationalist government did not carry out substantial reforms in the military area itself. Taking the period of Nationalist control as a whole, one must say that too little was done to improve the condition of the average soldier, to improve the practices of recruitment or the relations between the military and the civilian population. . . .

It should also be noted that during the period from 1931 to 1937 the Nationalist government was unable to take full advantage of the patriotic anti-Japanese sentiment of the intellectuals and students. It was the considered view of the leadership that it was futile for China to attempt to confront Japanese power before carrying out military unification at home. While this policy may again on the surface appear eminently sensible, the campaigns against the Communist areas and against local militarists provided the unfortunate spectacle of Chinese fighting Chinese rather than fighting the common Japanese enemy.

It is within the context of this situation that the Maoist strategy of revolution gradually emerged. The development of this strategy on the part of Mao and others was a gradual and groping process, there was no preexistent blueprint. . . . The emergence of rural bases, the emergence of a concentration on peasant support, on the creation of peasant military forces and on guerrilla warfare was precisely a response to some of the Nationalist weaknesses mentioned above.

The Kuomintang was the weakest in the countryside and in an environment of military disunity, the Communists in a sense took on the coloration of their environment.

The Nationalists, indeed, often referred to them as a peculiar breed of warlords. Yet they were neither warlords nor "agrarian reformers." From their communism they derived a profound faith that history was on their side and they on its side. They also derived the concept of the Communist Party as the instrument of history, as a monolithic group united by an iron discipline and a fixed purpose. Their image of the future was also profoundly influenced by Soviet communism.

By the forties, Mao Tse-tung and others succeeded in creating a Communist Party which corresponded in the main to this ideal type. Land reform played a considerable role in their program but this does not mean that their policies were uniformly popular with the peasantry or that their dreams for the future were in any way determined by the perspectives of the peasants. . . .

Above all, I would stress some of the policies which they developed in the military area. They paid enormous attention to the political indoctrination and morale of the average soldier and, within the limits of the situation, to his physical well-being. They also laid constant stress on proper relations between the military and civilian population. In accounting for their victory after 1945, I would be inclined to place more weight on this factor than on the efficacy of land reform as such.

Having pointed out some of the weaknesses of the Kuomintang and some of the strengths of the Maoist strategy of revolution, as I see them, I should immediately add that had there been no Japanese assault on China, it is not inconceivable that the Kuomintang might have survived and that the Maoist strategy might have failed. In the course of time, the Nationalist government might have achieved a decisive preponderance of military power in China. Whether this would have led it to cope successfully with all its other manifold problems we shall never know, but we do know that governments often survive without solving all their problems. . . .

The Japanese war against China after 1937 proved, however, to be like a disease which attacks a frail body at its weakest points. The net effect of the war was to aggravate the weaknesses of the Nationalist government. All thought of achieving the military control of north China had to be abandoned. . . .

The Communists, on the other hand, were able to apply their considerable experience in organizing rural areas to the situation in north China. . . . They were now able to make a strong appeal to nationalistic sentiment (which they undoubtedly shared) and to call for support among many elements — particularly intellectuals and students who were deeply impressed by their anti-Japanese activities. . . .

The Nationalist government carried into the postwar period its overwhelming concern with the immediate achievement of military, political, and even economic unification. Yet the factors which had made for low morale in both its political and military establishment had not been overcome during the course of the war.

They had, in fact, been aggravated.

One is tempted to speculate in retrospect on what might have happened if the Nationalist government had concentrated during the years between 1927 and the later forties in depth within the areas under its firm control rather than on the will-o'-wisp pursuit of the military unification of the whole of China. . . .

In considering some of the general implications of this story, I think it must be emphasized that the success of the Maoist strategy in China must be explained in terms of the specific history of modern China and not in terms of vague generalities about underdeveloped countries in general.

The political and military fragmentation of modern China, the whole phenomenon of "warlordism," the failure to carry out military reform even in those armies under firm government control played an enormous role in the ultimate success of Chinese Communist strategy.

Furthermore, as a result of the Japanese aggression, the Chinese Communists were able to wed their rural strategy to a genuine national appeal. In the eyes of many Chinese, they were able to make themselves the spokesmen of a genuine Chinese nationalism even while remaining Communists. [pp. 181–185]

The Chairman: Was the government of Chiang Kai-shek less authoritarian than that of Mao Tse-tung?

Dr. Schwartz: In the sense that it was either unwilling or unable to exercise control of every facet of human life, which seems to be the ambition of Mao's government. In this sense we can draw a distinction, perhaps, between the authoritarian and totalitarian. . . .

The Chairman: It is just a matter of degree, the extent of it?

Dr. Schwartz: Well, it can be a matter of degree. I do believe that as an authoritarian government the Kuomintang was not very effective.

The Chairman: Was not. Was it very effective as a democratic government?

Dr. Schwartz: No.

The Chairman: Then it was ineffectual in all respects, is that correct?

Dr. Schwartz: I would again add that many of the reasons for this ineffectiveness are not simply to be sought in the faults of the personnel of this government. There were many external factors beyond its control which contributed to this ineffectiveness. [p. 195]

Sen. Sparkman: Very briefly, if it can be given, what was the cause of the breakdown of the Nationalist forces right after they had done such a good job against the Japanese? By the way, were the Communists and the Nationalists allied in a common cause against the Japanese?

Dr. Schwartz: Supposedly allied throughout World War II. In actuality, I think full of cordial mistrust of each other. I think they both had lethal intentions regarding the other for the postwar period. So the alliance, I think, was a very frail thing.

Now, you mentioned, Senator, the Kuomintang effort during World War II. . . . It seems to me that basic reform of the military establishment was not undertaken, that nothing much was done to improve the morale of the average soldier.

Many of the deplorable practices of the warlord period had survived. I think there are reasons that may explain this. There was a great necessity to maintain the loyalty of the officers. But I would stress very much this area of activity. It was an area to which the Communists did devote a great deal of attention and to which the Nationalists did not devote a great deal of attention. . . .

Sen. Hickenlooper: There is opinion, based upon a considerable amount of evidence, that the Red armies were in fact receiving a substantial amount of assistance and encouragement and support from Russia during that period which had a great deal of effect on bolstering their morale and consolidating their organization, and that we went through a period where political figures in this country advanced the Reds as merely agrarian reformers and we didn't do much to really materially help the Kuomintang. . . .

Dr. Schwartz: Well, here we are reviving old quarrels, of course, and I can only give you my own opinion. It is my understanding that we were helping the Nationalist government materially. As far as the Communists were concerned, I do think they may have derived a certain amount of moral support from the Russians. I don't think that on the organizational side — particularly on the matter of organizing an army, they were necessarily learning very much from the Russians. In fact, there is some evidence that Stalin himself did not basically believe in the kind of strategy that they were pursuing. He did not believe that this would lead to success. This does not mean that he did not support their victory. They did get some arms from the Russians later in the civil war. I would still tend to ascribe their victory basically to their own abilities to organize themselves. [pp. 200–201]

Part Two

THE NATURE OF
THE COMMUNIST REGIME
AND ITS FOREIGN POLICY

3   POLITICAL STABILITY

Testimony of A. Doak Barnett

Mr. Barnett: [Prepared Statement] Communist China in 1966 is a very different country in many respects from China in 1949.

Perhaps the first thing that should be noted about the political situation in China is that the Communists have created a very strong totalitarian apparatus that has unified and exercises effective control over the entire China mainland, and they have used their power to promote uninterrupted revolution aimed at restructuring the nation's economy, social structure, and system of values.

While the impact of the regime has been harsh and painful for millions of Chinese, the Communists have built a strong base of organized support, partly on the basis of appeals to nationalism as well as promises of future accomplishments. They have also demonstrated a remarkable capacity to make and implement decisions and an impressive ability to mobilize people and resources. Not surprisingly, however, there are many tensions in the society and, in my opinion, fairly widespread — even though largely unarticulated — dissatisfaction with numerous Communist policies and methods of rule. But there is no significant organized opposition and no foreseeable prospect of its development. In short, the regime is not a passing phenomenon. In time it may change its character, but it will continue to exist, as we will continue to have to deal with it, for the predictable future. . . .

The biggest question about the future arises from the fact that Communist China is on the verge of an historic transition period in which virtually the entire top leadership will pass from the scene in a relatively brief period of time. . . .

When Mao and other top leaders die, therefore, I would expect China to enter a period in which there could be a great deal more fluidity and uncertainty about both leaders and policies than in recent years. It would be reasonable to expect, I think, that the outcome of the competition between leaders and policies that is likely to occur, and the resulting balance between what one might call radicals and moderates will be definitely influenced by the perceptions that the new leaders have of the international environment as it affects China. While it may not be possible for outsiders to exert very much influence on the outcome, our hope, certainly, should be that the balance will in time shift in favor of technical bureaucrats promoting relatively moderate policies. [pp. 7–8]

51

Sen. McCarthy: You expressed the opinion that as new leaders come into positions of power in Communist China that you expect a change in policy. What direction is that change likely to take, especially if we were to change our policy with reference to isolation? . . .

Mr. Barnett: . . . I am inclined to think that . . . even now you can find in domestic policy in China a mixture that reflects the pressures of two groups . . . and, crudely speaking, there is one group of people who are preoccupied, I think, with political control, with keeping up political tension and revolutionary momentum, and so on, keeping up ideological fervor. Then there is another group of people who are more preoccupied with the practical problems of running the economy and other aspects of the country. I think that when there are changes at the top, there will tend to be a crystalization of these groups, and there will be competition between them, and pressures in differing direction. . . .

My own guess and, as I say, it is very speculative, is that over a period of time those I call the technical bureaucrats or the managers would begin, in effect, determining large areas of policy in China. [pp. 51–52]

Testimony of John M. H. Lindbeck
and Benjamin I. Schwartz

Dr. Lindbeck: [Prepared Statement] The regime is solidly entrenched in China. By the regime I mean above all the Communist Party, but also the large administrative and economic institutions and mass organizations created by the party and staffed by officials who are party appointees. There is no good evidence, so far as I can see, that the continuity and basic stability of the regime is likely to be jeopardized in the foreseeable future. Even should there be a succession crisis when the present top leaders die, with a sharp struggle for power between competing groups in the party, it is unlikely, I believe, that the authority and control of the regime over the country will be seriously impaired. Contests for power are likely to be confined to groups within the party. The contestants, as influential party officials, will have a vital stake in the survival of the system and of the party as an organization. None of them is likely to seek the support of forces opposed to the regime to win power.

The strength and stability of the regime are a result of several factors. Above all it depends on the unity and efficiency of the Communist Party and the armed forces over which the party exercises particular control. . . .

The basic source of political tensions in China is the relationship between the regime, or party, and the people. . . .

The range and degree of resistance varies. The party leaders are skilled in trying to limit popular dissatisfactions and keeping them down to manageable proportions. Occasionally, protests have broken through the bounds of control, as they did during the brief hundred flowers period in 1957 when a policy of liberalization of thought and speech to win greater support from intellectuals led instead to a burst of attacks on the party and its policies; or again among farmers during collectivization and communalization when slaughtering of livestock, passivity, and other types of resistance appeared and forced readjustments in the regime's policies and patterns of incentives. During the worst of the post-Leap depression, sporadic armed protests occurred. Among the non-Chinese minority groups, antagonism to the regime periodically has taken a militant form.

. . . The party politicians are responsive to a degree to popular attitudes. They are well aware of the dangers of being alienated from the masses, as the people are called. Where resistance is localized and limited to a small sector of the population, coercive means can be used. But in other, more politically significant cases, the party seeks to use persuasion which is socially, politically, and financially less expensive — rather than physical force to gain compliance or public support. In extreme cases of resistance it has retreated, as from the communes, and reintroduced economic incentives, such as the private plots and free markets, and reinstated the family as a social, housekeeping and child-care unit. . . .

Broadly speaking, some groups in the party favor policies and procedures which are at least somewhat responsive to popular desires and needs; others are more inclined to push the pace of social change and economic development and to ignore public opinion. We have seen intra-party struggles between provincial and regional party groups and the top leadership in Peking. Some contests have probably been the result of personal rivalries, others have stemmed from policy differences. . . .

Will the new economic, political, and social institutions imposed by the Communist leaders of China increasingly be accepted and become domesticated? If the country's leaders maintain the relatively moderate and gradualist economic and social policies they have pursued during the past few years, this is likely to be the case. Over 300 million Chinese are children of the post-1949 era. Those twenty-five years and under have little or no memory of a non-Communist past. On the other hand, the experiences of the period from 1958 to 1962, when China underwent the mad pressures of the Great Leap, the disorientations of the communes, and economic recession, were undoubtedly traumatic for most Chinese, young and old, but some of the uncertainties and fears of that period are being forgotten with the passage of time. If routinization and continuity of life patterns and social work schedules are encouraged, this too will change the political atmosphere and context in which the regime operates, producing an increased sense of stability and confidence. [pp. 187–192]

Sen. Sparkman: Dr. Lindbeck, you referred to the internal weaknesses in the case of the present Chinese government. We know from time to time through the years the Nationalist Chinese on Formosa have talked about, or the Generalissimo has talked about, going back to China and that the populace would rise up to support them. What is your opinion with reference to that? Could there be a successful invasion of the mainland by the Nationalist Chinese?

Dr. Lindbeck: It is my feeling that there isn't any likelihood that the Chinese Nationalists could make a successful return to the mainland.

If there is to be a disintegration of the present regime on the mainland, it would seem to me that this would be the result of competitive forces at work in China itself. I should guess that if the Chinese Nationalists were to try to get back to the mainland, even competing groups in China would tend to unite against an attempt to reimpose the external power of the Nationalist Party on China.

The Chinese Nationalists, it seems to me, have many handicaps. One is that the Communist regime on the mainland has been very efficient in rooting out Nationalist supporters throughout the country; this is one of its chief concerns — to make sure that Taipei has no allies on the mainland.

Secondly, the image of the Nationalists on the mainland, I think, has not been significantly improved since 1949; it may be that it has become even less challenging or appealing as time has gone on.

In China, furthermore, one is dealing with a political system in which communications and information are carefully controlled by the top elite, by the regime. The Chinese Nationalists, so far as I can see, have not been very successful in penetrating the communicational system and reaching large numbers of people and thus successfully mobilizing support within the country. . . .

Sen. Sparkman: Do you feel there is any likelihood of uprising inside of China in the foreseeable future that would promise success?

Dr. Lindbeck: The quick answer is "No." This does not mean that there will not be persistent and future resistance to many of the policies of the regime. It depends on what measures the regime adopts in various fields.

If it goes through another period of driving the people as during the Great Leap, it could produce an economic depression similar to that experienced between 1959 and 1962; then I think we might again see the emergence of protest — and, as you probably know, this protest took violent form in 1961. At that time, for example, there were thirteen counties in one province where the militia turned against the government, and regular army troops had to be brought in. Again, as the Chinese have tried to step up the pace of their transformation of life in minority areas, there have been a series of armed uprising against the Communists. All of these have been manageable protests.

One of the problems facing dissidents is that resistance forces in China have virtually no opportunity to organize on a nationwide or even a regional basis unless, of course, regional party leaders were able to foster resistance. So, resistance is likely to be sporadic, unorganized, a local phenomenon.

Regarding the broader question of whether the regime can be overturned, I should say that unless the party itself undergoes tremendous disintegration, is riven by rivalries, it is hard to foresee at the moment any opportunity for major resistance forces to emerge in the country.

Sen. Sparkman: Dr. Schwartz, do you agree generally with what he has said?

Dr. Schwartz: Yes, I agree with almost everything that Mr. Lindbeck has said. [pp. 197–198]

Sen. Church: You don't think Chiang Kai-shek would be greeted on the shores as a liberator by the Chinese?

Dr. Schwartz: Here again I would like to associate myself with Dr. Lindbeck. I think there are many tensions on the Chinese mainland and there may be change in the future. I really do feel that while the Nationalist government has performed with some degree of efficiency on Formosa, in a sense, to use the old Chinese phrase, "It has lost the mandate" on the mainland.

New formations may emerge but I think they will be formations that we can't foresee now.

Sen. Church: You think, then, on the basis of the present evidence, Chiang Kai-shek has not retained any significant following in mainland China?

Dr. Schwartz: Well, here again, I don't have access to all the grass-roots feelings, but on the basis of everything I have been able to learn, I doubt that he can really prove to be a great rallying figure in China. There will have to be new rallying figures, it seems to me. [p. 204]

Sen. McCarthy: [It] has been pointed out by both of you along the way that there have been rather critical periods during which there was popular resentment sometimes involving the whole populace, sometimes the military and sometimes the intellectuals in China. If there were to be a significant change and a kind of revolt, what sort of government might emerge? Would it simply be another Communist government, a change of leaders, or would it involve a basic shifting in policy to meet the regional or class protests?

Dr. Schwartz: Are you talking about China now?

Sen. McCarthy: Yes, China.

Dr. Schwartz: I can conceive of a moderation of the extreme policies of the present government which may be caused by pressures from within that government itself. I do not think — contrary to certain stereotypes about Asians — that Asians take to totalitarianism in its extreme form any more than Europeans. I believe that the Chinese population would very much welcome a relaxation of some of the more extreme, fanatical policies of the present regime at this time. I must say, however, I am not inclined to overstress the possibility of an actual overthrow of this government.

Sen. McCarthy: What would be the kind of government that would replace it, another Communist government? The question I really want to ask is whether or not in your judgment or Dr. Lindbeck's, there is a possibility of overthrowing communism in China in the reasonably near future.

Dr. Schwartz: I do not place much stock in this possibility myself.

Dr. Lindbeck: My reaction is that there is very little chance of overthrowing the regime we have there. If there were a sharp division within the regime and one group undertook to unseat another group, it seems to me that the rebel group or coup group would still be basically Communist in its orientation. Potential rebels who are non-Communist in orientation are so scattered, discouraged, and impotent that unless there were a very protracted period of turmoil in the country, these elements would not be able to organize and seek power. Any groups now seeking power, it seems to me, already would be linked with the party and organized institutions in China. [pp. 261–262]

The Chairman: This is not relevant, but I am curious. Let us take India and China, one country larger than the other. One has a form of democratic government and the other a totalitarian. Do you have any view as to the relative political stability of these two large Asian societies?

Dr. Lindbeck: Well, I do not know how one measures it. There have been a number of studies and, I believe, a study done some years ago for this committee, on relative economic progress and the stability of political institutions in China and in India. . . .

My general impression is that the Chinese have been more efficient and sweeping in the ways they have tried to organize their resources for developmental purposes, but that in certain areas of economic and social development the Indians have probably gone ahead of the Chinese. The Chinese may have been more sweeping and perhaps efficient in organizing the overall development of their national resources than have the Indians.

The Chairman: I see.

Dr. Lindbeck: . . . Looking at them [China and India], however, as agricultural societies — and I suppose this is a key point about them — my impression, without knowing anything about India, is that the Chinese probably have done better than the Indians in developing their agricultural resources.

The Chairman: Do you wish to comment on that?

Dr. Schwartz: Well, I would accept that. But I do think, that we should have one caution here. India gives an impression of great turmoil. The turmoil is on the surface. One thing that impressed me in my brief visit to India was the tremendous variety of the country, whereas China gives this impression of monolithic unity. I am not sure that this monolithic unity, which is based really on a suppression of diversity, in all respects, makes China stronger than India. . . . In other words, the monolithic appearance of China should not necessarily be taken as proof of their infinitely superior strength in the cultural areas, let us say. [pp. 267–268]

Testimony of Walter H. Judd

The Chairman: Dr. Judd, is it your view that Mao is a puppet regime?

Dr. Judd: No, I don't think he is a puppet, except that by act of his own will and choice he is dedicated unwaveringly to the same world objective and program as the Soviet Union. All Communists so far as I know are united on the necessity for world revolution. They differ, as in the quarrel between Mao and Moscow, over how to accomplish it and when. [p. 461]

Sen. Sparkman: Do you believe that the Nationalist Chinese on Taiwan stand a fair chance of ever invading the mainland?

Dr. Judd: They have never used the words invade the mainland. They use the words liberate the mainland.

Sen. Sparkman: Or liberate?

Dr. Judd: They want reunion with their brethren on the mainland.

Sen. Sparkman: You believe the uprising would come from within?

Dr. Judd: It has to come from within but it ought to be supported immediately with assistance from without. You can't defect if you don't have any place to defect to. . . . Many students believe that if there were a place on the mainland, to which the Chinese there could defect, millions would do so. As long as there is a Taiwan where Chinese are free, their hope will continue.

I think that given some kind of a disruption or defeat or explosion within Red China, followed promptly with assistance from Taiwan and establishment of a beachhead, you could get a real shift, much more quickly than people realize. Almost all the Chinese dynasties went down when nobody expected them to. [p. 465]

Testimony of David N. Rowe

The Chairman: You said, I believe, that the regime in Peking is not representative of the Communist people. Would you elaborate on that? What do you mean by that?

Dr. Rowe: Well, I think I am talking about the same thing that Secretary of State Rusk talked about a number of years ago when he said our position is that this government in Peking does not represent the Chinese people. They do not represent the best things in Chinese civilization. They do not have the support of the Chinese people. It is my conviction, based upon a good deal of study of this matter, and not just a subjective thing, that 90 percent of the Chinese people would welcome the departure of Mao and all of his henchmen any time they could get rid of him.

The Chairman: How does one determine this?

Dr. Rowe: I cannot determine it.

The Chairman: I do not know.

Dr. Rowe: I give it as an opinion. I cannot prove it. But all the evidence I have leads me to believe that this is so. I have gotten this viewpoint or this opinion, as I call it, by talking to many refugees from Communist China.

The Chairman: Have there been any demonstrations in the last two years, that you know of, in China against the Peking regime?

Dr. Rowe: Well, sir, the regime itself states every once in a while, it states how many revolutionaries, subversives, remnants that seem to hang around forever of the former regime it uncovers every year, and these are very large numbers.

The Chairman: Does the regime also state how many protests there have been against the regime in the last two or three years?

Dr. Rowe: There undoubtedly have been rebellions against the regime.

The Chairman: Have they reported it or what is the source of this information?

Dr. Rowe: This information comes out through Hong Kong. It is very hard to hide.

The Chairman: I would think it is hard to hide. Although I am not a specialist on China, I have not read in the papers recently much about revolts against the regime.

Dr. Rowe: They have had them, Senator.

The Chairman: They have had them?

Dr. Rowe: Yes, sir.

The Chairman: Can you remember when and where?

Dr. Rowe: They have been scattered around through China in various places. In fact, one of the interesting features of the situation inside Communist China is the ease with which the Chinese Nationalist government in Taiwan can send guerrilla forces in there and find hospitality for them. These forces are flown in and dropped in, and they find hospitality among the local people.

The Chairman: Has that been true in the last two years?

Dr. Rowe: Yes, sir.

The Chairman: Where did this happen? I didn't know this.

Dr. Rowe: It happens in scattered regions up and down the China coast. I can get you the whole catalogue. . . .

The Chairman: And you say the Nationalists have dropped in guerrillas who have found a favorable ——

Dr. Rowe: Hospitable welcome.

The Chairman: Are they still there or what happens to them?

Dr. Rowe: They go in and come out.

The Chairman: How do they come out?

Dr. Rowe: They get picked up on the coast by small boats sent to meet them. It is a regular feature in the situation.

The Chairman: They are like the Scarlet Pimpernel, they have ways of getting out.

Dr. Rowe: Oh, yes, sir; in and out.

The Chairman: I should think that would be rather difficult. I really do not know.

Dr. Rowe: It is difficult. I have no doubt of that.

The Chairman: This question of a regime being representative of the people is a difficult one where there are so many countries with one-party regimes; is it not?

Dr. Rowe. Yes.

The Chairman: Do you think that where there is a one-party government that it is representative of the people, or can only a two-party, multiple-party regime be representative?

Dr. Rowe: No, I can conceive of a one-party government or a virtual one-party government that is representative of the will of the people and has their support.

The Chairman: Where they have no alternative except to vote for the party?

Dr. Rowe: Where some of them do not really care about any alternative. You and I might care about that but some people do not.

The Chairman: I do not know how to classify a regime as representative or not. I know a great many regimes that are not like ours. But unless there is an active and violent revolution against it, and as long as it functions and is in control, I suppose that it is representative of the people. . . .

Dr. Rowe: Would you like me to illustrate what I am talking about on the basis of which I come to my conclusions as to the representative or nonrepresentative character of the Chinese Communist regime?

The Chairman: All right, yes. Would you do that, please, sir?

Dr. Rowe: I am sure you have heard of the Chinese commune system, the Communist Chinese commune system. . . .

Now, they went about it whole hog. They did not hesitate and they did not compromise and then went right down the line on it. They razed the villages to the ground, built up new dormitories, separated the husbands from the wives and the children from their parents, told the peasant he did not own anything, even the clothes on his back, could not have anybody cook his food for him, but ate in a communal kitchen. . . .

Now, why didn't this system work? And it didn't — it was a total flop: It didn't work because the Chinese peasant is, was and is, still the backbone of Chinese agriculture. It is what the agricultural economists call a highly labor intensive agricultural system, which means that you raise the crops up out of the ground by the sweat of your brow and you do not have any fancy machinery to do it with.

So you say, here is the instrumentality, the Chinese peasantry, and you tell these people, "For the good of something, the state and the future, you sacrifice everything. We don't give you anything."

This peasant then starts, as the Chinese always have, and hopefully always will, to ask the inevitable question, which is, "What in the world is there in this for me?" And the answer is so obvious that, of course, he does not refuse to march out to the field at dawn; he does not. All he does is to lean on the hoe, and when you get a lot of these peasants doing just that and not putting in any work, the system, the agricultural system, grinds slowly but inexorably to a halt. That is what happened. . . .

Now, at that point, it was not 90 percent of the people but all the peasants who were in active opposition and resistance to the regime. . . .

But these are just the symptoms. . . . we could go on all day enumerating the evidences of the general lack of real support on the part of the public in China for the regime. These are the types of things I am talking about. [pp. 526–531]

Testimony of Robert A. Scalapino

Dr. Scalapino: [Prepared Statement] The question is often asked, "Can we anticipate major changes in China in the near future?" If by major changes, one means an overthrow of the Communist Party, the chances seem to me remote, barring global war or some other major and unforeseeable crisis. This is not because dissidence is absent in China. We have no accurate method of measuring such dissidence, but I am inclined to believe that if one could measure the total spectrum of opposition — from the most passive "grumblers" to the active or potential "subversives" — it would be relatively high, despite the fact that certain groups have clearly benefited from the revolution and are grateful.

The point, however, is that Communists more than most modern rulers have mastered the science of power. Consequently, dissidence can be relatively high and still pose no serious threat to a regime such as that of Peking because the dissidents cannot find or develop an organizational outlet. . . . Thus if change is to occur in China, it is most likely to come through communism, and via top party circles. . . .

There is a growing struggle which in its essence poses the primitivism implicit in Maoist political-military doctrines against the professionalism that is implicit in the whole modernization program. Already, some military men have been placed in major opposition to party leaders. As it unfolds, however, this struggle will involve the bureaucracy in all of its aspects, civilian as well as military, and it is likely to be settled within the party, especially since most of the key disputants will either be in the top echelons of the party or have access to these. I cannot easily envisage a situation where the military and the party would enter into struggle as separate, self-contained units.

Thus, in all probability, the most meaningful question is that so frequently posed recently, "Will a younger generation of party leaders diverge considerably from the group of old Bolsheviks currently holding absolute power, so that the resulting changes, while taking place within the party, will nonetheless be profound and, in general, in the direction of realism and moderation?"

This is a crucial question, and one that cannot be answered with any complete certainty. My own belief is that such changes will occur, but that the critical element of timing will depend heavily upon both the internal and the external environment. Even under the best of circumstances, I am inclined to feel that the struggle for a more pragmatic, realistic, and moderate political elite in China will be long and arduous, extending considerably beyond one generation. But the rate and nature of change will certainly be affected by the degree to which a wide range of subtle external pressures and alternatives can be developed. [pp. 562–563]

4 ECONOMIC PERFORMANCE

Testimony of A. Doak Barnett

Mr. *Barnett:* [Prepared Statement] The economic performance of the Chinese Communist regime to date has been a very mixed one, characterized by some notable successes, some serious failures, and some basic unanswered questions. When the Chinese Communists first came to power they were impressively successful in bringing order out of economic chaos, and in initiating an ambitious development program. During their first five-year plan, under a Stalinist-type program, China's annual increase in GNP — about 6 or 7 percent — was as rapid or more rapid than that of any other important underdeveloped nation at the time. But the momentum of growth started to decline by 1957, the last year of the first plan — as a result of the lag in agricultural output, the steady increase in population, and the ending of Soviet credits.

And in 1958 Peking's leaders embarked on their radical and reckless Great Leap Forward and commune program, hoping to achieve the impossible by unprecedented political and ideological mobilization.

The failures of the Leap produced an economic crisis of major proportions in China, which lasted from 1959 through 1961. The result, in effect, was a Communist version of a great depression. It compelled the regime to abandon many of its most extreme policies and ambitious goals, and Peking redefined its economic policies to include some sensible elements, showing realism and pragmatism.

Emphasis was placed on the need to promote agriculture, various sorts of incentives were restored, needed food was imported from the West, major industrial projects were postponed, and in general more modest goals were adopted.

Since 1962 there has been a slow but steady recovery of both agricultural and industrial production in China, and today overall Chinese output is comparable to what it was just before the Leap — although it is still not that high in per capita terms. The primary stress on development agriculture [*sic*] continues, and its results, plus continuing grain imports, have greatly eased the food situation.

This year a new five-year plan, the third, has begun, and even though no details on the plan have yet been published, undoubtedly there is renewed growth in industry — although at a more gradual pace than in earlier years.

In any overall assessment of the Chinese economy since 1949, several things would have to be noted. The Communists have not yet converted China into a major industrial power, but they have begun to build a significant industrial base.

At one point, in 1960, steel output was claimed to be 18 million tons; production now is below peak capacity but is probably between 8 and 10 million tons. Moreover, since the regime decides how output will be used, current production fully supports the nation's military power and further industrialization. There has been no appreciable overall increase in living standards in China since 1949, but, except during the worst post-Leap years, the regime has met the population's minimum requirements, distributed available goods fairly equitably, and kept the economy running — a not insignificant accomplishment in China. [pp. 8–9]

Sen. Williams: What progress is being made by the Communist leadership to solve their food shortages and their food problems? How successful has that been?

Mr. Barnett: Well, since 1962, there has been a definite improvement; there was a very critical situation in 1959, 1960, and 1961. There was widespread malnutrition in China during those years. I think there was very little real outright starvation, because they have a fairly good method of distribution, fairly equitably, what they have got, but they spread thin what they had at that time, and there were three bad agricultural years, plus the very bad effects of the communes. And so their grain supply was extremely short, and there was widespread malnutrition.

Since 1962, the situation has improved a great deal. One does not now hear evidence of malnutrition. On the contrary, people coming out of China whom I talked to last year when I was in Hong Kong reported that the diet was reasonably good for most people. . . .

I would guess that agricultural output at the moment is — I don't know, this may be difficult to say — I was going to say output will keep up with population growth, but it is not now greatly above population growth.

The fact is that our data are pretty slim, and these estimates have to be based on all kinds of detective work, aimed at trying to piece together what limited data there are. But I would say the general picture is one of a reasonably stable situation in food supply, and slow, but steady improvement in domestic output. [p. 34]

Testimony of Alexander Eckstein

Dr. Eckstein: [Prepared Statement] In appraising the potency of economic instruments in the conduct of Chinese Communist foreign policy, it is important to start with a brief analysis of the present state of the mainland economy, its strengths and weaknesses, its accomplishments and its unresolved problems.

Undoubtedly the most fundamental and intractable problem facing economic policymakers in China is that of population and food. On the basis of highly fragmentary and rather unreliable data, mainland China's population is supposed to be growing at an average annual rate of 2 percent or more. As a result the population is increased annually by about 15 million. Maintaining such a rapidly growing population just at the prevailing standards of living entails heroic efforts. It requires an annual rate of growth in food supply of 2 to 3 percent; it places a heavy demand on investment resources for housing, school construction, hospitals, and other education, health, and welfare facilities.

This population has high birth rates and fairly high death rates — that is, it is a preponderantly young population with a high ratio of consumers to producers. These characteristics are conducive to high consumption and low saving. Furthermore, a sizable share of savings needs to be channeled into investment in social overhead rather than production facilities.

These relationships pose a series of dilemmas, which are common to all economies subject to acute population pressure. At the end of the first five-year plan period (1957), it seemed that China might be on the way to breaking out of this vicious circle of backwardness. Seen from the perspective of 1965 or 1966, one can be much less certain of this.

There is no doubt that the Chinese Communist leadership is fully conscious of the problem and is trying to attack it from two directions simultaneously. It has in recent years accorded high priority to agricultural development. At the same time, it has embarked on a program of family planning, thus far largely confined to the urban areas.

Present indications are that this two-pronged attack has produced some recovery and progress. However, unless there is a miraculous boon in the form of unusually good harvests or foreign aid on a large scale, further economic growth and advance in China may be expected to be significantly slower than in the 1950's. Correspondingly, the Chinese Communist vision of becoming a top-ranking industrial nation may have to be postponed for a long time to come.

This prospect could be altered if Communist China were to gain access to foreign credits or grants. In this respect, China is in a unique situation, for it is perhaps the only underdeveloped country today that has no long-term credits or foreign aid to draw upon. On the contrary, since 1955 it has been a net exporter of capital. These capital exports have been used to amortize the Soviet loans and to finance Chinese foreign aid programs. It would seem that in contributing to rising Sino-Soviet tensions, the Chinese Communist leadership must have chosen to buy increasing self-reliance and freedom of action in foreign affairs at the price of economic development at home.

China's development prospects could also be altered markedly by changes in domestic policy. In recent years, the Chinese Communists have pursued a prudent and more or less conservative economic policy — easing the tax and collection pressures on the peasantry, trying to foster a generally more favorable incentive system for agriculture, keeping the savings burden down, and channeling a large share of investment to agriculture and agriculture-supporting industries. However, this policy yields a pattern of resource allocation which runs strongly counter to the ideological and programmatic commitments of the leadership. It tends to produce a lower rate of investment and a lower rate of industrial growth. Therefore, the current economic policies are in many ways distasteful to the regime — so much so that they become a continuing source of tension between what the leadership desires and hopes for and what it considers possible and necessary. This tension may in turn tempt the leadership to resort once more to bold measures to break out of the vise [vice?] of backwardness. Such attempts could easily lead to another economic breakdown and crisis. Consequently, one of the most serious problems for the leadership is to curb its own sense of impatience. . . .

China's imports were crucial for the expansion of her industrial plant, the relief of her acute shortages of food after 1960, and the modernization of her defense establishment. During the period of the first five-year plan as a whole, about 20 to 40 percent — depending at what exchange rate the dollar figures for imports are converted to yuan — of the equipment component of investment was imported. In the absence of these imports, Communist China's economic growth might possibly have fallen from an average annual rate of about 7 percent to 3 to 5 percent. Moreover, a cessation of imports would have greatly retarded technological progress and modernization of the economy, most particularly of industry. It would almost certainly have stifled the development of the iron and steel, electric power, chemicals, and other technically complex industrial branches.

Since 1960 this type of import has greatly diminished in importance for the construction of new plants has been drastically curtailed. Because many industries were operating below capacity, imports of equipment were confined to those branches which have continued to expand throughout the depression, that is, chemicals and petroleum extraction and refining.

As capital goods imports diminished, food — particularly grain — imports gained greatly in importance. Although such imports have only increased China's total grain supply by 3 to 4 percent, they have greatly eased the distribution burden, reduced the collection pressures in the countryside, relieved the transport system of a heavy load, and provided the cities with a guaranteed food supply. As late as 1965, indications were that Chinese Communist policymakers and planners intended to continue importing grain for at least the next two to three years. Whether such imports will become a longer term feature of Chinese Communist trade policy is impossible to forecast at the present time. . . .

There is no doubt that imports played a crucial role in the modernization of the Chinese Communist military establishment. While there are no data on the quantity or value of Chinese military imports, some crude guesses about the relative importance of these purchases from abroad can be made on the basis of certain assumptions. In these terms it would seem that imports of military equipment and material constituted at least 20 to 40 percent of the total defense expenditure. In any case, the import component of defense was sizable enough to be of considerable significance regardless of what the precise figure may have been. [pp. 331–334]

The Chairman: Could you give us a little information on their trade with Japan. I notice you say they have mutually relaxed their regulations. They have acceded to the Japanese terms. Is this a substantial trade?

Dr. Eckstein: Yes. Trade with Japan has been now increasing very rapidly in the last two years. In 1964 it was more than doubled as compared to 1963, and it has increased again very much. . . . Since the Sino-Soviet break the Chinese have increasingly reoriented their trade toward the non-Communist world, and the principal beneficiary of this reorientation has been Japan.

The Chairman: Could you indicate about how large this is in dollars?

Dr. Eckstein: I think last year the total turnover was over $450 million. . . .

The Chairman: You mentioned foreign aid. How much do you estimate they gave in foreign aid?

Dr. Eckstein: This is a very interesting question because there is a very considerable gap between Chinese foreign aid extensions, commitments, promises, and actual deliveries. The totality of Chinese foreign aid commitments, both to Communist and non-Communist countries, through 1964 or 1965, is close to $2 billion cumulatively.

The Chairman: Yes.

Dr. Eckstein: Of this, over half was to Communist countries. Most of these commitments, that is, to North Korea, North Vietnam, and Albania primarily, have been met, with some temporary lag. On the other hand, not much more than 10 percent of the actual commitments to the non-Communist world have been met. . . .

The Chairman: Were these aid grants or loans?

Dr. Eckstein: This varies. They are both grants and loans. To some countries only grants, to some countries it is only loans, to other countries yet it is a mixture of grants and loans. Some of the loans are completely interest-free; other loans carry a low or nominal rate of interest. The terms partly depend on what the situation is in that particular country as far as U.S. aid programs and, particularly, Russian aid programs are concerned. The Chinese tried to compete with the Russians in Africa, particularly, and in many cases they tried to outbid the Russians as far as terms are concerned. They are not capable of outbidding the Russians as far as levels of aid are concerned, but they try to outbid them as far as the terms of aid are concerned.

The Chairman: Would it be fair to say they are about 50–50, grants and loans? I do not think it is very significant, but I am curious.

Dr. Eckstein: I would say I would have to check on this, but my recollection would be it would be roughly about 70-percent loans and about 30-percent grants, something like that.

The Chairman: Could you indicate very briefly the nature of the goods? Were they mostly consumer goods or capital goods?

Dr. Eckstein: Well, they take a variety of forms. For instance, I just recently came back from Nepal, where the Chinese have a foreign aid program. In Nepal they are building a road, building a road from Katmandu to the Chinese border, which is now jeepable, and you can [go] from Katmandu to Lhasa in fourteen hours by jeep. This, of course, is a road of very great strategic and military significance. They are also building a warehouse in Nepal, for instance. They are going to probably build some other roads.

In Yemen they built a road — to Cambodia they have exported textile plants. Thus, Chinese aid has gone into roadbuilding, some capital goods, and also some manufactured consumer goods. . . .

Sen. Morse: You say . . . that China has been importing a considerable amount of military equipment and material. You suggest a figure of maybe 20 to 40 percent of their total defense expenditure comes from that route. Could you tell us two things: First, what countries have they been getting that military equipment from, and what is the nature of the equipment.

Dr. Eckstein: Well, on the first: prior to 1960, most of it — this statement refers to the situation prior to 1960 — if not all of this, came from the Soviet Union and from other East European countries.

What the particular items were I would not know in detail. I could only speculate but, of course, Senator, some items we know about. There were some planes, some MIG's for instance. There was artillery, airplanes of various kinds. That is, these were weapons and materiel designed to help the modernization of the Chinese ground forces.

There was also a certain amount of assistance by the Soviets prior to 1960 for the development of China's peaceful atomic capabilities which, of course, the Chinese could also use for eventual production of nuclear devices. . . .

Sen. Morse: Does China suffer from any oil shortages as the result of the Soviet embargo or does she have a sufficient supply of domestic oil, or is she getting oil from other sources?

Dr. Eckstein: Prior to 1960 the Chinese already possessed their own manufacturing and extraction facilities and capabilities in petroleum, but they were not self-sufficient. They depended quite heavily on the Soviets.

Fortunately for them a new set of oilfields were discovered in Manchuria, and this greatly increased their crude oil extraction, so that they became fully self-sufficient in crude oil, and then in recent years also self-reliant in some of the refined products. Thus their petroleum imports have been falling year by year. I think, in 1965, there were still some petroleum imports from the Soviet Union, but much less than before. . . .

Sen. Morse: When I was over there in Hong Kong I saw great exportation of food supplies out of Red China. We went down to the railroad yards and saw the trains come in just laden with food, and we know she exports a great deal of rice. Would you say that the main reason for exporting rice is for foreign exchange purposes?

Dr. Eckstein: Actually China's rice exports are not all that large. In the past the highest level in any one year was 1.6 million tons. I think it then dropped during the crisis to negligible levels. It has been recovering since.

As you suggest, the principal reason for these exports is that if you trade rice for wheat, you have a foreign exchange gain there; that is, rice carries a higher price in the world markets than wheat. If you can substitute wheat for rice and export rice, then you have made a foreign exchange gain, and I think this is part of the explanation. . . .

Sen. Case: On the first page of your statement . . . you speak of the result of the high rates of investment being the great expansion of the Chinese war-devastated plant. Where did they get the capital to do this?

Dr. Eckstein: Well, as far as capital goods are concerned, in the fifties these were obtained from the Soviet Union and from Eastern Europe. In effect the Soviet Union and also some East European countries exported complete plants, complete factories, turnkey projects, to China.

As far as the financing of it is concerned the preponderant bulk of it came from internal savings, largely generated by agriculture. That is what we would call involuntary or forced savings.

Sen. Case: You mean they squeezed it right out?

Dr. Eckstein: Yes. And then a certain part of it, a small part of it, came from Soviet loans.

Sen. Case: Is the rate of investment and rate of forced savings comparable to anything we know anything about or in other parts of the world?

Dr. Eckstein: Toward the late fifties, for which we have data, investment reached about 25 percent, that is gross investment. This is higher than it is in most Western countries, but it is not unprecedented. It is not higher than it is in Japan, and it is comparable to that of the Soviet Union.

It is almost certain that in recent years it has been significantly less than that. How much less is difficult to say. The estimate of those of us who are trying to study this is that it is probably now somewhere around 10 to 15 percent.

Sen. Case: Now that the pressure has been eased.

Dr. Eckstein: Right.

Sen. Case: Is this because of their desire to ease it or because they feel it is wise to ease it?

Dr. Eckstein: I think it is because they feel it is wise and necessary to ease it to permit agriculture to recover.

Sen. Case: Not because they like the peasants but because they want the agriculture.

Dr. Eckstein: That is right. . . .

Sen. Carlson: Well, of course, I assume China is like other countries. Unless they do deficit financing they have to depend on the money they have, and if they are expanding their nuclear, military operations very extensively, which are quite expensive, I am sure, they are going to have to parcel out their money, whether it is going to go to fertilizer plants or other improvements for the production of food or to build military machines or as you say, you say they have not expanded the steel production. That also is very important in an industrial economy. I can see they might have some problems. My thought is can we expect any great improvement in China in the next ten to fifteen years?

Dr. Eckstein: I think you are pointing to a very real problem, sir, that, in a sense, they are trying to do now three things simultaneously. They would like to improve the economy, continue developing it at a fairly rapid pace. They would like to develop an atomic capability, they want to continue to modernize their conventional military establishment.

Whether they are able to do all these things I personally tend to doubt. I think this is one of the reasons why their rate of investment has been reduced as compared to the 1950's. [pp. 339–356]

5   MILITARY CAPABILITIES

Testimony of Samuel B. Griffith
and Morton H. Halperin

Gen. Griffith: [Prepared Statement] The armed forces of the Chinese People's Republic stand today at an overall strength of some 2.5 million. The vast majority of men wearing the uniform of the PLA [People's Liberation Army] serve in the ground forces, in infantry divisions. Estimates as to the number of these divisions vary from a low of 105 to a high of about 120. If a figure of 110 be presumed, there are approximately 1,800,000 now serving in the infantry arm.

The current PLA infantry division is well balanced in terms of organic weapons, but is short on service, maintenance, medical and communication personnel. As yet, the divisions lack sufficient motor transport to move them or to keep lower echelons continuously supplied in fluid situations.

For motive power, the PLA's infantry must still rely on the legs of its tough soldiers. As marching standards are far more rigorous than in Western armies, shortage of motor transport is a matter of less concern. Still, despite their remarkable march capability, Chinese infantry formations would be at a grave disadvantage in rapidly moving situations in reasonably open terrain where cross-country mobility of tracked-vehicle task forces would greatly exceed theirs.

On the other hand, in tropical jungles or mountainous country they could exploit proven cross-country march capability against a road-bound enemy. . . .

The PLA's Armored Command is small, but its four to five armored divisions are formidably equipped with 80 to 100 Soviet model T-34 and T-54 tanks (or Chinese copies) plus a number of JS-2 heavies. The T-54, a well-designed, high-performance medium tank, mounts a high-velocity 100 millimeter gun and has excellent cross-country capability. The JS-2, a 50-ton low-silhouette, widetrack tank, carries a 122 millimeter high-velocity gun, is well armored and has good cross-country performance.

Problems of replacement and maintenance of this and other modern equipment of Soviet design plagued the PLA during 1960 and 1961. Whether or not Chinese industry can yet replace obsolescing tanks, or even provide sufficient spare parts to keep what the PLA has in operable condition is questionable.

In early 1962, the MAC [Military Affairs Commission] directed the PLA to establish and operate its own spare-parts replacement program. Obviously, this was one of the areas critically affected by the withdrawal of Soviet aid. As the Chinese have no doubt discovered, this problem cannot be solved by traditional handicraft methods and "backyard" operations. The need to maintain aircraft, motor vehicles, armor, self-propelled artillery and other heavy and complicated equipment of Soviet origin obviously puts a very serious strain on Chinese industry, which must also simultaneously satisfy many other equally important requirements. One may conjecture that purchase abroad of heavy equipment such as locomotives, road machinery (one list of equipment wanted named excavators, rock crushers, small, medium and heavy tractors and bulldozers) is in part designed to release personnel and plant for the manufacture of airframes, armored vehicles, artillery and military prime movers.

The personnel strength of the air force can be approximated only by using some sort of a data measure which we shall call "crewing levels." If we assume that 60 to 70 officers and men are required to crew one aircraft we arrive at a figure (based on 2,500 combat aircraft) of 150,000 to 175,000.

The latest for naval strength — 135,000 — may be somewhat low. The navy supports a small air arm. Presumably, this component would be employed in coastal, short and medium range overwater reconnaissance and mine laying. There is also a small landing force.

In estimating the strength of ground force supporting arms and services we are again in the cloudy realm of uncertainty and speculation. There are, we know, a small number of lightly equipped mountain divisions at a manning level of 8,000 to 10,000 and border guard formations. These units are well equipped and demonstrated their combat capabilities in October and November 1962 against the Indians. In the North East Frontier Agency (NEFA) the Chinese moved rapidly and executed combat maneuvers with skill and precision.

Additionally, there are a number of security police units deployed throughout the country. No estimates can be made of their strength. There are several cavalry divisions, possibly two airborne divisions and some separate brigades and regiments. It is probable that these special units are trained in guerrilla operations.

The status of the PLA's air force is a major enigma at the present time. What was described in 1952 by Gen. Hoyt Vanderberg, then Chief of Staff, U.S. Air Force, as a "formidable air force" has obsolesced critically in the past fourteen years.

During the Korean war, MIG 15's and 17's formed the bulk of the Chinese Air Force. At present, the MIG 17 is the standard interceptor.

A few — possibly as many as one hundred — MIG 19's were acquired from the Russians prior to 1960. There have been unconfirmed reports of PLA interceptors similar to MIG 21's sighted by Nationalist air patrols south of Shantung Province. There was another such report of MIG 21's in the *Washington Post* this morning, I believe, sighted on air fields in North Vietnam.

If these reports are correct — and we would be prudent to assume they are — a limited capability to produce airframes, jet engines, weapons, and control systems has been developed. One must not underestimate the Chinese determination to create a modern jet air force.

An important step toward this goal was taken in December 1964 when the 7th Ministry of Machine Building was established. The appointment of a very senior office [officer?], Wang P'ing-chang, former deputy commander of the air force, as Minister, is significant. But how deeply the Chinese will commit themselves to a manned interceptor program cannot now be estimated.

To date, surface-to-air missiles (SAM) deployed in North Vietnam have not proven particularly effective. According to a good source — Mr. Khrushchev — the Russians "gave" the Chinese "some rockets" prior to 1960. It is reasonable to speculate these "rockets" were SAM and air-to-air types, and that working model guidance systems were provided. As early as 1951 the Chinese were operating excellent Soviet-made radar-controlled antiaircraft equipment in Korea, and heavy concentrations of AA have been spotted for defense of critical areas in North Vietnam.

It is a reasonable assumption, therefore, that the early warning and air-defense system designed to protect critical target areas in China proper is fairly effective, and that its continuing development is receiving a very high priority.

Peking announced the shooting down the other day of a U.S. — they said it was a U.S. — nonmanned aircraft, presumably overflying China for photographic purposes or to gather weather data.

The air force is generally credited with about 400 to 500 Russian IL-28, known as "Beagle," twin-jet bombers. This must still be considered a very good aircraft. The Chinese have also a few TU-4 (Bull) four-engined propeller bombers. (Some of these are reported to be configured for long-range reconnaissance.) This Soviet copy of the U.S. B-29 of World War II has long been obsolete in Western air forces. This slow and highly vulnerable aircraft has little strategic value except as a possible launching platform for "standoff" missiles or a fueling plane. . . .

If there are any specially trained amphibious troops in the ground forces, they (unlike the U.S. Marines) receive no publicity. It has been reported that the navy has a relatively small landing force. Possibly the function of this force is to operate landing ships and craft, provide underwater demolition personnel, "beach-jumpers," and similar specialists. The existence of such a force has been reported but cannot be confirmed.

Shortly after the Korean war the People's Republic began to pay some attention to naval requirements, and with Soviet assistance and advice a rudimentary naval force was established. From the first, emphasis was laid on submarines and coastal defense craft.

How many long-range diesel-powered "G"- and "W"-class submarines the Soviets sold the Chinese is unknown; estimates are in the range of thirty to forty, of which at least one "G"-class boat has been identified. This class boat is equipped with three launching tubes, so that it is capable of firing missiles from a submerged position. I do not agree with my friend Hanson Baldwin of the *New York Times* that one such boat affects the balance of power in the Pacific. But I would agree that five to six such boats, equipped with nuclear-armed ballistic missiles, would definitely do so. The type of fleet I conceive the Chinese to be constructing, together with the missiles described, would provide them with a credible deterrent, probably by 1972, if not before.

A conventional submarine force of the size postulated would pose a substantial threat to traffic in the far Pacific from Korea to Indonesia. A capability for some of these boats to surface launch short-range missiles (say 300 to 400 miles), is probably already developed.

The submarine force described would thus constitute a respectable — and less vulnerable — variant of the French *force de frappe*. Further — and perhaps unexpectedly rapid — growth of a sophisticated submarine fleet must be assessed as an almost certain development for the near future.

For defense of coastal waters the Chinese rely on high-speed motor torpedo boats and defensive mining. The U.S. Navy discovered to its dismay in the fall of 1950 at Wosan that Russian mines and mining techniques were extremely good, and prudent assumption must be that the Chinese learned from the Russians both how to manufacture mines of various types and how to sow them in effective patterns.

One aspect of an amphibious capability has been mentioned. The Reds inherited a few landing ships and craft from the Nationalists, I think in all, maybe sixty. Press photographs have shown landing ship tank (LST), landing craft tank (LCT), and landing craft vehicle and personnel (LCVP). Amphibious ships and craft of these types are relatively cheap and not too difficult to produce in quantity, and could be augmented by motor junk and towed barges.

Taiwan is the obvious target for an amphibious operation but air superiority over the Strait and the landing areas would have to be guaranteed. Given the present state of the PLA's air force, such a capability seems remote. . . .

As approximately 6,500,000 males reach the age of eighteen every year, the PLA can afford to be selective, and to apply very rigid standards in respect to the mental, physical, psychological, and political attributes of prospective servicemen. As a matter of principle, the PLA prefers

to induct young men only from families with poor peasant and proletarian backgrounds. The party presumes, probably correctly, that this
will preserve the ideological purity of its armed forces.

The same family background criterion is applied to aspirants to
"leader" (officer) status. Young men with bourgeois or landlord parents
are systematically excluded from opportunity to become leaders. In this
manner the party hopes to create a leadership corps which is "class
conscious," animated with revolutionary zeal, dedicated, obedient, and
of unquestioned loyalty to it.

The context of the martialized life provides the party opportunity
to observe an individual's career in its children's and youth's organizations and in lower and middle schools, and to spot those who tend to be
too individualistic, cynical, or skeptical, or who do not otherwise enthusiastically conform to its conceptual and behavioral norms. With equal
facility the party can distinguish progressives at an early age. Thus the
entire organizational structure may be seen as consisting of a series of
built-in filters. . . .

In its propaganda the party consistently emphasizes that the primary
mission of the PLA is to repel imperialist aggressors and to foil the
nefarious plots of the Chiang bandits. The theme of defense of the
motherland is repeated in practically every speech made by a member
of the military hierarchy. There is no reason to believe that the PLA
would not loyally respond to any challenge directed against the Chinese
mainland.

Its behavior in a frustrating and prolonged combat situation outside
China's borders would naturally depend on many factors, notably the
degree of control the party can exert. A primary objective in any combat
situation must be to erode the party's mechanism in the army. Until
this happens the PLA should be expected to perform in peripheral areas
as creditably as it did in Korea.

The party has admitted that about 5 percent of the population follows its lead only with the greatest reluctance, and that another un-
named but significant percentage consists of "wavering elements."
Selective induction and promotion processes will, it obviously hopes,
exclude these unreliable elements from ever attaining a dangerous foothold in the PLA. But some termites are already in the woodwork, according to General Lo [Lo Jui-ch'ing], who warned that they were infiltrating
the PLA, "trying to grab the official seats from us (the staunch party
men) in certain fields."

It is statements such as this which lead some people to question the
loyalty of the PLA. On Taiwan it is one of the articles of faith that the
PLA is only superficially loyal. But facts do not lend any support to this
view. In the great exodus during the spring of 1962, over 125,000 main-
landers came into the Crown Colony of Hong Kong (including the
"new territories"). As far as is known, not one of these was a serving

officer or soldier. Some few were demobilized ex-officers or noncommissioned officers, several of whom had, so their questioners discovered, been dismissed from the PLA. Surely, had dissatisfaction been as rampant in the armed forces as Taiwan sources insist it is, a great many serving soldiers would have thrown away their rifles, put on peasants' clothing, and crossed over. The brief Sino-Indian border war also refutes the claim advanced in Taiwan. There, no Chinese soldier "turned his hat around." The Indians took one prisoner. He was lost and blundered into an Indian outpost.

Despite huge offers of money, coupled with promises of complete immunity and good treatment, the Nationalists have induced only a few Red flyers to desert to them. Red pilots are under surveillance which would naturally be more strict than that exercised over their colleagues in the ground or naval forces. And — although there are no figures to confirm this — one may suspect that the great majority of air force "leaders" and senior enlisted men are party members. Nevertheless, if a trusted pilot planned to desert with his aircraft he would find means of doing so.

What I am trying to suggest here is that we should not be deluded by the hope that in a crisis the PLA leadership would necessarily issue a Latin American type pronunciamento. The possibility seems remote. The party did away expeditiously with Marshal P'eng Teh-huai in in 1959. P'eng was one of the three army men at the top of the heap. The PLA is, in my opinion, a highly motivated, loyal, and dedicated instrument. [pp. 275–283]

Dr. Halperin: [Prepared Statement] Since 1946 the Chinese have been concerned about American possession of atomic weapons and have attempted to calculate the damage that the United States could do to China with these weapons. When Mao in 1957 in a widely quoted statement stated privately that 300 million Chinese would be killed in a nuclear war, he was apparently reporting the results of a calculation and not expressing any lack of concern that such an attack would seriously damage the mainland of China.

Their perception of the damage which would be done to them in nuclear war has led the Chinese to a determination not to provoke a nuclear attack on China. While the Chinese have been and are prepared to risk such an attack when the survival of the Communist regime in China was at stake, they have attached a very high priority to avoiding a nuclear war. In short, there is no reason to believe that the Chinese want a nuclear war or are not as determined as any political leadership to avoid a nuclear attack if possible. Nevertheless, as I have said, the Chinese believe there is a real possibility growing out of an attack in the Vietnam conflict.

Given their current military preparedness, the Chinese see no way of blunting the initial American first strike which they expect will destroy Chinese military installations, including their nuclear production facilities and industrial urban centers. The Chinese expect the United States to follow this attack with a ground invasion designed to conquer and control China.

There has apparently been considerable debate between the Chinese military and the top political leadership about how to deal with such an invasion. The strategy proposed by the military and rejected, it appears, by the political leaders would have relied on professional military forces to attempt to meet and destroy the invasion. Chairman Mao has preferred to rely on the same strategy of "people's war" which he urges on other groups of insurrectionists. If the Chinese expect an imminent nuclear attack, the political leaders of the country will retreat from the main cities and return to rural areas. The People's Liberation Army similarly will retreat from population and industrial centers and withdraw to the interior of the country.

The people's militia, which is now undergoing intensive military and ideological training, will be expected to bear the brunt of the invasion and to engage in "people's war" against the American forces. In these circumstances the Chinese believe the most important thing is to instill an ideological fervor in the Chinese people so that they will engage in guerrilla activities against the American troops. The Chinese hope that if they can make this strategy credible it will succeed in deterring an American nuclear strike by making clear that the United States will not be able to invade and control China.

While they are confident that this strategy could succeed in enabling the Chinese Communist Party to survive and to begin slowly to rebuild, the Chinese place far too high a price on their ideological, political, and economic progress to be willing to take any actions that would provoke an American attack.

The intense Chinese drive for an operational nuclear capability is, I believe, related to their longstanding fear of an American nuclear attack. At a fundamental level, the Chinese desire for nuclear weapons is simply a logical extension of their intention to become a great power. However, the priority given to the effort, the resources devoted to it is, I believe, attributable to their belief that they need to develop a deterrent against American nuclear attack. The development of such a capability will leave the Chinese freer to press their efforts to establish their hegemony in Asia and to give such support as they can to "people's wars."

In addition, the Chinese believe that they will get some increased prestige in the third world and within the Communist bloc from their development of nuclear weapons. [pp. 285–287]

The Chairman: General Griffith, I know it is a very complicated subject, but would you compare the relative military strength of China and the United States. Have you attempted that?

Gen. Griffith: Well, sir, I would like to preface what I say by the remark that except in regional terms China is, to use her own expression "a paper tiger" and is likely to remain one for, in my opinion, probably five or six years; let us say, in terms of projecting power other than nuclear, perhaps a decade or perhaps more, probably two decades.

It isn't really possible to make comparisons between the Chinese military power and our own. We are, without any question, the greatest military power in the world; we have a tremendous flexibility in our forces. This is evident in the fact that we conduct the type of operations we can in Vietnam and support them across thousands and thousands of miles.

The Chinese did not even have the capability to support a sustained operation in the North East Frontier Agency or in Ladakh in 1962. I would say in summary that, well, I would hate to put that statistically, but I would say it is in a ratio of 10 to 1, Mr. Chairman. [p. 289]

Sen. Morse: You said that the Red Chinese military forces have two and a half million men. What do you think they would be capable of mobilizing in case they should involve themselves in a land war with us on the China mainland?

Gen. Griffith: Well, Senator, I cannot conceive of us getting involved in a war on the China mainland in conventional terms. I believe General MacArthur testified many years ago that anyone who advocated such a thing or took such a step should have his head examined. I believe those were the words he used, and I agree. I did not always agree with General MacArthur's statements, but I certainly agreed with that one.

Sen. Morse: It seems to me it is obvious. But I cannot dismiss the danger of our becoming involved in a land war with China even on the basis of your testimony this morning, if we follow a course of action that would cause her to move against us. We would have to meet her on the land because I think our administration has made perfectly clear to this committee and others that we cannot defeat her with bombing. We can do great damage to her, but if we get involved in a war with her, we will have to meet her on the land. I think it is also well known publicly that within our plans toward China we have manpower forces contemplated to move in if we get involved in a war with her.

My question, based upon that possibility, and I think it is a real possibility, is how many men can she mobilize, and the next part of my question is how many men will we be able to mobilize to meet her in a land war in Asia?

Gen. Griffith: Well, Senator, if I may just preface my attempt to answer that with a reiteration of my statement that I would not anticipate this at all; that is, the commitment of American ground forces to the Chinese mainland. But I will make it hypothetical. If, then, they were to be committed, I think that the People's Liberation Army is eminently loyal to the party. I do not think that we could for a minute hope for defections. I think that the People's Militia would be very effective. This numbers something — of the militia — numbers something around 10 million of whom at least half are ex-servicemen who have been demobbed. I think this militia would probably be very effective.

Again I say I am discussing this, Senator, purely from a hypothetical point of view, because I cannot see an American strategy that would conceive of an invasion of the Asian land mass by our own forces.

Sen. Morse: Could I ask, along this line of questions, Dr. Halperin, suppose we supported, as there are those who would have us support, the Nationalist Chinese Army on the mainland of China. Do you think they would be welcomed with internal support from within China, from the population?

Dr. Halperin: I think there is no reason at all to think they would receive any support at all from the mainland. [pp. 301–302]

Sen. Church: General, in response, I think, to questions put to you by Senator Morse, you indicated it would be a kind of folly to intervene on the mainland of China with American troops in the event of a war between our two countries. Should that kind of war come about, do you think that it could be finished by bombing alone, even nuclear bombing?

Gen. Griffith: No; I do not. I do not think the war would be finished. The Chinese just simply would not surrender and we would still be faced with this gargantuan task of going in and occupying Asia, and if it is costing us $10 billion a year now for the effort we are putting forth in South Vietnam, one must presume it would cost us, well, twenty times that much.

Sen. Church: And if I may ask, Professor Halperin, because your statement mentions Chinese strategy, in such an eventuality as being one of falling back on guerrilla tactics, wouldn't that mean we would have to undertake to occupy, and then attempt to pacify, all of China?

Dr. Halperin: I think that is right. We should not expect, as the General suggested, that they are going to surrender to us and let us come in and peacefully occupy the country. [p. 308]

Testimony of Alexander Eckstein

Sen. Morse: Let us assume that the war did start and China did move into the war. Then, as the economic expert that you are, would you give us an estimate as to the degree to which China could economically fight that war within her own country, and to what extent she could fight it for a prolonged period of time? Would she continue to fight or do you think if we moved in with all the war power we are capable of pouring on her she would surrender?

Dr. Eckstein: I find it very difficult to visualize an all-out war between the United States and China. I hope that neither side is seriously contemplating this as a possibility. But if you posed this, let us say, as a theoretical or hypothetical contingency, I would imagine if it should ever come to a point of total conflict between China and the United States, that the Chinese would fight in a very determined way, that they would try to mobilize the total population and would probably have the support of most of their population regardless of whether they are Communists or not; that they would be able to mobilize all of the nationalistic and patriotic appeals, at least for a while; that they would probably try to fight a defensive war in which they would, in a sense, maximize their capabilities and minimize their disadvantages; try to fight a land war while we would probably try to fight a naval and air war and, of course, it would be presumptuous of me to predict what the outcome would be. I think it would be a disaster for us even if we win.

Sen. Morse: You see because I do not share your views that this is not a very real possibility, I think that is exactly what we are leading into if we continue to escalate the war in Vietnam.

Suppose that we wreaked this devastation on China. Have you given any thought as to whether or not we would have to maintain large forces in China after her capitulation, assuming that she capitulated, to police and maintain order and maintain our control in China for a good many years to come?

Dr. Eckstein: Well, I should imagine that kind of a contingency would involve a very similar type of thing as what the Japanese got involved in in China, and I think it would be an endless thing. [pp. 364–365]

6   GOALS AND MOTIVES OF CHINESE POLICY

Testimony of A. Doak Barnett

Mr. Barnett: [Prepared Statement] In examining Peking's general foreign policy, the first thing to note is that China's leaders obviously have very ambitious long-term goals. Moved by intense nationalism, they aim to build a strong base of power at home and to strengthen China's security; they also hope to recover what they consider to be "lost territories" (including Taiwan); and they are determined to play the role of a major power on the world stage.

At the present time, they view the United States as the major obstacle and threat to many of their aims and interests — and call, therefore, for the removal of American power from Asia — but they also regard the Soviet Union at present as a serious obstacle to Chinese aspirations and therefore compete with it, too, whenever, and wherever feasible.

As first generation revolutionary leaders, and true believers in the Maoist version of Marxism-Leninism, Peking's leaders are also dedicated to the promotion of revolutionary struggles, especially in the underdeveloped world. Their public pronouncements now tend to concentrate on this aim and in at least some areas, such as Vietnam, they are prepared to give significant support to revolutionary forces, even though they have avoided direct Chinese military intervention.

While it is important to recognize Peking's ambitious goals, it is equally important to note that, on the basis of available evidence and Communist China's performance to date, the Chinese Communists do not appear to think primarily in terms of spreading their influence through direct military and territorial expansion; they appear to recognize the limits to their capabilities for military action outside of China's borders; they have usually been quite realistic in assessing the power balance in concrete situations; they have generally been calculating and even cautious in avoiding military "adventurism" and limiting their risks; they have tended to think in long-range terms about their most ambitious goals; and they have repeatedly been flexible and pragmatic (at least until recently) in adapting their strategy and tactics to fit changing situations in pursuit of their short-run goals. [p. 10]

Sen. Sparkman: Does the question of additional living room have anything to do with China's movements? I am thinking now of reports that

80

we have heard from time to time of trouble between China and Russia on the north; China and India on the south. Is it an effort to push out, to get more room?

Mr. Barnett: My own personal view is frankly no. I don't think so.

Sen. Sparkman: In both directions?

Mr. Barnett: I do not think the Chinese Communists are thinking in terms of territorial expansion to solve their domestic problems. Where they have exerted strong border pressures, these have been in areas where China, from Peking's point of view, has had some kind of territorial claims, and I see no evidence myself that the Chinese are thinking in terms of general territorial military expansionism.

If — and this is very "iffy," since as I have just said I do not believe that there is evidence that this is the basis for their policy — but if they were to think in terms of expansion for population reasons, or because of food problems, I find it very hard to conceive that this pressure could be north, for a whole variety of reasons. This would involve a direct challenge to the power of the Soviet Union, that is obviously now, and will be for a long time, much more powerful than China. Beyond that, I don't think that most of the territory in the north is attractive to Chinese agriculture, for example. So that if there were any such pressures they would be to the south rather than to the north.

But I see no evidence that this is a basic motivation behind Chinese policy, and I don't think it is likely to be in foreseeable future.

Sen. Sparkman: And that would apply to southeast Asia as well?

Mr. Barnett: Yes, that is what I referred to by south. . . .

Sen. Hickenlooper: Mr. Barnett, I think your discussion this morning has been quite comprehensive and certainly very interesting. I would like to ask you, if a definition or an outline can be given in a few words, what you think about the overall basic philosophy and motives of the present regime in China, possibly differentiating from the characteristic different attitude of the Chinese people. Would you say the present regime is an inward-looking program devoted to more intensive nationalism within its own borders or do you say that it is influenced strongly by expansionist policies such as, let's say, the world conquest theory of international communism? What are they trying to do? I know this is not an easy question to answer in one sentence.

Mr. Barnett: No, it is a very complex question and Chinese policy is a very complex mixture, I think, of elements that play on the Chinese leaders in their thinking about the world.

I would not say that they are inward-looking. If I were to contrast them with traditional regimes, I think traditional Chinese regimes tended in many respects to be inward-looking. As long as the Chinese Empire, as they traditionally conceived it, was filled out, then the tendency was to keep contacts with the outside world to a minimum.

I would say that the ideological component of the Chinese Communist view of the world leads them to be very much outward-looking. If I could just pursue that a moment.

Sen. Hickenlooper: Yes, go ahead.

Mr. Barnett: But you used the term "world conquest." Now this can have many meanings, I think, in many different people's minds but I do not think the Chinese Communists are outward-looking in the sense of old-fashioned military conquest. I think that they feel that the world is going through a revolutionary process. I think that they, in some respects, are very sensitive to changes that are going on in the world. In some respects, [they] overestimate and misestimate changes [that] are going on in the world. But projecting from their own revolutionary experience in China, as they look on the world, they see actual or potential revolutionary situations in a great many areas, and they feel that they should support these revolutions but that the term support ——

Sen. Hickenlooper: Well, to that purpose?

Mr. Barnett: Well, I think they are strongly motivated by the desirability of a Communist world as they would see it. But in terms of their concrete ability and willingness to support revolutions, they think primarily in terms of giving moral support, giving ideological leadership, of encouraging struggles.

Incidentally in the Lin Piao statement that has been cited many times, one of the messages that I think is overlooked often, is that they stressed to the Vietnamese, to the North Vietnamese, and the Vietcong, that their revolution was important, that China's path pointed the way, but that they had to be self-reliant — and don't rely on concrete external support. I think, in effect, one thing they were saying to the Vietnamese in this speech was, "This is an important revolution, keep it up, but you have got to do it yourself essentially." . . .

Sen. Hickenlooper: Do you think the rapidly expanding population in China on the mainland, and the problems that it creates so far as food is concerned might strongly motivate them to try to get control of the rice bowl in south Asia?

Mr. Barnett: I don't.

Sen. Hickenlooper: To augment their food?

Mr. Barnett: I must say that the population question in China is one of the great conundrums, and it is very hard to see what is going to happen. They have introduced a birth control program, but there is very little evidence that it has had much impact in the rural areas. It is having some impact in urban areas. I think they are aware now of the population problem, will be working to try to get it under some control, but I think one has to recognize that their ability to cut down their population growth rapidly is probably limited and, therefore, population is going to grow fairly rapidly for sometime to come.

But there is no indication — that is all I will say — to date there is no indication, that they are thinking in lebensraum terms of getting territory in which their population could go, or in which they would have a kind of breadbasket. Looking at the dimensions of the problem, there is no doubt that southeast Asia is of some marginal importance, actually and potentially, to them in food terms, but it is marginal.

China's overall food output now is about 186 million tons. I don't call to mind immediately the total output in southeast Asia, but I think if my memory is right at the peak its exportable surplus was perhaps 3 or 4 million tons. This 3 or 4 million tons could be a significant margin in relation to the food problem in China, but it is a marginal one. But physical, territorial control of southeast Asia is not a prerequisite for developing relationships in which China could benefit from southeast Asia's food surplus. She is as you know now, importing 4 million-plus, 4 or 5 million, tons of grain a year, largely from Canada, Australia, and so on.

I think over the long run, I would expect the Chinese to want to be an importer of grain and food from southeast Asia. But I see no indication that there are compulsions to establish direct territorial control over the area for this. [pp. 23–27]

Testimony of John K. Fairbank

Sen. Hickenlooper: [What] is the motivating drive of the leaders of Red China?

Dr. Fairbank: I think that we have in this country studied their words — we have had many people working many hours for many years on what they put out and what they say. And we try to deduce from that what are their motives and intentions, what makes them tick. I think we have led ourselves astray by looking at the words and not studying Chinese history, and this is an ex parte statement from a Chinese historian, of course: You need more Chinese history if you are going to deal with the Chinese.

The point is that they are using words which sound like and are in many ways identical with those of the international Communist movement, which they join and in which they believe. . . .

Sen. Hickenlooper: [With] all the problems they have at home, they have found it convenient and apparently necessary from their viewpoint to send thousands of people, especially to the underdeveloped countries, to either become proselytizers, or what have you, for the international Communist cause. For example, Africa where they have sent people to each state to subvert the governments, if possible. They have sent them to Cuba, they have sent them, in fact, to most of the developing states so far as I know. That is expansion to me which indicates a militancy along that line.

Dr. Fairbank: On that, I think, if you balance up the internal activity with the external, you will find that they spend very little of their attention on external affairs.

Suppose you have a quarter of the human race and send out a few thousand people. We have got several millions abroad with only one-sixteenth of the human race. In other words, the comparison is always in their favor when we are talking about expansion and troops abroad and all such things.

Sen. Hickenlooper: Yes; I understand the comparison in numbers. [pp. 116–118]

The Chairman: Have the Chinese been successful in their external adventures in creating other countries in their own image, in Africa or Latin America, Cuba?

Dr. Fairbank: They have been successful in what we call the Chinese culture area, that is, the countries like North Korea and North Vietnam which are next door to them.

The Chairman: Outside of that?

Dr. Fairbank: Outside of that they have really fallen on their faces recently. It is amazing how they have stubbed their toes in so many places.

The Chairman: Could you, for the record, name them, you know most of them.

Dr. Fairbank: The Afro-Asian Conference idea, where they wanted to dominate it and throw out the Russians, backfired. There were several African countries where Chou En-lai came on a great mission of goodwill and made speeches saying, "We colored people must stick together and you also must have your social revolution." Since they had just become new nations they took this amiss.

The Chairman: Yes.

Dr. Fairbank: And then there is Indonesia where they made an egregious error in apparently backing the Communist effort.

The Chairman: In Ghana most recently, Ghana is most recent. They thought they had a foothold in Ghana, didn't they?

Dr. Fairbank: Yes, and the same in Cuba. Now, the Chinese have 20,000 ethnic Chinese or something like that in Havana, overseas Chinese. There is a community there. You would think that would give them a foothold that they could really work on, and yet the whole thing has backfired. It is an amazing example of being too doctrinaire.

The Chairman: I do not think it is to be unexpected. I am not too amazed. I think it is a wholly realistic thing to expect and unfortunately, I think there are setbacks also on our part to a great extent. . . .

Dr. Fairbank: Yes. The whole principle of nationalism is once you rescue it, it turns against you.

The Chairman: That is right. I think it is very important for us to remember. [pp. 133–134]

The Chairman: I wonder if we could return to some of the points that were touched on briefly this morning. I have in mind particularly the proper way to interpret Lin Piao's speech, which has been referred to by members of the administration and others as a basis for a judgment on the attitude and policy of China.

Dr. Fairbank: I tried in my earlier statement there to hit on that, of course, very briefly. I think the main point is that in the Chinese cultural scene there is a different function performed by words, and we have to really stretch our imaginations to look at this situation. The Chinese use words to express what ought to be, in their view, and if you do not follow the right words, then your conduct is not correct.

In other words, the expressions that they use are part of their conduct, and if you have a correct doctrine, as they believe they do, about world revolution, Marxism, and so on, then you should express that correct doctrine, and if you doubt that doctrine you are letting it down, you are a traitor, you are really unreal, because that is a true doctrine, and you always ought to put it forth.

Well, now, Lin Piao's statement is an expression of a true doctrine, the revolutionary thing, about how revolution will triumph, and it shows the peculiar parochial nature of the Chinese Communist movement in that it is used in a peculiarly inappropriate way from our point of view, it is remarkably unrealistic.

You see, they came to power in their development in China by taking over the cities from the countryside, surrounding the cities, making them impassable from the countryside, and no food could come in, and gradually controlling the population and winning. Now they apply this to the world scene by that argument of an analogy which, I think, is so inaccurate — the cities in this case are the industrialized nations — that they will take them over through the underdeveloped countries. This leaves entirely out of account the communications systems between the two. When they controlled the roads that led to the cities in the countryside they strangled the cities. How are they going to control the sea lanes of world commerce? This whole thing does not make sense.

Now, this kind of statement of Lin Piao's, to my mind, is an abstraction, a testament of faith, a reassertion of faith in the revolutionary belief that he has. And, I think, it is put out exactly for the opposite purpose to what some people seem to think. It is put out, in my mind, to compensate, to say, "Look we are having trouble. We always have setbacks, but still we believe in this revolution," and that is all it says. It is not a blueprint for taking over the world, in my view, at all; that is, of a practical nature. It is not a timetable, it is nothing of that sort. It is merely a profession of faith by a revolutionary who is still a revolutionary.

The Chairman: The way you describe it is a kind of ritualistic gesture. There is no meaning as far as reality goes.

Dr. Fairbank: Well, I really think there is that element in the Chinese scene that we cannot appreciate because we are accustomed to speaking very realistically as a way of dealing with things. They believe that people should behave properly, that there is a proper way, and that if everybody agrees in that proper way then people can have a harmonious society or, at least, a developing one as they now have. Now, this means that the proper form of words is, you might almost say, a sort of religious thing, that is, their faith is in the revolution, and when you say the right word you are expressing your faith. Chairman Mao spends a lot of time getting everybody to say the right word. You cannot say the wrong words and get away with it. [pp. 147–149]

The Chairman: Do you feel that the Chinese think that war with us is inevitable?

Dr. Fairbank: I have sometimes tried to catch the attention of the audience by saying that I was afraid we were on a collision course. But in recent months in thinking it over, I rather doubt it because I do not see how we are going to effect the collision in any sensible way. I mean, for them to attack us is not very sensible. There is that danger. For us to attack them is, I think, not very sensible, but there is that danger. I am myself inclined to think that the attitude we have is an important factor in this whole situation. In other words, we have got to calm down our fears and try to calm down their fears.

The Chairman: Yes.

Dr. Fairbank: If we do not, why, the fears on both sides can escalate, and that is even more dangerous than military action.

The Chairman: The only comment you tempt me to make is that there are very few wars I can think of that were very sensible. Beginning, say, from the First World War, it never made much sense to me; did it to you?

Dr. Fairbank: Well, there are wars that have been sensible on one side, not on the other, perhaps.

The Chairman: Perhaps, but it seems to me war is essentially an irrational activity.

Dr. Fairbank: On the other hand, I would suggest that war is part of modern history, if I may refer to that.

The Chairman: Yes.

Dr. Fairbank: And that it is unlikely that we are going to get rid of it in some form very soon because it is a highly developed institution which we all very dearly love.

The Chairman: That is right. That is why it is hard to reconcile that thought with your statement that you did not think that the Chinese would go to war. I had no fear, I think it all depends on how we act or what we do or how wisely we conduct ourselves. It may or may not be. There is no inevitability about it, but it is very important. That is why I think these hearings are important. The education of our own country as to their attitude, what should be an intelligent attitude in approaching this problem. So I do not accept it as being inevitable.

On the other hand, I think it is quite probable if we follow irrational policies.

Dr. Fairbank: It is perfectly possible for us in this situation in this particular period of months to go ahead on assumptions that they will not respond in certain ways and make a fatal mistake.

The Chairman: That is right.

Dr. Fairbank: This is perfectly possible, and that calls for, therefore, everybody having the greatest caution and thinking not twice but three times. [pp. 176–177]

Testimony of John M. H. Lindbeck and Benjamin I. Schwartz

Dr. Lindbeck: [Prepared Statement] From listening to public discussions and reading newspaper articles about China, one might gain the impression that China's Communist leaders spend much, if not most, of their time thinking about promoting revolutions around the world and plotting to extend their control over China's neighbors. In actual fact, China's leaders are preoccupied with Chinese domestic issues and the country's internal problems and development. . . .

China's Communist leaders are specialists in Chinese domestic politics, but amateurs in the field of international politics. However harsh the methods or technically and professionally primitive some of the major programs and policies they have adopted, these men applied themselves with energy to developing and using military force for achieving power within China; to consolidating their control over the country; to modernizing the use of China's human and natural resources; and to overhauling radically China's economic, social, and political systems. If power, organized skill, and the introduction of radical programs of economic development and social modernization are criteria for success, then they have considerable achievements to their credit.

By contrast, for a regime that is professedly internationalist in orientation, relatively modest amounts of attention and resources are allocated to activities relating to external relationships. Apart from the attention and resources devoted to the country's military forces — and these were brought into being for domestic purposes and still have domestic as well as external functions — the number of people working on foreign political, economic, and cultural relations; budgetary allocations for foreign affairs; and the amount of time devoted to international affairs by governmental bodies and in annual official reports represents a small proportion of the total. Instead of the firm grasp the country's leaders seem to have of Chinese realities, if not of modern science and technology, these men seem to me to reveal oversensitivity to prestige and ideological considerations, ignorance, and misconceptions; lack of experience and sophistication; and narrowmindedness in their handling of China's relations with its external environment. [pp. 186–187]

The Chairman: Dr. Lindbeck, I will address one question to you. In your statement you state rather clearly that China's present government is preoccupied with domestic affairs. This came as quite a shock to me. We read primarily of its aggressive nature. Statements in our press indicate the Chinese are greatly concerned with their international relations and give priority to them. Would you expand upon what you meant by saying their preoccupation is with domestic affairs?

Dr. Lindbeck: If one looks at what the governmental leaders do, the way in which they develop their budgets, the kind of programs which they debate at great length and which they implement, one gets a very different impression, at least I get a very different impression than that presented in our press, about how these men spend their time, and where they allocate China's resources.

Now, it is very natural that we should be concerned about China's foreign policies because these policies impinge directly upon us and on China's neighbors. But looking at the programmatic documents of the Chinese rulers and looking at their behavior, the main issues on their minds relate to the successes or failures they achieve in pushing programs of industrialization, in extending political control, in transforming the social and political climate in China.

One might use several measurements to see where people spend their time, and to determine the subject of main concern to them; it seems to me that by applying several criteria or measurements of attention spans and activity, Mao Tse-tung and most of his top associates appear to have become increasingly specialized on domestic issues rather than foreign problems.

Now, of course, it is true that a few of the leading members of the ruling group are specialists on relations with other Communist Parties and obviously spend a good deal of time thinking especially about this. There also is a small group of men who are concerned with foreign economic relations, foreign political relations, foreign military relations — who, in other words, specialize on overseas activities. But if you take the elite as a whole, the bulk of its members have become increasingly specialized on what is going on in China, and the whole business of trying to make China into a going concern.

The Chairman: Finally, would you comment on Lin Piao's speech which has been much discussed in the press and referred to in these hearings?

Dr. Lindbeck: Well, this speech has been, of course, interpreted in many ways. It seems to me that none of the major elements in the speech are novel. Lin Piao is summarizing and restating ideas which were propounded or developed in earlier years by others in the party, including Mao Tse-tung. Some of the ideas, for example, were set forth by Mao in his visit to Moscow in 1957, where, in effect, he laid out the concept of contracting of the imperialist world through the expansion of national liberation movements and the emergence of a larger number of neutralist countries; these movements finally would hem in the United States and make it less and less influential in international affairs. So, the first point I would make is that Lin Piao's speech is not a new major programmatic document.

Now, the second point to be considered, I suggest, is why this speech was made at all. Was it intended primarily for a domestic audience or for a foreign audience? My own inclination is to believe that it was addressed primarily to a domestic audience, a restatement of great ideals as visualized by the Communists; it was a statement of reassurance to the Chinese people that the great vision of the transformation of the world had not come to an end, but that this process of change would continue to take place under the workings of the large forces of history. . . .

Dr. Schwartz: I wonder if I might say something — is this permissible — about the Lin Piao statement.

The Chairman: Yes, sir.

Dr. Schwartz: This is a favorite subject of mine. It seems to me that the Lin Piao's [sic] statement does reflect what I would call the highest hopes, you might say, the optimum vision of the regime. What their hope consists of is that history will move in the direction of their vision. I think they are quite ready to help history if it moves in that direction and perhaps to intervene with advice and aid when circumstances emerge in various areas — as in the Congo, when a situation developed which seemed to be favorable to their vision. In such cases, they will try to support it, but the basic faith is in the movement of history itself. I also would add that the Lin Piao document in itself is a contradictory document if one examines it carefully.

While it projects this optimum vision it has in it certain saving clauses. For instance, the optimum vision involves the notion that the only real national liberation movements are movements led by Communist parties, and I assume by now they would mean Communist parties oriented to Peking; that any government that comes to power under the leadership of other elites is not a genuine revolutionary government. In fact, such a government might almost be called a puppet of the imperialists.

This has not led them to attack all the existing governments of Asia, Africa, and Latin America. In fact, they continue to cultivate these governments and to describe some of them as "progressive." So that you might say that while the Lin Piao statement contains the maximum vision, it also contains what might be called dilutions of this maximum vision which reflect adjustments which they have actually had to make to a world which has not corresponded on the whole to their maximum vision. [pp. 196–199]

Sen. Church: Do you think, as an expert on China, that Mao Tse-tung today is comparable to Hitler, that is to say, that he does seek a Chinese conquest of Asia as Hitler clearly sought a German conquest of Europe?

Dr. Lindbeck: I think that the motivations of the Chinese Communist leaders, compared to Hitler's motivations, are quite different. It seems to me that Germany under Hitler was seeking control over other economies and political systems in order to bleed them of their resources for the benefit of Germany.

The external interests of the Chinese Communist[s] it seems to me take quite a different form. Ideologically they are committed to the notion that history is producing major changes in the globe that tend to favor them and the kind of system they represent. With reference to Mao's and his colleagues' interest in extending Chinese influence, they are talking about and thinking about the emergence of states dominated by Communist parties in Asia but not necessarily under the immediate control of German-type gauleiters sent from China. The Chinese traditionally have a very different relationship with their neighbors than the Germans had with the countries of Europe and with Russia. This, too, colors and makes a difference in the way in which the Chinese sense and approach or think about their neighbors. . . .

Sen. Church: Do you think then that the prospect for success or failure in any given guerrilla war outside of China will have more to do with the indigenous situation within that country than it will have to do with such assistance as China can give?

Dr. Lindbeck: This is the main point in Mao's doctrine about national liberation wars. It is the constellation of political and social forces in a given arena or country that will determine, he says, the success or the failure of a national liberation movement. . . .

A corollary part of the doctrine is that a national liberation war cannot be run successfully solely or primarily on the basis of outside resources. There must be adequate indigenous resources to bring it to success.

Sen. Church: I think from what you have said that the character of the Chinese threat in Asia is clearly very different indeed from the character of the Nazi threat in Europe. [pp. 205–207]

The Chairman: Would you comment on the Chinese entrance into the Korean war as being an example of aggression?

Dr. Schwartz: No.

The Chairman: It has been cited as an example of aggression.

Dr. Schwartz: No; I would think not, because it is still quite conceivable to me that they might actually not have intervened; I think they really did sense a direct threat to their national interests there. . . .

I am not convinced that before our march toward the Yalu they would have come in. It is not at all clear that they would have come in. After all, they were, at the time, just organizing their internal regime and were confronted with a host of economic problems, so that I don't think that this particular instance is a good case. . . .

The Chairman: If you have anything to add, Dr. Lindbeck, why just intervene. . . .

Dr. Lindbeck: I would agree on the Korean points.

The Chairman: You agree on that?

Dr. Lindbeck: With Dr. Schwartz. I can see how one might make an indirect case of the Chinese being military aggressors in Korea because they were aiding military aggressors. The North Koreans can be stigmatized because they were aggressors; but this is a type of circular reasoning and not, I think, the real estimate of original Chinese intentions. . . .

The Chairman: What about Tibet? Is this a valid example of aggression?

Dr. Schwartz: Well, here you have a much more difficult question. I think that the Chinese are expansive nationalists in the sense that their conception of what the proper borders of China are is a Maximalianist [*sic*] conception. Almost anything that had any brush with the Chinese empire in the past is part of "China irridenta," if you will, and, by the way, they differ probably in no great respect from the Nationalist government in this conception of the great China.

I think a case could be made for the notion that Tibet could very well be an independent country; that it has a separate culture, and that the Chinese control of Tibet in the past was one of a kind of a loose and poorly defined suzerainty. But the Chinese are here behaving as extreme nationalists — here we get into the order of questions that we deal with, let's say, regarding the American expansion in the West.

Was there aggression or not aggression? I think in some sense it was aggression, but it is a kind of aggression that you often find in modern nationalism; that is, it is an aggression that takes the form of having a very large conception of what the proper borders of the nation are. . . .

The Chairman: Was Tibet an independent country recognized as such by any other country? Did we recognize Tibet, for example, as an independent country?

Dr. Lindbeck: No, we did not. . . .

The main objection of the Tibetans to the Communists has been to what might be called their social and cultural aggression. Previous Chinese rulers, in general, respected the religious and social institutions the Tibetans had developed. When the Communists began to carry through their transformation of Tibetan society, they produced violent resistance which finally took explosive form. So we should make a distinction, it seems to me, between different types of Chinese policies in Tibet. The Nationalists had a political commissioner in Lhasa who had very little real power. The Ch'ing Dynasty also kept a commissioner in

Tibet for much of the time. These men did not directly control the internal operations of political, religious, and social institutions, but exercised supervisory influence. This supervision was acceptable in that when China was strong there was little trouble with resistance in Tibet even though the Tibetans were usually somewhat uneasy about what the Chinese might do.

However, when the Chinese Communists introduced sweeping political, economic, and social changes, the Tibetans became combative. I might add here — on the first point Mr. Schwartz made — the Chinese Communists in the first constitution they adopted in 1932 set forth the principle that non-Chinese peoples in China would be allowed to be autonomous, or independent of China, separate countries. Only after the Chinese Communists came to power did they take over the principle, which had been clearly stated by the Nationalists, that all peoples living in territory claimed by China, or who had been under Chinese administrative control were to be citizens of China. The principle of the right to political independence of ethnic and cultural minorities was abandoned. The common program of 1949 and the constitution of 1954 embody these Chinese claims. I am saying that the Communists took over the Nationalist attitude, once they assumed responsibility for the governing of China.

The Chairman: Do you conclude from that, that this is evidence of a military aggression or a tendency to military aggression on the part of the Chinese or not?

Dr. Lindbeck: No.

The Chairman: You do not. What do you think?

Dr. Schwartz: I wouldn't want to draw any conclusions from the Tibetan experience for the world as a whole. . . . I should note that Tibet did exist as a separate political entity in the Middle Ages. In fact, it was a powerful political enemy. The Chinese empire was at times actually very much afraid of the Tibetans.

The Chairman: How long ago was that?

Dr. Schwartz: Back in the T'ang Dynasty, thereabouts.

The Chairman: When was that?

Dr. Schwartz: Let's say the seventh, eighth centuries. The Tibetans also, I think, have had a strong sense of difference from the Chinese.

All I would urge here is that I doubt very much whether one can draw a distinction between, let's say, the attitudes of the Nationalists and the Communists on this issue. It is an extreme — I mean they are both extremely nationalistic, and I don't know that I would want to say more, but it is a different case from aggression against a country clearly outside of the Chinese orbit.

The Chairman: Yes. What about India? Could you describe that? The three cases that have been cited to us, I believe by the Secretary of Defense, are India, Tibet, and Korea, where the Chinese are militarily aggressive and this is a justification for policies which we are following. How do you describe the Indian affair in Ladakh and along the northeast area? . . .

Dr. Schwartz: Well, my sympathies tend to lie more with the Indians in this instance even if one can assume that the Chinese have a case on the border issue. Their claim that this line was established by imperialism strikes me as somewhat hypocritical. After all, much of the Chinese border was established by Chinese imperialism. I don't think that such drastic measures were necessary to correct their grievances as they understood them. I am sure they had other motives in view in undertaking this. Perhaps they wished to reduce the image of India in the world at large. . . .

Sen. Church: In connection with the Indian boundary dispute, did the Nationalist government on Taiwan take the same view and support the position taken by the Communist government in Peking?

Dr. Schwartz: That is my understanding, yes.

Sen. Church: So that, whatever the claim was, it did not derive from the Communist character of the regime?

Dr. Schwartz: No, I would derive this from — well, maybe in part from the Communist interest of Peking. That is, if one of their motives was to discredit the Indian government, this may have had something to do with it.

Sen. Church: Yes, but the basis for their claim lay in Chinese national history.

Dr. Schwartz: Yes.

Sen. Church: And as to the nature of the claim both Chiang Kai-shek and Mao Tse-tung were in agreement?

Dr. Schwartz: Yes.

Sen. Case: May I just interject and comment at that point, you do not put much stock in the three arguments, specific arguments, that the Secretary of Defense cited to the committee as basic justification for our concern with Chinese expansion and aggression, but you still have some concern yourself about Chinese expansionism and aggression, and concur in the general need for containment, I take it, as part of our policy?

Dr. Schwartz: Yes.

Sen. Case: I wish you would just go into this, because I know we are just all trying to get enlightenment here.

Dr. Schwartz: I haven't seen the transcript of the Secretary of Defense's testimony, but I was left with the impression that much of that dealt with the whole Lin Piao projection which to my mind is something else again — this concerns the Communist side of Chinese policies rather than the strictly Nationalist [nationalistic?] side. Here I would tend to lay much less stress on the importance of this document than does the Secretary of Defense.

The Chairman: Professor Lindbeck, do you have anything else to add?

Dr. Lindbeck: I should like to add that I believe the Chinese are prepared to use military force if they think they can gain real advantages from this. . . .

The Chairman: I wonder if at this time before we recess you could sum up about China being aggressive militarily, particularly disassociated from the idea of her reclaiming a suzerainty power. There is very little basis for this; is that correct?

Dr. Schwartz: I don't think that they are likely to take any wild aggressive measures.

The Chairman: Be militarily aggressive?

Dr. Schwartz: Militarily aggressive measures. I do think that one cannot debar the possibility that in some cases they might be willing to resort to military force on their borders. But the question, even if this is true, the question is how does one deal with this? In this the Chinese are not unique.

The Chairman: I know that comes next, but you see we have been told as a justification for our policies, and the vast sums appropriated, tax bills and so on, is because the Chinese are militarily aggressive and we must be very frightened of their military aggression. I am only trying to clarify some of the points that are advanced. Then I come again to the question of the ideological success they have had around the world. Would you say they have been very successful ideologically?

Dr. Schwartz: Not so far.

The Chairman: Then why is it we seem to be so very fearful of them. Are you fearful of them? Should we be fearful of them?

Dr. Schwartz: In the ultimate sense I am rather optimistic and not so fearful. I do think that ultimately they can be brought into a framework of world order, and that their most grandiose ambitions may subside. Of course, I don't think they will settle for anything less than being recognized as one of the world's great powers.

The Chairman: Oh, yes. [pp. 222–230]

Testimony of Samuel B. Griffith
and Morton H. Halperin

Sen. Sparkman: By the way, the opinion has been expressed here that China is not expansionist. Will you express an opinion on that, either of you?

Gen. Griffith: Well, Senator, I think that I wouldn't be quite as dogmatic in my opinion as whoever made the statement. I think China is expansionist to a limited degree. I don't believe that, and I want to make myself as clear as I can on this, the Chinese do not, I believe, have the slightest intention of physically occupying southeast Asia. All they want in southeast Asia is to exercise a benevolent, if you will, hegemony over that region.

They want their influence to be felt in that region for the reasons that I have stated, and I don't believe that the present Communist government is acting — is feeling — any differently in this respect than a very powerful Nationalist government might feel. These are traditional areas of Chinese culture, they have always been traditional areas of Chinese influence, and I feel that this is only natural for the Chinese to want to have fruitful relations in which they play perhaps a dominant position with these smaller countries. But I don't think that they propose to go in there and try to run those countries. That would be my reaction.

Dr. Halperin: I think I would accept that. I would add only two points. One is that Taiwan is an exception. The Chinese look upon Taiwan as a part of China and they would use military force to take Taiwan if they thought that could be successful.

Gen. Griffith: Right.

Dr. Halperin: The second point I would add, I think, the Chinese want to expand their influence not only throughout southeast Asia but throughout the world. They aspire in the long run to be a world power playing a role in supporting revolution and what they see as left-wing Communist groups throughout the world. But they are not expansionist in the sense of having plans to use their own armies to march into countries and conquer them. . . .

Sen. Hickenlooper: General Griffith, I am somewhat confused by these statements this morning. I don't know whether they attempt to create the idea that China is a big benevolent grouping of people and not expansionist really, that they have enough to do at home, and merely want to extend some influence here, there or the other place. There is another school of thought that believes that the present leadership in China is almost diametrically opposite from the ancient leadership in China following the Confucian philosophy, and that really China is following the idea of eventual domination of the world by centralized communism. I don't think the two are quite compatible. There is the old statement, I think credited to Lenin, that the way to Paris was by way of Peking on the encirclement theory. That the way to squeeze off Europe was to encircle them and come in through south Asia, establish their influence and control in that area, move on to India, move on to Africa and eventually squeeze Europe out like popping a seed out of the inside of a fruit. Now, that is rather crudely put but what about those philosophies?

Gen. Griffith: Well, I think, Senator, what they want to do is, and I agree with Mr. Halperin, to expand their influence in the world, and they hope, they would like to do this by using Lin Piao's theses of national liberation wars. If I could address myself ——

Sen. Hickenlooper: To help widen the field of answer a little bit, in extending their influence, do you consider that it is to extend the influence of mainland China or is it to advance the cause of universal international communism eventually?

Gen. Griffith: I think it is both. It would be hard to separate the strands there. But I think China has announced repeatedly that she has a rightful position as a great power in the world and she proposes to assume this position. She knows this is going to take a long time. Now, this implies a depreciation of American power, and she hopes by encouraging these wars of national liberation wherever she can, to depreciate American power.

Sen. Hickenlooper: Do you see any indication that the mainland Chinese leadership wants to establish and expand their position as a world power by cooperating with other nations of all kinds in the world or by exclusive Chinese power through the process of wars of liberation? . . .

Gen. Griffith: I think she wants to — this is sort of a paradox really, Senator. She does want to, I think she would like to establish friendly relations with some countries selectively, but yet it is difficult to reconcile this, as you have intimated, with the actions of the leadership during the last five or six years.

Let's say she has completely antagonized a very large part of the American public. She has antagonized the American government, she has antagonized the Soviet government, she has antagonized the Indian government, and she managed to achieve this all in a very short space of time and as one of my friends says, believe me this takes some doing, to antagonize the three very powerful governments, two of whom are contiguous to her. . . .

Sen. Hickenlooper: I can see arguments to support, from the standpoint of the mainland Chinese, reference to the fact that we are considered to be alien meddlers, but do you consider that the mainland Chinese are alien meddlers in other places?

Gen. Griffith: Oh, very definitely. They are going to be alien meddlers wherever they can. They have attempted it in Africa. I think five or six African countries have learned that the Chinese are precisely alien meddlers, and I think that this whole doctrine of national liberation wars indicates quite clearly that they are going to be alien meddlers wherever they think they can be successful. . . .

Sen. Hickenlooper: The Chinese activities are quite widespread wherever they can foment and lead so-called liberation movements. . . .

Gen. Griffith: But this, if I may say one other thing, I agree with Dr. Halperin that this doctrine of national liberation wars is not really a credible or realistic one. We could go into that at greater length later. I don't think it is truly going to stand up.

Sen. Hickenlooper: Well, it may not stand up in the long run, but it is a very real fact in the present time, and has been for some time in the past, hasn't it? I refer to the attempt to sponsor disruption in various countries by this so-called wars-of-liberation process.

Gen. Griffith: Oh, yes, but apparently they never know when to stop, if we may believe what Major [*sic*] Castro has said.

Sen. Hickenlooper: He has made some very caustic remarks about China. What does either of you think the impact to be of such situations as have occurred recently in the last few weeks in Jakarta, in Africa, and other places? What do you sense at the moment to be the impact on the present Red leadership in China of those events?

Dr. Halperin: I think, Senator, it has led them to be very discouraged about the possibility of friendly and cooperative relations with regimes other than those that are run by a Marxist-Leninist Communist Party. I think it has led them to reaffirm that only revolutionary regimes can be true opponents of the United States and I think it is going to lead them to pay less attention to trying to have friendly relations with left-wing but non-Communist regimes.

Sen. Hickenlooper: Do you think that it will have any long-range or material effect upon their attitude or will they say, "Oops, we stuck our nose in the wrong door crack here and got it pinched, we will back out and try someplace else."

Dr. Halperin: I think it is going to lead them to concentrate primarily on trying to support the small Communist groups which exist in these countries and, on the other hand, concentrate on their own revolution in China. [pp. 295–299]

Testimony of Alexander Eckstein

The Chairman: Do you think their failures in various underdeveloped countries which we have witnessed recently in Africa and in Cuba, have had the effect of turning their attention more to their own domestic economic and political and social concerns?

Dr. Eckstein: Yes. I very strongly subscribe to some of the views expressed here earlier that the evidence for Chinese expansionism is extremely limited; that is, the Chinese are very expansionist at the verbal level, but very cautious at the action level. In recent years; that is, since 1962, at least, the Chinese have in actual fact been preoccupied with internal problems, with problems of internal recovery.

They had to face up to the task of formulating a third five-year plan, and must have asked themselves, "Where do we go from here; we have gone through an acute economic crisis, how do we overcome this crisis, how do we cope with our long-run development problems, with our long-run population problems?" I think these considerations had definite priority over expansionist aims. This, of course, does not mean that foreign policy goals were sacrificed; only that these goals were pursued by political means and in ways which did not require commitments of economic and military resources on an appreciable scale.

Stated more positively, I think, certain foreign policy objectives did in fact loom large. For instance, Taiwan was undoubtedly a matter of utmost importance to the Chinese Communists all of the time, and there might be some other matters close to their borders which may be of the greatest importance to them. But I think their posture in these respects is defensive rather than offensive.

The Chairman: Defensive.

Dr. Eckstein: Yes. [p. 339]

Sen. Hickenlooper: What is the controlling policy of China now? . . . Will China give up a substantial measure of internal economic development in order to advance the ideological development . . . of the wars of liberation and the advancement of international communism abroad; or will she give up the theory of the war of liberation in order to enhance and speed up her internal economic policy? Which will, in effect, control China? They are both involved, I know. But if they had to choose, which would they sacrifice?

Dr. Eckstein: It seems to me that the first priority is the survival of the Chinese Communist regime. That is, that the first claim will be to maintain the political stability and viability of the government. Beyond this, I think the Chinese are likely to pursue a cautious foreign policy; that is, a policy which would not involve major military risks and would not entail major commitments of economic resources for war purposes.

On the other hand, if political gains can be obtained, such as national liberation wars through proxy, without major risk of military entanglement and without large-scale commitment of resources, I think they would tend to encourage that. But I think that if they have to choose between economic development at home or getting involved in a major adventure abroad which might really risk a major war and also basically and profoundly undermine their capabilities for economic development, they would very much shy away from it. [pp. 346–347]

Testimony of Donald S. Zagoria
and Harold C. Hinton

Dr. Zagoria: [Prepared Statement] [The] Chinese Communist regime today faces the most serious and far-reaching foreign policy crisis it has ever confronted. This crisis is largely the outgrowth of rigidly dogmatic postures assumed in recent years by Mao and his closest collaborators.

The crisis is of such magnitude as to have seriously weakened Peking's influence in the underdeveloped countries, cast doubt on the legitimacy and viability of even the regime's reasonable international aspirations, and greatly sharpened existing divergencies among Communist movements all over the world. It is a crisis which will not be resolved without basic changes in Chinese Communist policy — changes which may not come until after Mao's death, but which could occur sooner and, in any case, in my opinion, are bound to happen in the foreseeable future.

The dimensions of this crisis are global — Indonesia, Cuba, Kenya — wherever we look in Asia, Latin America, and Africa, the Peking regime stands accused of unwarranted intervention and arrogance, its representatives are asked to go home, and its intentions are viewed with growing suspicion.

Within the international Communist movement, where Peking a year or two ago could count on some twenty allies and sympathizers, and seemed ready to set up a new Communist international alliance of Afro–Asian–Latin American parties, Chinese influence is now at an all-time low. Even the intransigent Albanians are beginning to have second thoughts about the wisdom of Mao's strategy and doctrine. Meanwhile the split with Moscow deepens.

The current crisis in Communist China's foreign policy has its roots in 1957 when Mao, incorrectly assuming that the development of Soviet ICBM capabilities had wrought a decisive change in the world balance of power, abandoned Peking's previous caution and embarked on a more militant course to achieve his primary foreign policy goals: elimination of U.S. military power from Asia, repossession of Taiwan, and international recognition of Communist China as a great power.

It soon became clear that the Soviet Union, on whose support Mao had unquestionably counted, was unwilling to back Mao's ambitious aims at the risk of war with the United States. Quite to the contrary, it soon made overtures for a detente with the United States. The "spirit of Camp David" and Khrushchev's subsequent efforts to persuade Peking to accept a modus vivendi envisaging Chinese Nationalist control of Formosa pressed home to Mao the fact that the Russians could not be depended on to help push the United States out of Asia. This difference of approach to the U.S. presence is among the fundamental causes of the Sino-Soviet split and explains the bitterness of Chinese feelings toward the Soviet leadership.

Peking then turned to the underdeveloped countries, encouraging nationalist and local Communist leaders in these countries to join in an anti-American alliance. Mao's plans could not be carried out without replacing Soviet by Chinese authority in the Communist and leftist groups of Afro-Asia and Latin America. However, Mao's gambit has fallen flat all along the line: radical nationalists receptive to Peking's game are disappearing from power, and Communist Parties in Africa, Asia, and Latin America are deeply divided and increasingly disenchanted with Mao.

What amounts, then, to effective containment of Communist China has been accomplished primarily by the Peking leadership itself. In a few short years, the Chinese leadership has split with the only other major Communist power in the world, it has alienated itself from the international Communist movement and from the emergent nationalist forces of the developing countries, and it has not only failed to attain most of its pressing national goals but it has even prejudiced them. The rumblings of discontent with Mao's policies are plainly audible in China today.

China's failures are essentially the result of its erroneous assessment of the forces at work in the Afro-Asian world. National self-realization rather than instant social revolution or an anti-American crusade is the immediate goal sought by the new countries, and Peking's product-mix of subversion, helpful revolutionary hints, and polemics on the evils of imperialism has inevitably found only a limited market where economic development and nation-building are the primary concerns. By the same token, Peking cannot compete with Russia or the United States when it comes to economic and military aid. . . .

The extent of the crisis facing the Chinese Communist leadership in the field of foreign policy is dramatically pointed up in the now-notorious statement made by Marshal Lin Piao last September. Ironically, there are two — and, in my opinion, only two — countries in the world where Lin Piao's revolutionary smorgasbord is regarded as some kind of magic weapon: one is China, and the other is the United States.

Two, in my opinion, equally erroneous interpretations of Lin Piao's statement are current, and both, it seems to me, miss the point. On the one hand there are those who dismiss it as Fourth of July rhetoric. On the other are those part-time Pekinologists who call this Lin Piao's *Mein Kampf*, blithely ignoring the fact that it is basically a rehash of what Chinese Communist leaders have been saying on and off since at least 1949.

The analogy with *Mein Kampf* comes, therefore, a little late, to say the least. But, more importantly, it is harmful and misleading because it equates Maoist and Nazi ideology in such a way as to evoke the specter of overt Chinese Communist military and territorial expansion in Asia. Neither in the Lin Piao statement nor in the multitude of similar statements made in the past is there any suggestion of Chinese Communist intentions to engage in direct, Hitler-style expansionism.

In fact, a cardinal point of Lin Piao's message is the Vietcong and other Communist revolutionaries throughout the world must make their revolutions on their own, that they should not count on Chinese or any other outside assistance. Far from giving notice of any intention to intervene aggressively, Lin Piao is rationalizing Peking's unwillingness to go to the aid of the Vietcong, in a struggle which — let there be no doubt —

the Chinese Communist regard as just and which is taking place on their very borders.

The difference between Hitler and Mao, then, is that *Mein Kampf* was a blueprint for what Germany herself, under Hitler, would do; Lin Piao's statement, on the contrary, is designed to tell other Communist parties what they should do, to recommend strategy. It is, thus, simply not Fourth of July oratory.

However, most of the Communist Parties now recognize that Lin Piao's advice is largely inappropriate to their local situations, and they are not about to act on it. The ingredients of the Chinese Communist revolutionary model — which has long been put forward as a do-it-yourself model for foreign Communists — are well known: a disciplined Communist Party, a broad united front, a protracted guerrilla struggle originating in the rural hinterland and based on armed peasantry — the whole led by Communists right from the outset.

How many foreign Communist Parties are in a position to implement the model? With the exception of Vietnam, the answer is none, as of this moment, and for very good reasons: Not one Communist Party in Africa, Asia or in Latin America has a strong base, either in the society in general or among the peasants in particular — an indispensable prerequisite for launching a Maoist-style guerrilla war. The one party which came closest to having such a mass base, the PKI [Communist Party] in Indonesia, has recently been decimated by the Indonesian Army and is unlikely to recover in the foreseeable future. . . .

Since the Chinese Communist leadership has in the past shown itself flexible enough to adjust policies when they go wrong, I see no reason not to expect that they will be able to recognize their plight and adapt accordingly. True, what we have thus far seen from Peking is not the sign of change in direction but rather the rationalization of past mistakes. But this cannot suffice. The Chinese will not stay indefinitely in the corner they have painted themselves into.

What options do they have? They could try to reach a rapprochement with the Soviet Union. But so long as Mao lives, this is unlikely. They could improve relations with the United States. It is interesting in this respect to note that a recent French emissary in Peking was told that the Americans were, after all, only an enemy, and a respected one, whereas the Russians were traitors and traitors could never be forgiven. The clear impression was that it might eventually, and I stress the word "eventually" because I do not expect or anticipate an early improvement in Chinese-American relations, that the clear impression was that it might eventually be easier to adjust relations with the United States than with Russia.

Thirdly, Peking could try to revive the "Bandung spirit" of the mid-1950's when it sought to portray itself not as a revolutionary power but as a friend of the entire Afro-Asian world. But it is not likely to do any of these things until the issue of Vietnam is decided because the old guard still cherishes the hope that a success in Vietnam could turn back the tide. [pp. 368–373]

Dr. Hinton: [Prepared Statement] The Chinese Communist Party came to power in 1949 determined not only to wipe out China's past humiliations at the hands of what it called foreign imperialism but to make China the leading state in Asia and a model and source of support for other Communist revolutions in Asia. The scope of its ambitions was soon broadened to include the whole of the underdeveloped areas and even the attainment of the status of the world power. The United States, which was tentatively moving toward diplomatic recognition of Communist China in the last months of 1949, found its intentions frustrated by the Chinese Communist determination to cast the United States in the light of the major enemy for reasons both foreign and domestic, including a desire to isolate Western-oriented Chinese and facilitate their reindoctrination.

A first step in Communist China's quest for influence was the acquisition of all territory claimed as Chinese. In 1936 Mao Tse-tung had said that Taiwan, or Formosa, should be independent after its liberation from Japan, but he changed his mind as the United States and Britain promised Taiwan to China in 1943, the Chinese Nationalists made it their main base and refuge after 1949, and the United States began to protect it in 1950. Shortly afterward Communist China intervened in the Korean conflict in order to keep American ground forces away from its Manchurian frontier. It succeeded in this, but its intervention, together with the developing Sino-American confrontation in the Taiwan Strait, led the United States to shift the emphasis of its military policy in the Far East from containment of the Soviet Union to containment, or as the Chinese would say encirclement, of Communist China.

Thus Communist China's overeager promotion of its own security and influence, although it enhanced its influence somewhat by creating in many quarters an exaggerated impression of its readiness to resort to force, also created a greater and continuing threat to Chinese security. Much the same is happening now as the United States constructs major air bases in Thailand in response to a Vietnamese crisis in which Communist China has chosen to involve itself to a limited degree.

Since 1950 a major deterrent to hostile action again[st] Communist China by the United States or anyone else is the widespread belief that China's large conventional forces, which it refuses to reduce under any international disarmament agreement, hold the non-Communist countries of mainland Asia hostage for the good behavior of its enemies. To a degree, therefore, Communist China can count on Asian countries as well as others to exert restraining pressures on the United States. In reality, Communist China's ability to invade other Asian countries is severely limited by logistics and is almost canceled by the threat of American retaliation and the political liabilities that would follow an actual invasion, as distinct from a mere threat or assumed capability to invade. . . .

China has done very well in its recent relations with the developed non-Communist countries, including Japan and excluding the United States, primarily because its revolutionary activities there are minor and ineffectual and it gives priority to its national interests, which stress trade with these countries, and [trade] with Japan and West Germany in particular, is trending upward. On the other hand, the Chinese interest in the developed countries is by no means entirely economic. China hopes to lure them away from the United States, and keep them away from the Soviet Union, in order to use them if possible against both. French recognition in January 1964 was a major diplomatic feather in China's cap, and shortly afterward the Chinese gave signs of an interest not only in signing a trade agreement with West Germany but in establishing diplomatic relations with it, not for the sake of harming East Germany but for the sake of putting pressure on Khrushchev, with whom their relations were almost unbelievably bad at that time. Nothing came of this Chinese interest in relations with West Germany, as it turned out.

Communist China's policy toward the underdeveloped areas consists essentially, although not entirely, of overtly inciting and covertly aiding Chinese-style armed revolutions, not necessarily Communist-led but aimed at "imperialist" influence in the country in question, within the limits of supposed feasibility. The purpose seems to be twofold: not only to promote eventually the spread of communism but to weaken the United States and distract it from the Far East by involving it in crises and brushfire wars elsewhere in the underdeveloped areas. The best known formulation of this strategy is Marshal Lin Piao's article of September 3 last on "people's war," in which he says that the Japanese army in China produced its own defeat by driving the Chinese people into the arms of the Communists, that the United States is now doing in the underdeveloped areas as a whole exactly what the Japanese did in China, and that the peoples of the underdeveloped areas, therefore, can and should imitate the Chinese people's example without relying for decisive aid on Communist China or any other external source. So central to Lin's argument, and yet so fantastic, is the analogy between imperial Japan and the United States that one is tempted, even before examining the evidence, to conclude that the Chinese hope for widespread anti-imperialist risings in the underdeveloped countries is poorly founded. [pp. 376–379]

Sen. Carlson: Mr. Hinton, what is your thought about the continuous alienation of India? Why did the Red Chinese invade India? What are your views on that?

Dr. Hinton: Well, as for the relations between India and Communist

China, the difficulties there go back quite a little time before they burst into the open.

A great deal of the Chinese Communist embracing of neutralism of Nehru, and so on, was a desire to get the neutrals into a mood friendly to Communist China and a mood to restrain the United States from putting pressures on it at a time when Soviet protection for the Chinese was becoming increasingly doubtful in the mid-1950's.

Then there came up the issues of Tibet, in which a very serious insurgency began against the Chinese in about the second half of 1955, and I would say the graph of Sino-Indian relations had risen and fallen almost with the graph of the rise and fall of insurgency in Tibet ever since, the point being that the Chinese are determined to keep any Indian army or any other element they regard as basically hostile away from any position from which they could establish direct contact with the Tibetan guerrillas.

Whether they achieved this or not would require detailed information which frankly I don't have. But I think it is clear this is the primary purpose. Beyond that, of course, the Chinese would ultimately like to see the ultimate Balkanization or splitting up of the Indian subcontinent into its linguistic components and hopefully the coming into power in all of these fragments of a left-wing Peking-oriented local Communist machine of some kind.

In fact, there is plenty on the Chinese side to guarantee there will be fundamentally poor rather than good relations with India over a protracted period of time, even though there may be temporary honeymoon periods. [pp. 397–398]

Sen. Lausche: Dr. Zagoria, can you identify the various places where Communist China's aggression has taken place since the Korean war? Now, we begin with Korea. It was an aggressor there. I would like to get them set forth here in the record.

Dr. Zagoria: I would like to say so far as Korea is concerned, the Chinese Communists did not initiate the Korean war. It was initiated by the Russians, and the North Koreans. I think there is pretty good evidence to support that view, and the Chinese Communists were very reluctant to intervene in the Korean war and did so only after General MacArthur crossed the 38th parallel and was marching towards the Yalu River, an act which the Chinese regarded as a threat to their own security.

It is true that the Chinese Communists were condemned by the United Nations for their intervention as an act of aggression and it is also true they supported an act of aggression because there is no doubt that the North Vietnamese [Koreans?] did initiate that action.

But I think that the assessment was a product of erroneous thinking that the Chinese Communists were part of a monolithic international

Communist movement and anything Stalin did they were naturally going along with, and I don't think that is correct. . . .

Sen. Lausche: [Was] there a Communist invasion of the Indian territory?

Dr. Zagoria: There was a Chinese Communist move into territory that the Chinese claimed was theirs, and the Indians claimed was theirs. So that in that sense, I do think, I think a clearer case can be made against China for aggression in India than almost anywhere else since the Korean war.

Sen. Lausche: All right. What about Quemoy and Matsu?

Dr. Zagoria: Once again, this [is] like Tibet. Well, first of all, the geographical position of Quemoy and Matsu is something like Staten Island and New York, and I think there is no doubt that the Chinese Communists want to get the Nationalists off those islands. The Nationalists do harass the mainland from these islands. But, the offshore islands and indeed Taiwan are areas which Communist China regards as Chinese territory.

Now, this is not to say that I condone any action on their part to recover those areas by force. But I do think that their efforts to recover territory that they regard as part of China and in which they claim they are supported by a great many things that one could point to — international agreements, for example; the great powers, I think at the Yalta Agreement, agreed that Taiwan was part of China. All I am saying is that their actions in cases such as that have to be differentiated from aggressive actions against another country on whom they have no such claims.

Sen. Lausche: I list them as Tibet, India, Quemoy and Matsu, with the specific statement by the Red Chinese that, even though Quemoy and Matsu were surrendered, that would not be adequate, because Taiwan belonged to them. [pp. 416–417]

Testimony of George E. Taylor
and Walter H. Judd

Dr. Taylor: [Prepared Statement] In my view it is safer to proceed on the premise that there is no world community, as the phrase goes, into which we can induce the Chinese to enter. Unfortunately we live in a world in which there are at least two violently opposed concepts of international relations, of political and social organization, and of world order. The dialog between them is still minimal. Everything we do with Communist China has to be seen in this context. Whatever the relations between Peiping and Moscow, as far as the world community is concerned, they share the same outlook. The problem then is one of how to define our relations with the Chinese section of the Communist world. It is clearly necessary, in this dangerous world, to do this.

Further to clarify my premises, I do not think, for example, that the evidence supports the fashionable view that the Communist world is falling apart and that Communist states have the same sort of foreign policy objectives as any other nation-state or can be expected to pursue them in the same manner. The social and political content of nationalism is determined by the institutional power configuration, and this is what is new and lasting about communism. It is because it is the nature of power that determines foreign policy — to put the matter very briefly — that I feel so little hope of any changes in Chinese Communist policies that are not forced on her. It is necessary to mention this because there is a great reluctance on the part of China specialists, perhaps because they love the Chinese so much, to admit that the Chinese Communists are really Communists.

The agrarian reformers of the forties are now the aging paranoids of the sixties, to be handled, it would seem, by group therapy. If they were really nationalists masquerading as Communists, then Chinese tradition as well as the humiliations of nineteenth-century imperialism would be relevant to their mood, but in my view the Communists represent a complete break with the past. Their world view is not conditioned by the imperial past, although they are willing to exploit it. A comparison with some real nationalists will point up the differences. It was the National[ist] government that won the ending of imperial privileges in 1942 [1943?] and lost the chance of building up a modern China largely as a result of the Japanese invasion. We might have difficulties with them if they were in power on the mainland, but I doubt they would be sponsoring the Vietcong or fomenting trouble over the rest of the world.

There is nothing about Chinese nationalism that calls for the hate campaign of the Chinese Communists against the United States, for the militarization of a quarter of the people of the earth, for the racial invective that pervades so much of their propaganda, even in Hong Kong, or for the support of revolutionary movements in southeast Asia, Africa, and Latin America spelled out in the Central Committee decisions of 1963 and reaffirmed in the Lin Piao statement. A true nationalism would call for attention to domestic problems and would certainly avoid a quarrel with a powerful neighbor. . . .

. . . Most have referred to the most recent statement of Chinese Communist political goals, the Lin Piao position paper of September 1965, but it is variously interpreted. The Aesopian dialog of the Communist world is not always easy to follow, and this effort was clearly designed to achieve several purposes at the same time. In my view it should be taken seriously as a general indication of the objectives and strategy of the Peking wing of the movement. It is not impossible that this strategy could be made to work. It is based on the assumption that the revolution is not going to occur in the great industrial states, that the Achilles' heel of the West is the third world, that the promotion of wars of national liberation in Africa, Latin America, and southeast Asia will distract and waste the energies of the Western powers, confuse their peoples, and demoralize their leaders.

Some believe that Communist China is too weak to carry out such a grandiose strategy, that in fact she is now reeling from shattering defeat. When the Soviets came to the assistance of the Chinese Nationalists in 1923 they were not a strong power, but they almost succeeded in taking over the Nationalist movement at a cost of one thousand advisers and about $3 million. The Chinese Communists were not very strong when they provided the Vietminh with the heavy weapons that made possible the conquest of Dienbienphu, nor when they intervened in North Korea, nor when they promoted a Communist attempt to take over Malaya in 1948. May I also suggest that the Chinese Communists were involved in the attempted coup d'etat in Indonesia last October and that it came very close to succeeding? If it had succeeded it would have been followed by an intensification of the war against Malaya, Thailand would have been caught in the pincers, and our position in Vietnam would have been very precarious.

The main question that the leaders and peoples of southeast Asia are asking is, "Who is going to win?" Under the above conditions it would have seemed that the Chinese brand of communism was in the ascendent; Lin Piao's statement would have looked like a curtain raiser rather than noisy bragging or defensive defiance. China is obviously in no position to seek a head-on collision with the United States and is most unlikely to give us the opportunity to declare war on her, but she is quite capable of fostering wars of national liberation wherever opportunities are provided. . . . [pp. 455–457]

The Chairman: How do you distinguish between a war of liberation that they speak of, and an old-fashioned war of liberation from colonial domination? What are the distinctive characteristics of these two types of wars?

Dr. Taylor: Yes. Well, a war of national liberation is one that has to be led by an indigenous Communist Party. I think that is the main distinction, sir.

In 1923 the Chinese Nationalists under Sun Yat-sen and Chiang Kai-shek were conducting what I think you mean in referring to an old-fashioned war of national liberation against colonialism. Sun Yat-sen described China, as you know, as a semicolonial power. Nobody controlled it completely but everybody had a bite of it.

. . . Then I would suggest that from the Communist point of view it became a war of national liberation for a period, anyway, certainly up to 1927 when the movement split again and Communists went one way and the Nationalists went another. [pp 459–460]

Sen. Lausche: You made further mention of there being a divergence of approach as advocated by Khrushchev and by Mao Tse-tung. My question to you is, has Mao Tse-tung gone so far in protesting the conduct of Red Russia, as to practically say that every means should be used to communize the world, even to indulgence in violence of the worst type?

Dr. Judd: Again the answer is "Yes." Mao Tse-tung proclaims that on every occasion. Power, he puts it, comes out of the barrel of a gun. Now I suppose he would say out of a nuclear missile. That is the only kind of power he admits. . . .

Sen. Lausche: Dr. Taylor, you mentioned aggression by Red China evidencing an absence of desire for peace. Will you follow me and see if I am correct? Have they been guilty of aggression in Tibet?

Dr. Taylor: I would think so, yes.

Sen. Lausche: In India?

Dr. Taylor: Yes.

Sen. Lausche: In Malaysia?

Dr. Taylor: Definitely.

Sen. Lausche: In Korea?

Dr. Taylor: Yes.

Sen. Lausche: In South Vietnam?

Dr. Taylor: We are accepting a fairly broad definition of aggression. Yes.

Sen. Lausche: In Laos?

Dr. Taylor: Yes.

Sen. Lausche: Thailand also, as mentioned by Senator Symington. Can either of you point out a single instance where Mao Tse-tung and the Communist Party have been the promoters of peace and brotherhood and good neighborliness, and not centering all of their intention [attention?] in trying to communize the world?

Dr. Taylor: Well, sir, I think to find such an example would be rather a difficult assignment. I would, if I may, Mr. Senator, suggest that my answers were predicated on a fairly broad definition of aggression. I do not think of military action with flags flying and bugles sounding as the only form of aggression. The peculiar type of subpolitical, social, economic, subversive activity in which the Communists have now excelled so well is possibly the more dangerous type [sic] that we have to contend with today, and I would think it very important to keep in mind that the Chinese threat is not the threat of large armies marching over small borders, but of powerful support of those who wish to subvert a society. [pp. 471–473]

The Chairman: Do you know, Dr. Taylor, how many soldiers we have outside our borders?

Dr. Taylor: No, sir.

The Chairman: About 600,000. Do you know how many the Chinese have?

Dr. Taylor: Abroad?

The Chairman: Yes, outside of their borders.

Dr. Taylor: I don't know. They have some, but I don't know.

The Chairman: Where are they, and how many?

Dr. Taylor: Well, they certainly have quite a few; these are not all soldiers, I wish to insist upon this.

The Chairman: First we will take soldiers and then non-soldiers. Do you know of any soldiers?

Dr. Taylor: Yes, they have them in Tibet, some 300,000 of them.

The Chairman: In Tibet?

Dr. Taylor: They have quite a lot.

The Chairman: You don't consider Tibet part of China?

Dr. Taylor: No. They have them in Inner Mongolia.

The Chairman: What is Tibet? What is its status?

Dr. Taylor: It is now supposedly an autonomous region.

The Chairman: What was it before 1957 or 1958? Was it an independent country?

Dr. Taylor: It has been an independent country.

The Chairman: Had we recognized it as an independent country at any time in its history? . . .

Dr. Taylor: So far as I know, no.

The Chairman: Do you know, Doctor?

Dr. Judd: I think not.

The Chairman: It was not. Was it by any country? It was never recognized as being an independent country, was it?

Dr. Taylor: It had a vague sort of status. . . .

The Chairman: Vague status. I accept that. It is true. So it is still very vague whether you can say those troops are outside of China or not, right?

Dr. Taylor: Well, yes, in this sense the Chinese do not have large numbers of troops abroad.

The Chairman: Why not? If they are determined to subvert everybody why don't they have troops abroad?

Dr. Taylor: For the very good reason it wouldn't be a very good way of subverting anybody.

The Chairman: No, it wouldn't. How many countries in Africa or Latin America do you consider they have under their domination or influence now?

Dr. Taylor: I don't think they have any under their domination. They have various areas of influence. Up until recently, they had a considerable influence in Indonesia, and up until last October one of the largest Communist Parties in the world, as well. Admittedly the Chinese have great influence. The Chinese have some support from the New Zealand and Australian Communist Parties. They are very proud of their influence in the Japanese Communist Party, very proud indeed.

The Chairman: In the congress of Communist Parties that opens today or tomorrow, how many countries have gone to Moscow indicating they prefer Moscow over China?

Dr. Taylor: Most of them.

The Chairman: How many have refused to go?

Dr. Taylor: Well, China, and I believe Albania.

The Chairman: Two of them. Out of how many?

Dr. Taylor: I can't give you the exact figures.

The Chairman: Well, approximately? Is it twenty or are there ninety? Do you know, Dr. Judd?

Dr. Judd: At the tricontinental conference they had in Havana in January, they said there were 600 representatives from Communist Parties in eighty-two countries.

The Chairman: Eighty-two?

Dr. Taylor: It is about a hundred.

The Chairman: Somewhere between eighty-two and one hundred. It doesn't indicate the Chinese have been very successful, does it?

Dr. Taylor: Yes, sir, they were very successful in Indonesia. They have been very successful in Vietnam, they have had considerable success in Japan, and I would say that they have been remarkably successful in changing the political climate in India where for a very small investment they have intensified the antagonism between Pakistan and India a great deal. They have brought people in to help bring about military coups in several states in Africa. Yes, sir, I would say they have been quite influential.

The Chairman: Well, I am completely misinformed. Do you consider the coup in Ghana as brought about by the Chinese Communists? That is an example. What do you have in mind that the Chinese Communists have brought about in Africa?

Dr. Taylor: Well, they had plenty of people there and I believe the sort of political actions that they encouraged there were designed to and succeeded in helping bring about the military coup. Nkrumah was very much given the red carpet treatment by Peking. I think there is plenty of evidence that they encouraged him in the policies that he followed, and that these policies led to, or shall we say, had something to do with, the coup.

The Chairman: Let me understand it. . . . Do you mean that, because Nkrumah was encouraged to, and did, follow policies advocated by the Chinese Communists, and these policies were so disagreeable to his people that they caused a coup, and that this is a sign of success of Chinese subversion?

Dr. Taylor: Yes. May I say ——

The Chairman: In other words, whenever they get someone to follow their policies which results in a coup that throws the followers out, that this is a sign of their success?

Dr. Taylor: Yes. For the very good reason that they wished to polarize the situation and succeeded in doing so.

Dr. Judd: Mr. Stalin said, "The mightiest ally of the Soviet Union is to have strife, conflicts, and wars in every other country." Wherever they are able to get conflict going and make people lose faith in themselves, divide peoples, convince Americans or others that after all our system has a lot of failures and shortcomings too, they are succeeding. [pp. 484–486]

Testimony of David N. Rowe

Dr. Rowe: [Prepared Statement] [The] prevention of a military showdown now between the United States and Communist China is the main aim of Communists everywhere. Why?

(a) If such a showdown came soon, it would destroy Communist China as such and constitute the single most catastrophic setback in history to the course of the Communist world revolution.

(b) If such a showdown can be prevented for five to ten years, the pro-Communist China and anti–anti-Communist elements in this country count on the development of Communist Chinese thermonuclear power to produce a standoff and make Communist China then invulnerable to U.S. destruction, by means of the retaliatory threat. They count on this stage lasting ten to twenty years during which either one and probably both of two things would happen:

1. The United States would prove unable to develop any effective deterrent to so-called "indirect aggression" and to "people's war" with the result that all of Asia would come under Chinese Communist domination and control, and the impact on Africa and Latin America would be disastrous.

2. Under the deterrent of terror the political and psychological pressures toward a détente with Communist China similar to present illusions along that line with the U.S.S.R. would engender a thorough and complete coexistence policy vis-à-vis the Communist Chinese.

The Communist Chinese need coexistence much worse than do the Russians. Why? The lack of massive external support and their huge and insoluble internal problems doom them forever to weakness and mediocrity and complete totalitarianism and military adventurism. They are trying their hardest now to soften our approach to them under the blackmail of aggression and war, to gain at no cost to them politically what they need in outside economic and technical support from the West, and particularly from the United States of America. This is why their friends in the United States are trying hard to soften the U.S. approach to Communist China. [p. 497]

Sen. Sparkman: In your opinion, is modern-day China expansionistic?

Dr. Rowe: I think there is no doubt about this. Communist China is expansionistic.

Sen. Sparkman: Do you believe that they want to either move into southeast Asia or to have that as their own sphere of influence?

Dr. Rowe: They certainly, as an absolute minimum, want to have that as their sole sphere of influence with all Western influence of any kind removed from it, and even removed from its neighborhood.

As to the question of whether they want to take over these countries and govern them as dependencies or assimilate them into the frontiers and the boundaries of Communist China, that is quite another matter.

There, their own tradition would lead them away from this . . . . there is not too much reason to debate the question as to whether they have real territorial ambitions here, because what they would have by way of complete control and domination would be just the same as if it were incorporated into their own territories from the foreign relations point of view, the primary purpose being the exploitation of the economic resources of southeast Asia. [pp. 513–514]

Testimony of Hans J. Morgenthau

Dr. Morgenthau: [Summary of Prepared Statement] Let me . . . take a look at the actual policies pursued by the Communist government of China in the last sixteen years. I think the first observation one must make is the impressive contrast between the extreme and almost mad statements Chinese leaders have made with regard to the outside world, and the extreme caution with which China has actually acted with regard to the outside world.

More particularly, if you look at the actual objectives which the Chinese government has set itself in foreign policy, the offshore islands and Taiwan, Korea, southeast Asia, Tibet, the India frontier, and Outer Mongolia, you realize that they are all within the nationalistic tradition of China, and it is not by accident that Chiang Kai-shek has supported all of them.

There has been no difference of opinion, for instance, between Chiang Kai-shek and Mao Tse-tung as to the fact that Taiwan constitutes an integral part of China. They only happen to disagree as to who shall govern China.

There has been no disagreement between Mao Tse-tung and Chiang Kai-shek concerning the claim that Tibet constitutes an integral part of the Chinese empire. Nor has there been any difference of opinion between them as to illegitimacy of the McMahon Line as the boundary between China and India. The verbal expressions of the Chinese leaders have all pointed toward the restoration of the Chinese empire as it existed about one hundred years ago, before the period of China's humiliation started and lowered the restoration of China's traditional influence on the Asian continent.

It is, of course, obvious that in actuality the Chinese government has gone farther than that. It has meddled in the internal affairs of a number of nations in Africa and Latin America by virtue of its Communist militancy. Here we are in the presence of an additional factor which the foreign policy of the United States must take into account. [pp. 552–553]

Testimony of Robert A. Scalapino

Dr. Scalapino: [Prepared Statement] What are the Chinese goals? Three have been oft proclaimed: To remove all Western influence from Asia; to encourage by a variety of means an ideologically politically uniform Asia cast in the image of "the new China"; and to enlist this "progressive" Asia in the global struggle against both the "revisionists" and the "imperialists." The words are those of the Chinese.

These are scarcely the goals of an elite that is primarily oriented toward defense, and posing its objectives in very limited terms. It is quite true, however, that these goals — and some of the actions that have accompanied them — have triggered a reaction, not alone from us but from many others as well. Thus today, China must calculate defensively because the United States, and in some degree the Soviet Union, will not permit her to calculate offensively on any significant scale.

Her defensive calculations undoubtedly include a determination in each specific instance as to what she can and cannot tolerate from the standpoint of her own national interests, and what risks, correspondingly, she is prepared to run. Personally, I do not believe that the Chinese Communists are prepared to take the risks of an open war with the United States at this time except under the most extraordinary of circumstances or under conditions where they misinterpret American signals. Specifically, I regard it as highly unlikely that China will intervene fully in the Vietnam war unless the obliteration of North Vietnam is threatened. Even then, it will be an extremely difficult decision for Peking because she knows she would be subjected to massive destruction, and such a war would run completely counter to her basic policy which has been aimed at provoking an American-Soviet confrontation in the course of involving the United States simultaneously in a series of "national liberation wars."

The fact, however, that China is forced to react defensively and partly from fear at this point should not obscure the very strong commitment which the current generation of Chinese leaders have had to global influence. From the moment they emerged into full control, these leaders committed themselves and their society to the cultivation of power in all of its forms: military, political, psychological, and economic. Contrast their attitude toward power and their actions, for example, with those of Nehru and Nehru's India. Nehru eschewed armaments, avoided alliances and, on occasion, seemed to shun even active political diplomacy. Mao and his comrades, on the other hand, were prepared to make major sacrifices for the sake of political and military power, including the development of a nuclear arsenal.

Since the Communist era began in China, no Asian state has been capable of matching Chinese power unaided, and it is wise to remember that there is not a pacifist bone in a Maoist body. The Chinese Communists, moreover, have consummated alliances large and small, undertaken aid and technical assistance programs far beyond their economic capacities, and engaged in a range of political activities throughout the world that caused most nations, friend and foe, to label China "major power designate." That is a significant accomplishment, incidentally, because such a status grants certain rights without conveying the requisite responsibilities.

When all of these activities are surveyed, I do not understand how anyone can regard Chinese actions or goals of the past decade as defensive, either in character or intent. The recent major failures of that policy, indeed, are due to precisely the opposite problem: the Chinese Communists sought to force the pace, undertaking actions in Asia, Africa, and Latin America that were interpreted by others as aggressive, ultranationalist and dangerous. As noted earlier, it is quite likely that Peking will now be forced to retrench in foreign policy as they have previously been forced to retrench in domestic policy. The basic ingredients — the fundamental source-springs — of Chinese foreign policy, however, are likely to remain. It will be important, therefore, to distinguish between short-run tactics and long-range goals.

What have been the major source-springs of Chinese foreign policy under the Communists? Three forces seem to me of central importance: tradition, nationalism, and MLM — Marx-Lenin-Maoism. In certain respects, the current Chinese leaders still think of their problem as how to handle the barbarians. They still divide the world into those who accept Chinese culture (now to be read "ideology") and those who live outside the pale. The former are the "civilized" or the "progressive" people, to use their terms; the latter are barbarians, be they "revisionists," "imperialists," or "neutrals." The barbarian must be handled by a combination of persuasion and coercion. One uses visits to the imperial capital, exchanges of gifts, and many other devices to awe and impress; and one uses strong words and, when necessary and possible, strong actions to cajole and coerce. Some of China's difficulties today are unquestionably due to a continuance among her present generation of mandarin rulers of an "imperial complex," an engrained sense of cultural superiority, and the attitude of condescension toward other peoples that invariably accompanies this.

The nationalist quotient in Chinese foreign policy is, of course, extremely high. In many respects, China is behaving in much the same fashion as have other major societies en route to power. First, she has sought to define and defend her boundaries as she interprets these; secondly, she has sought to create a buffer-state system around her; and finally, she has sought hegemony in the world in which she lives: the Asian world, the non-Western world, and the Communist world.

In pursuit of these objectives, the Chinese Communists have been no more able to follow a totally consistent foreign policy than the leaders of other major states. The main thrust of Chinese Communist foreign policy, as suggested earlier, has been characterized by revolutionary fervor, global commitment, and relatively inflexible division of the world into comrades and enemies. The line has been hard, advanced by practicing ideologues fiercely impatient with the existing order and anxious to challenge it in radical fashion. And yet, for tactical reasons and out of necessity, these leaders have adopted a great variety of approaches. On occasion, they have not hesitated to consort with "feudalists" and support "reactionary" regimes; sometimes, they have used the soft line, as at the time of Bandung; not infrequently, they have been caught in such un-Marxian stances as making an appeal to race. Indeed, one is forced to conclude that the one element of major consistency is that which runs through the policies of all nations: the consistent expression of what appears to the political elite as in their national interests. And it is precisely this fact that offers hope of some flexibility, even among hard-core ideologues. . . .

The final source-spring of Chinese Communist foreign policy, I have labeled MLM. The Maoists think of themselves as orthodox Marxist-Leninists, indeed, as the only legitimate leaders of the world Marxist movement. At the same time, however, they pride themselves upon having "applied Marxism-Leninism creativity" to the conditions of China. Perhaps it is accurate to define the Maoist element in Chinese Marxism as the practical development of a five-stage revolutionary progression which places heavy reliance initially upon intellectual leadership and a peasant-based radical movement that has its roots in the countryside.

The Maoist revolutionary formula begins with the creation of a Com-

munist Party which must never lose control of the revolutionary movement. That party proceeds to guide the creation of a united front, using
nationalist and socioeconomic appeals, but relying heavily upon organization, and using freely the instruments of coercion as well as those of persuasion. When the front has been prepared, the movement into guerrilla
warfare is the next stage, and then the advance to positional warfare.
When military victory has been attained, the so-called People's Democratic Republic is established under the complete control of the Communist Party.

Long before Lin Piao's speech of last summer, it was clear that the
Chinese Communists regarded this revolutionary formula broadly appli-
cable to the world scene — from the Congo to Vietnam. In very high
degree, indeed, the old Bolsheviks of China, so strongly isolated from world
reality, have seen the world mirrored in their own ideological-revolutionary
image and history. The need for a true Communist Party means
that one must fight such false Marxists-Leninists as the Russians. The
united front with its emphasis upon a union of peasants, workers, intellectuals, and national bourgeois under the leadership of the vanguard
party spells out the Chinese determination to unite the world peasantry
(the Afro-Asian societies) and certain susceptible bourgeois elements
(clearly France was once in mind) under Peking's banners.

Thus, MLM makes Chinese Communist foreign policy something more
than merely another expression of nationalism in action. It defines both
the scope and the techniques of policy in a unique way. China is interested in Albania as well as Korea; in Mali as well as in Vietnam. The
definition of national interest, the conceptualization of problem, the
vocabulary of dispute are all colored by MLM. It would be as dangerous
to underestimate the Marxist quotient in Chinese foreign policy at this
point as to accord it total influence. [pp. 565–569]

7   THE SINO-SOVIET DISPUTE

Testimony of A. Doak Barnett

Mr. Barnett: [Prepared Statement] The Sino-Soviet dispute as it has evolved in recent years is clearly one of the most important developments in the international politics of the 1960's — just as the formation of the Sino-Soviet alliance was in the 1950's. There can be no doubt that the conflicts between Peking and Moscow now are very real, very bitter, and very deep. The dispute has involved basic clashes of national interests as well as major ideological differences, and it has resulted in worldwide competition between the two countries.

In a fundamental sense the Sino-Soviet dispute has weakened Peking's international position, which has been to our advantage in many respects, since it imposes increased restraints on the Chinese Communist regime. But not all of the results of the dispute have been good from our point of view. It appears, for example, to have been a significant factor reinforcing Peking's tendency in recent years to maintain a highly militant posture.

We cannot, moreover, rely on the dispute to solve our own basic problems in relations with the Chinese. In certain situations, Soviet interests and policies may run parallel to ours, as appears to be the case even in Vietnam today, to a very limited degree. But we cannot expect such parallelism to be dependable or believe that it will result — as some suggest — in a kind of Soviet-American anti-Chinese axis. Even when a degree of parallelism does exist, it cannot be expected to resolve all the difficult problems of dealing with the Chinese. Furthermore, although it is difficult to see in the predictable future any full restoration of the type of Sino-Soviet relationship that existed in the early 1950's, it is certainly possible that Communist China, particularly under new leaders, might decide to try to repair at least some of the damage that has been done to the alliance in recent years. In any case, the United States will itself have to work toward a solution of at least some of our problems with Communist China; the Sino-Soviet dispute will not solve them for us. [p. 12]

Sen. Williams: I noticed that Communist China simultaneously alienated the United States and the Soviet Union in India. Would you care to comment on this? Why does she pursue such a belligerent course?

117

Mr. Barnett: Right. In some sense this does raise baffling questions — as to why the people of Peking decided they were prepared to have hostile relations with both of the two largest powers. But I think that there are explanations . . . as to why the Chinese became so concerned with the Soviets' policies that they were prepared to pursue the policies which helped to exacerbate the split. I myself regard the period 1954 to 1959 as crucial in the whole development of the Sino-Soviet split, and I believe that certain issues which the Chinese looked on, above all, as national interest issues, rather than ideological issues, were at the root of the dispute. I think, to simplify, that there were at least three developments in that period in Soviet policy that were terribly important from the Chinese point of view and help to explain why they ended up where they did in their position in relation to the Soviets.

One of these was the failure of the Soviets to give the Chinese Communists as much support as they had hoped in the offshore islands crisis of 1958, in regard to Taiwan. . . .

A second was the neutral position assumed by the Russians regarding the India border issue in 1959. At the time the Chinese Communists said this was the first time that a Socialist state has not backed up another Socialist state on this kind of an issue.

And the third was the complicated field of nuclear relations between the two countries. As you probably recall in 1957, late 1957, an agreement was signed between Moscow and Peking in which the Soviets promised support in the nuclear weapons field — although there never had been data as to the precise nature of this agreement — and then in 1949 the Soviet Union broke this treaty, dissolved this agreement. And the Chinese involved ——

The Chairman: 1949 or 1959?

Mr. Barnett: 1959, excuse me, 1959. Now, I think that the Chinese were impelled to conclude that the Soviets wanted to try to prevent Communist China from becoming a nuclear power, and this became absolutely clear, of course, in 1963 when the test ban was signed. This was a point after which the Chinese really escalated their verbal attacks on the Soviet Union.

In other words, I think that issues of this kind, and the general move on the part of the Soviets toward — in the direction, at least, of — a limited détente with the United States, from Peking's point of view, made it look as if the two major powers were trying to freeze the status quo, that the Soviets would not back up what Peking thought were some of its major interests, and that, therefore, any kind of a policy on the part of the Soviets moving in this direction would add increased obstacles to the Chinese achievement of their goals, would be highly undesirable from Chinese national interest point of view, wholly apart from ideology.

There were many ideological issues involved, some of these quite real, but I myself think some of these underlying factors were more important. [pp. 32–33]

Sen. Clark: Would you comment on the interrelationship between our policy with the Soviet Union and our policy with Communist China?

Mr. Barnett: Yes. I would like to, because I know some people raise questions as to whether any moves of the sort I have suggested toward China would tend to complicate the détente with the Soviet Union, and maybe force the Soviets to move away from it.

Personally, I very much doubt that, and I do not think it is likely because I think that the Soviets' moves toward a limited détente with us are not because of the Sino-Soviet dispute. The Soviets were willing to risk the Sino-Soviet dispute, as great a blow as this was to their relationship, because there are basic factors they thought were overriding: the danger of nuclear war, the danger of small conflicts getting out of hand and growing into big conflicts; I think these factors are still going to operate.

So that it seems to me that these are the basic reasons that explain why we have been able to move toward some agreements with the Soviets, and if we move . . . in some of the directions I have suggested toward China, it is not going to change these basic factors. I think they are still going to operate, and I think it is important for us, somehow, at some future point, to begin to get into this kind of a dialog with the Chinese, and begin to help the Chinese realize that there are greater dangers of a large-scale conflict than they are now prepared to accept. [p. 44]

Testimony of Benjamin I. Schwartz
and John M. H. Lindbeck

Sen. Hickenlooper: From all of the press information we get, [the Sino-Soviet] split seems to be quite violent, and quite broad. But in view of the fact that we have seen Communist propaganda blow hot and cold and at convenience a short time later change and reverse its field, what do you think about Russia and Red China being able to compromise their differences very quickly if one of them gets in trouble? . . .

Dr. Schwartz: I think one cannot even now bar the possibility of limited cooperation between Russia and China on various issues. I myself happen to think that the split between them is extremely deep — that one cannot talk about communism in general any more. One must talk about the Chinese and the Russians. . . .

I think that the Chinese at this point are dreaming of a new Communist order centered on Peiping, and that therefore communism as an ideology in a way aggravates the split. It leads both protagonists to try to maintain supreme ultimate power in the world Communist movement and these claims are conflicting.

I regard the split as very fundamental, indeed. I think that one of the regrettable results of our recent involvement in Vietnam is that our consciousness of the crisis has receded into the background. One of the things that fascinates me about the Chinese press is that even when discussing Vietnam they devote almost as much attention to their relations with the Soviet Union — to their exasperation with the Soviet Union — as they do to their relations with us.

But here again, if I may refer again to my initial statement, I do not attribute to the Communists an inexhaustible fund of diabolical cleverness. I don't really believe they are much more clever than we are.

Sen. Hickenlooper: There have been occasions when I could say that almost anybody is more clever than we have been. I hope we are more clever in the long run than most people.

Dr. Lindbeck: I don't know what the Russian experts would think Moscow's decision might be. The reverse situation — i.e., if the Soviet Union and the United States directly threatened each other's existence and if Moscow were in danger of going under — I suspect that the Chinese would act. Now how they would act and precisely in what form, of course, I don't know. I think they also would try to take advantage of any dispute or any conflict between the two superpowers.

But barring Armageddons of the kind we are discussing, it seems to me that the differences between the two countries now are really quite deep and great. They go beyond ideology. A notable aspect, I suppose, of the depth of this difference is that each country is trying to hurt the other. Once you start injuring somebody, it usually is very difficult to heal the injuries. The pain the Russians are causing the Chinese is, I think, felt in Peking as being very painful indeed. The Chinese are extremely annoyed, for example, by Russian strategies in international politics. Russia's refusal to support specific Chinese interests against the United States makes the differences between them very important and keenly felt in Peking.

Sen. Hickenlooper: Does that lead one then to the speculation that both the Chinese and the Russians would consider their own long-run nationalist interests rather than support the other country? Or would they consider that the basic ideology of whatever type of communism they may follow is much greater against the Western world?

Dr. Lindbeck: My formulation of the question would be a little different. That is, I think both governments act on the basis of national considerations. They interpret their national interests in the light of their ideology — their ideology informs their assessment of trends in the world; their weighting of priorities is also related to their conception of history, the direction of changes over the globe as a whole. By virtue of the fact that they do share some sets of common perspectives provided by Marxist-

Leninism, they probably would tend to agree on a number of vital issues. But the point I would like to make is that both elites, the Russian and the Chinese, look out from their national bases of power in making the decisions forced on them by international developments. [pp. 202–204]

Sen. Church: While we are talking about boundaries, I wonder if I could ask a question about the 7,000 miles of common frontier between China and the Soviet Union. Do you think that Russia may have less to fear or as much to fear or more to fear from China than the United States?

Dr. Lindbeck: What time period are you talking about?

Sen. Church: I am talking about the present and looking toward the future.

Dr. Schwartz: Well, in in terms of actual military power, of course, the Russians are much stronger than the Chinese. But I do think that in actuality they have great fears, that they are very much concerned, so I would say at least as much to fear.

Sen. Church: Then, following on, if they have as much to fear from China as the United States, this derives, does it not, from the long common boundary, and from the fact that the Chinese do have claims, territorial claims, that historically they have raised, and may later press against the Russians, is that not true?

Dr. Schwartz: Yes, that is true.

Sen. Church: So that the nature of the present difficulty, the rift between Russia and China is not confined to ideological differences in their respective interpretations of communism, but is at least partially grounded on old-fashioned national antagonisms between the two countries based upon conflicting territorial claims?

Dr. Schwartz: Well, the way I would be inclined to put it is as follows: that as long as the ideological alliance between them was firm, all of these issues, which were certainly there in the background, were more or less swept under the rug. We now know that even Outer Mongolia is an issue in the Chinese view, but it was suppressed. It seems to me that now that the crisis has grown between them, these issues have had a chance again to come to the fore, to surface again.

I think it would not be cautious to assume they would necessarily go to war next week over these issues but they have had a chance to resurface.

Sen. Church: Yes.

Dr. Lindbeck: I would, I think, differ with Mr. Schwartz' initial reaction. I should think that the Russians have less to fear than we do, in one sense. The situation in southeast and south Asia concerns us. Boundaries in this direction are much softer and this area is more vulnerable than on other sides of China. The Russian boundary line, even though it is 7,000 miles long, is much sharper and better controlled. I would think it is in the long run that the Russians feel that the Chinese might be a great threat.

Dr. Schwartz: I think I would accept that correction.

Sen. Church: Yes. Presently the threat may not be as serious as that posed to us in southeast Asia.

Dr. Lindbeck: Right.

Sen. Church: But eventually it may grow into a very serious threat, is that your position?

Dr. Lindbeck: This depends on the broad trend of international developments. The outcome could be more difficult for us if Russian and Chinese antagonisms grow instead of stabilize and southeast Asia became a major point of conflict between them. [pp. 228–229]

Testimony of Harold C. Hinton

Dr. Hinton: [Prepared Statement] For a number of reasons that included its determination to confront the United States in Asia, the Chinese leadership chose to ally itself with the Soviet Union in 1950. The alliance was seriously strained by the Korean crisis and still more by the massive retaliation doctrine and the entry of West Germany into NATO, which riveted Soviet attention on Europe more than ever and reduced almost to the vanishing point Soviet willingness to take serious risks on behalf of China, even in defense of its security and still less in support of its offensive ambitions, such as the taking of Taiwan. In 1956, therefore, Communist China decided that it must have nuclear weapons and delivery systems of its own. It succeeded in getting substantial Soviet technical aid and equipment toward this end in exchange for acquiescence in Soviet efforts to achieve a test ban agreement. A Chinese demand for the turning over of finished Soviet nuclear weapons as an interim measure seems to have foundered, however, on a Soviet counter-demand for joint defense arrangements that would have amounted to Soviet controls. The Soviet Union canceled its nuclear aid, and China in return withdrew its support for a test ban agreement, its objections rising to a crescendo when the Soviet Union actually signed such an agreement in 1963. Over and above the specific issue of the test ban, China objects to any sort of American-Soviet détente, because it diminishes still further the Soviet incentive to give China active support against the United States without reducing Sino-American tensions in any way.

Undaunted, Communist China has continued its drive to become a nuclear power. Indeed, there is strong evidence that it is the only country in the world that is seriously trying to join the United States and the Soviet Union as a thermonuclear superpower. The current Chinese leadership apparently intends to use whatever pressures and exact whatever sacrifices are necessary to put China at least over the hump on the way to thermonuclear weapons and suitable delivery systems, just as Stalin did for the Soviet Union, and is greatly worried that younger Chinese may not share its taste for hardship and nuclear status symbols. The Chinese quest for nuclear weapons as well as Chinese pressures on the Soviet Union within the framework of the international Communist movement, that are at least partly in retaliation for what the Chinese regard as Soviet betrayal of the Sino-Soviet alliance, have contributed heavily to a deterioration of Sino-Soviet relations that since 1963 has occasionally taken on dramatic proportions. One manifestation of this deterioration has been a border dispute that has sometimes approached the level of at least local war. [pp. 377–378]

Testimony of George E. Taylor

Sen. Case: What is your conception of international communism? What are the institutions that hold it together, give it continuity? Who defines its philosophy, determines its actions, if it acts — just what is this thing? . . .

Dr. Taylor: Very briefly, Mr. Chairman, it is a new type of society with a new basis for power, and I think the basis for that is fairly well known by the American public today. . . .

I suppose what it comes down to is that there is no viable international political organization holding Communist states together. On the other hand, I think it is very dangerous to assume that the Communist world is becoming a pluralistic world. . . .

I think it is very dangerous to think it is a pluralistic world. The term "polycentrism" has been used to suggest this. I think the Soviet Union still has enormous power, naturally, over those Communist states nearest to it. What is going on now between Peking and Moscow, I think, is an organizational struggle fought with organizational means. The Chinese have fought with ideological weapons and have had considerable success. The Chinese have succeeded in getting quite a few states, Communist Parties or parts of Communist Parties in various parts of the world, to support their general line, the one I referred to, the Lin Piao line, and they have done this deliberately in order to get organized support for getting their own way and power within the so-called bloc.

I feel very strongly that we should assume that this is the Communist way of struggle. This is their way, the only way they know, of dealing politically with each other. It is very interesting that the Communist Chinese have called the Russians all the same names that the Russians have called the Chinese. And although there is a difference, I think, in their emphasis and the way they want to go about it, they are still struggling for domination within the same general Communist world. [pp. 478–481]

Testimony of Robert A. Scalapino

Dr. Scalapino: [Prepared Statement] At its roots, the Sino-Soviet dispute itself is closely connected with the phenomena of nationalism. We now know that nationalism has not only survived communism, but in many respects triumphed over it. The Sino-Soviet cleavage illustrates the fact that two nations supposedly sharing a common ideology but differing substantially in cultural traditions, timing of revolution, stage of development, generation of leadership and degree of power are almost certain to have different views of the world and of their own needs. Hence, they will have different concepts of national interest which, in the case of Marxists, will be translated into different interpretations of what is truth; namely, what is orthodox Marxism-Leninism. . . .

The Sino-Soviet dispute centers upon the issue of how to treat the United States, although there are other significant issues as well. The Soviet Union basically believes in nation-to-nation competition with the United States, counting upon the ultimate superiority of Soviet productivity and power. Thus it argues that the appropriate method of confrontation is peaceful coexistence, meaning all-out economic, political and social competition but the avoidance of nuclear war. . . .

China, on the other hand, not being able to conceive of the possibility of nation-to-nation competition with the United States in the near future, and having no basic responsibility for the maintenance of peace or the prosecution of a nuclear war, argues the classical Bolshevik thesis that America must be challenged by the technique of unfolding the world revolution. The Chinese theme is that primary emphasis must be placed upon mobilizing the non-Western world for a rapid, continuous assault upon the "capitalist West, led by the United States." Thus the Russians are rebuked for their refusal to take massive risks on behalf of global revolution, and they are now charged by Peking with active collaboration with Washington for purposes of world domination. . . . [pp. 567–568]

Part Three

AMERICAN POLICY
TOWARD CHINA

8 CONTAINMENT WITHOUT ISOLATION?

Testimony of A. Doak Barnett

Mr. Barnett: [Prepared Statement] I would like, right at the start, to state my own belief that there is a need for basic changes in the overall U.S. posture toward Communist China. For almost seventeen years we have pursued a policy that might best be characterized as one aimed at containment and isolation of Communist China.

In my view, the element of containment — using this term in a very broad sense to include both military and nonmilitary measures to block threats posed by China to its neighbors — has been an essential part of our policy and has been, in some respects at least, fairly successful. Our power has played an important and necessary role in creating a counterbalance to Communist China's power in Asia, and we have contributed significantly to the task of gradually building stable non-Communist societies in areas that lie in China's shadow. But the U.S. attempt to isolate Communist China has been, in my opinion, unwise and, in a fundamental sense, unsuccessful, and it cannot, I believe, provide a basis for a sound, long-term policy that aims not only at containing and restraining Chinese power but also at reducing tensions, exerting a moderating influence on Peking, broadening the areas of non-Communist agreement on issues relating to China, and slowly involving Communist China in more normal patterns of international intercourse.

I strongly believe, therefore, that the time has come — even though the United States is now engaged in a bitter struggle in Vietnam — for our country to alter its posture toward Communist China and adopt a policy of containment but not isolation, a policy that would aim on the one hand at checking military or subversive threats and pressures emanating from Peking, but at the same time would aim at maximum contacts with, and maximum involvement of, the Chinese Communists in the international community.

Such a policy would involve continued commitments to help non-Communist regimes combat Communist subversion and insurrection, as in Vietnam, and continued pledges to defend areas on China's periphery, including Taiwan. But it would involve changes in many other aspects of our policies.

127

While continuing to fulfill our pledge to defend Taiwan against attack, we should clearly and explicitly acknowledge the Chinese Communist regime as the de facto government of the China mainland and state our desire to extend de jure recognition and exchange diplomatic representatives with Peking if and when it indicates that it would be prepared to reciprocate.

We should press in every way we can to encourage nonofficial contacts. We should, instead of embargoing all trade with the China mainland, restrict only trade in strategic items and encourage American businessmen to explore other opportunities for trade contacts. And within the United Nations we should work for the acceptance of some formula which would provide seats for both Communist China and Nationalist China. In taking these steps, we will have to do so in full recognition of the fact that Peking's initial reaction is almost certain to be negative and even hostile and that any changes in our posture will create some new problems. But we should take them, nevertheless, because initiatives on our part are clearly required if we are to work, however slowly, toward the long-term goal of a more stable, less-explosive situation in Asia and to explore the possibilities of trying to moderate Peking's policies.

Some people believe that a policy combining the differing elements I have suggested, that is, containment but also increased attempts to deal directly with Peking — would involve contradictory and inconsistent elements. I would argue that, on the contrary, in terms of our long-term aims the seemingly contradictory elements would in fact be complementary and mutually reinforcing.

Others argue that a change of posture such as the one I have suggested might be interpreted as a sign of weakness and irresolution on our part, and therefore be dangerous, particularly if taken while we are engaged in a major struggle against Communist insurrection in Vietnam. I would argue that our commitments and actions in Vietnam make it wholly clear, to both friend and foe, that we are not acting out of weakness and that while we search for areas of possible agreement and accommodation we will also continue in our determination to protect the interests of ourselves and our friends, to oppose violence as a means of political change, and to assist in the growth of viable, progressive, non-Communist regimes, in Asia, as elsewhere. [pp. 4–5]

As a part of our effort to increase unofficial contacts with Communist China we should, in my opinion, end our embargo on all trade and permit trade in nonstrategic items. The present significance of our embargo, it should be stressed, is wholly symbolic, since no other major trading nation maintains such an embargo, and Peking is able, therefore, to purchase in Japan, Germany, England, or elsewhere any goods that are denied to it by us. The ending of our embargo might well be largely symbolic, too, since the Chinese Communists are likely to prefer trading with countries other than the United States. Nevertheless, it is conceivable that over time some limited trade contacts might develop, and be desirable from our point of view. . . .

Our aim, certainly, should be to work toward eventual establishment of normal diplomatic relations, but it is likely to be some time — even if we alter our own overall position — before that is possible. We can and should, however, clearly indicate now — in much more explicit fashion than we have to date — that we do recognize the Peking regime in a de facto sense. One might argue that our frequent ambassadorial meetings with the Chinese Communists in Warsaw already constitute a form of de facto recognition, but officially we have refused to acknowledge any sort of recognition — de jure or de facto — and we should now do so. [p. 15]

Sen. Case: I think it is necessary and desirable to have an impartial witness like you, if you will, give the arguments for containment which is the basis of our policy, because I gather from the whole sweep of your statement and your answers to the questions which I have heard so far, you support this administration and its policies as you see them. . . .

Mr. Barnett: Right. There is a variety of states on China's periphery, and there is a variety of attitudes toward China. But I would say that a great many of the small states on China's periphery have a real sense of uneasiness about China's power. . . .

My own feeling would be that if we did not inject our power into the equation of power in Asia, what would be likely would not be that the Communists would just take over Asia, as some people fear, in a physical or military sense. What I would see would be a steady and fairly rapid and, perhaps, fairly extreme process of accommodation to China on the part of small states whose leaders feel that they have to go very far — to protect themselves without any external protection — in adapting in a variety of ways, their policies to fit Peking's general outlook and general goals.

I do not want to seem critical of Cambodia and Burma, but I think Cambodia and Burma have gone quite far, as I would view it, in accommodating to China, and I think that if the whole region was there, without any counterbalancing force, and there were these trends and forces toward accommodation, this would impose, in a real sense, real limitations of action on these countries, and have a great many influences on them that would not be what they would desire.

So that I think it is essential to have this reassuring backing up, supporting, of the small, apprehensive countries, by U.S. power. [p. 39]

Sen. Symington: The British and the Pakistanis felt they have not obtained much in the way of improved relationship by recognizing Red China. I do not argue the case, I am merely asking for your comments as to what would be the answer to those who put forward that position. . . .

Mr. Barnett: Yes. The British and the French have quite clearly been disappointed with the Chinese Communists in Peking; their relationships have been minimal. But they still argue, and I have not run into British diplomats who do not still think, that despite all the frustrations in dealing with the Communist Chinese in Peking, it is of great value to have representation there. I think the position of all of these powers, including India, incidentally, despite all their problems with China, is that on balance it is better to have the Chinese Communists in the U.N. than out.

It is fairly convincing to me. One's expectations should not be too great. I think this is very important. [p. 43]

Sen. McCarthy: In your statement you said you thought if we moved away from our policy of isolating China these countries [in southeast Asia] would be somewhat more confident of our position and of their own. In other words, they would not feel they were put in the middle in quite the same way they are now.

Mr. Barnett: This is complicated, too, I think some countries would applaud a move away from a policy of isolation, and I think there would be some other countries that would be apprehensive about it, about what its implications were. I think, therefore, that any move in this direction would have to be accompanied by a conscious effort to reassure those countries who might be apprehensive that a shift along the lines I have suggested did not mean that we were disengaging from the area. . . .

Sen. McCarthy: It is not so that an aggressive public position on our part tends to strengthen the hands of the more radical group [in China]?

Mr. Barnett: I think an aggressive — well, let us say an isolation policy and a policy of pressure on China tends to strengthen those I would call the people concerned primarily with ideology and politics. A policy posture that tried to involve China more in the international community, I would say, would present more options to them and would strengthen, tend to strengthen, those I have called the technical bureaucrats. [pp. 51–53]

Sen. Symington: [What] would you do today, if you were the President of the United States, to improve what you and I consider vital, the relationship of the United States with China? I am sure everybody would be interested in your frank opinion. . . .

Mr. Barnett: I would like the President to make a major speech on China in which he shifts our posture, as I said — in which, while indicating that we are not going to abandon a containment policy, we do recognize that the Communist regime is the regime on mainland China, which we have not yet done at all, and that we are going to do everything possible to explore means of bringing it into the international community, instead of trying to keep it out.

Now, I think that from such a major statement would follow a great many of the specific things I tried to mention this morning; they would then be logical, whereas at the present time they are not logical within the framework of our present policy. Within the framework of our present posture, it is quite logical to try to keep them out of the U.N., to try to do a great many other things. . . .

The Chinese have communicated things to us [through ambassadorial meetings in Geneva and Warsaw]. As a matter of fact, not only do I think we consider them important, but the Chinese also consider them important. At one point when we were considering downgrading the talks from ambassadorial discussions to discussions between diplomats at a lower level, the Chinese protested and insisted that they be maintained at the ambassadorial level.

So that they have a value, but the value has been limited, and the context has been limited, and the framework for discussion has been limited — and inevitably so, in terms of our posture which is: When necessary, we will deal with you, but we don't accept the fact that you are the government, for the long run, of China, and we don't accept that for the long run that you are the government of the mainland of China, and that we don't want you in international bodies.

Now, you are right, we have modified this to some extent and on the arms control issue we have been moving in the direction of changing our posture and inviting them into arms control discussions. I think this is very wise and sound as far as it goes. But I think it would be sound to push this to the logical point, which is a redefinition of our posture in a broader sense. [pp. 71–72]

Testimony of John K. Fairbank

Dr. Fairbank: [Prepared Statement] My conclusion is that the alternative to war with Peking, over Vietnam or elsewhere, lies along two lines of effort — one is to achieve a better balance between destruction and construction in our own efforts in Vietnam, so that the non-Communist model of nation-building there can compete more effectively with the Chinese Communist model of nation-building. The other line of effort is to defuse or dampen Peking's militancy by getting China into greater contact with the outside world, more connected with the international scene and more interested in participating in it like other countries.

How to get the Peking leadership into the international order, instead of their trying to destroy it according to their revolutionary vision, is primarily a psychological problem. Therapy for Peking's present, almost paranoid, state of mind must follow the usual lines of therapy: it must lead the rulers of China gradually into different channels of experience until by degrees they reshape their picture of the world and their place in it.

The remolding of Chairman Mao, the greatest remolder of others in history, is not something I would advocate as feasible. But I think it is high time we got ourselves ready to deal with his successors and with their successors in years ahead.

In practice this means getting Peking into a multitude of activities abroad. China should be included in all international conferences, as on disarmament, and in international associations, both professional and functional, in international sports, not just ping-pong, and in trade with everyone, including ourselves, except for strategic goods. One thinks naturally of the U.N. agencies and participation in the Security Council as well as the Assembly. Yet all this can come only step by step, with altercation all along the way — not an easy process but a lot more constructive than warfare.

American policy should work toward a gradual shift from trying to isolate Peking, which only worsens our problem, to a less exposed position where we can acquiesce in the growth of contact between Peking and other countries and let them suffer the impact of Peking's abrasiveness.

In gradually manipulating Peking into an acceptance of the international world, as an alternative to trying to subvert it, we must motivate Chinese behavior according to China's needs:

1. One of these is the craving for greater prestige in the world to redress the balance of the last century's humiliations. For China to be in the center of the world's councils would seem to a Chinese patriot only right and proper.

2. We can also use the Peking government's need for prestige to maintain itself domestically. It is still true that the virtue of the rulers, as advertised in their acknowledged achievements, is a vital element sustaining any regime in China.

3. In addition, the Chinese people positively need certain kinds of aid through exchange of technology or of goods, like all developing countries.

4. Peking may also be motivated by the opportunity to manipulate foreigners against one another. This traditional way of dealing with outsiders can be attempted in any conclave like the United Nations. But any number can play this game, and, in fact, it is the essence of diplomacy.

As these types of motives come into play, we may expect the Peking regime to be involved in bilateral relationships and be influenced by others whose desire is for peace rather than violence. In the end all this may make coexistence more attractive and feasible.

Opening the door for China's participation in the world scene is only one part of an American policy. The other part is to hold the line. The Chinese are no more amenable to pure sweetness and light than other revolutionaries. Encouraging them to participate in the U.N. and other parts of the international scene has to be combined with a cognate attitude of firmness backed by force. Military containment on the Korean border, in the Taiwan Straits, and somehow in Vietnam cannot soon be abandoned and may have to be maintained for some time. But containment alone is a blind alley unless we add policies of constructive competition and of international contact.

In short, my reading of history is that Peking's rulers shout aggressively out of manifold frustrations, that isolation intensifies their ailment and makes it self-perpetuating, and that we need to encourage international contact with China on many fronts. [pp. 106–107]

Sen. Case: Would you justify your belief in containment as a part of the dual program of containment plus de-isolation?

Dr. Fairbank: Well, my justification as a historian is usually conservative, thinking about what actually has happened, and I put this in a framework which satisfied me to some extent, that we have an international world in the process of development, that we are trying to aid this, that for this purpose we believe nations have the — should have the opportunity to develop their national life on the basis of self-determination. This is where that point comes in.

We also have this belief that contact, open society, pluralism, the international trading world is a more fruitful way to modernize in these backward areas or underdeveloped areas. This is something we have to keep watching because we can easily, you know, have a cover for this in our minds which is a great rationalization.

The facts may be somewhat different. But on the basis of the world scene, I see this general movement going ahead. [p. 124]

Sen. Gore: . . . I think the Doctor has made an extremely important observation with respect to the bilateral negotiations between the two powers in the most direct confrontation. Would you [the Chairman] mind his going one step further and suggesting how this might be originated?

The Chairman: Not at all. That is what this hearing is being held for.

Dr. Fairbank: Well, this dreaming about the future is a game any number can play, and I am happy to indulge. This is wish fulfillment.

Sen. Gore: Isn't it something about which men must think?

Dr. Fairbank: Yes, indeed. The problem is to think in practical terms of getting from here to there, and these practical terms include maintaining a stiff position as an inducement. They include dealing with other parties, working through other parties — middlemen. Now, the people in Japan are very eager to be middlemen between East and West. They feel they are in an in-between position. They have learned from both China and America. They are very upset, very concerned, about this whole situation.

The Japanese government is working with us. (The Japanese intellectuals are dead against us, on the whole.) But in Japan you have a third party [—it] is a very considerable country of great power and potential. One thing ought to be discussion with them. I do not doubt this has been going on. Ambassador Reischauer is there.

But working around the periphery of China you also have the Soviet Union, and we have made our efforts there. They are involved in their own problems. It is very difficult for us to expect them to help us in any way. Perhaps we can find aims from which we would have a common benefit.

I think that, perhaps, the primary thing for all of this is to develop in this country an attitude which is right-hand and left-hand both, the tough guy–soft guy approach, the carrot and the stick; this combination — peace and war, negotiation and fighting.

If we can develop a concept of this kind, we will exert our maximum influence. But if we leave ourselves with the concept of just fighting, why then, we can get ourselves into a real disaster. If we leave ourselves with the concept that you first stop fighting and then you negotiate, again we are unrealistic because the Chinese do both at once perfectly well — other countries can, too. [pp. 158–159]

Sen. Symington: If you carry the spheres-of-influence concept to its conclusion, then it would be very difficult for us to hold a position at all in the Far East; would it not?

Dr. Fairbank: It seems to me consigning the Far East to somebody else's sphere of influence is asking for trouble, and having any part of the rest of the world that we claim is entirely our sphere of influence is, perhaps, asking for trouble too. In other words, dividing the world into spheres is really setting up competing groups, if you follow that line of thought.

I would say that the cultural difference between us and East Asia is part of our problem, but it does not mean that we lay off, that we avoid contact, that we withdraw.

The fact is that we have been in East Asia just as much as we have been in Europe. In fact, the Americans have been more active there in some ways. The Europeans, in the first place, were just as active in Asia as they were in the Americas. So I think the smallness of the world means that you cannot separate these exclusive areas.

Sen. Symington: Some argue, feeling that we are culturally closer to Europe, that Vietnam is beyond our proper realm of concern. I do not agree. I certainly agree with you. I do not agree that we should have nothing to do with the Far East because we do not have as many ancestors from the Far East, or some reason of that character.

Dr. Fairbank: The power balance, I think the power balance — the stability of international relations — getting great powers who have the destructive capacity into situations where they feel they are viable and not filled with resentment and explosive — it seems to me that is our problem.

In the case of China, that means not that China must have a sphere of influence that covers all of East Asia, at least not yet; and we may emerge eventually with a China that has gradually built up so strong that it may have more and more influence in adjoining areas. But we want a situation in which that influence is on its own merits — financial, commercial — cultural, not just military, and the idea of military domination in the new international world is a more and more dangerous one. We are trying to get the Chinese, it seems to me, off the tack of world revolution as their main effort.

Sen. Symington: Right.

Dr. Fairbank: That is why I think we have this new look in the American policy — which is not to isolate China but to get it into contact. . . .

Sen. Symington: If you had the authority to decide policy, as the President does, what do you think he should do now with respect to improving our position in the world, specifically with respect to improving our relationship with Red China?

Dr. Fairbank: The list of items that Mr. Barnett mentioned appealed to me. I mean, they are technical steps. Allowing travel — this is in the morning press. I think the administration sees this. Exchanges of all kinds. Trade not in strategic goods but otherwise all right. And I would be interested particularly in efforts that give the Chinese some feeling of acceptance, if ever they will accept any preferred efforts, particularly in connection with the United Nations.

The problem of the Chinese having, as you would say in the treaty port, some face — this is a very real problem because Chinese life is organized in such a way, and has been for so long, that a person is adjudged by his conduct and his status — how he behaves, and the status he is in — and when the Chinese are not in the world councils it just does not accord with the fact that they see all around them; namely, that they are a great country and a great people and should be in the center of things. We have to cross that hurdle. [pp. 171–173]

Testimony of Benjamin I. Schwartz
and John M. H. Lindbeck

Sen. Case: . . . I would like to ask you, as I asked Mr. Barnett and Dr. Fairbank, if you would develop your reasons for favoring the containment side as well as the de-isolation side of the proposition. You generally take this position, I take it.

Dr. Schwartz: Well, I support it but I would like to add certain remarks to it. It seems to me one of the reasons why our containment policy in Europe was successful is because we had many living and viable societies which were cooperating with us in this containment policy. There was a desire on the part of most states in Europe to contain the Soviet Union.

Sen. Case: For fear that they couldn't.

Dr. Schwartz: Fear that they couldn't, but also a desire to do so. I do feel that even the bulk of states in Asia desire to contain China and I think we can collaborate with them in the military sphere.

Now, so far as containment of subversion is concerned, this is a somewhat different proposition. Here we require the active cooperation of many elements in the society itself. Therefore, I say that the problem of containment, as applied to Vietnam, is a very agonizing and perplexing one and to simply say that we should contain the Communists in Vietnam by no means enlightens us in any way about what we should do in Vietnam.

Sen. Case: Nor how to do it.

Dr. Schwartz: Nor how to do it.

Sen. Case: But it does go to the soundness of our objectives basically.

Dr. Schwartz: Well, I believe that as long as the Chinese do have faith in what I call their optimum vision, this means that they would perhaps try to impose their model on any other society which they would be able to control, and to this extent I believe that they must be contained.

Sen. Case: Is this generally your thinking about this, Dr. Lindbeck? . . .

Dr. Lindbeck: It seems to me we have partly imposed upon ourselves the need for containment. Encouraging, for example, the Japanese not to move into the military field has left one part of Asia very vulnerable. In a sense, there is a normal obligation on our part to compensate for this lack of military force on one margin of China.

If the Japanese had power and influence in Asia in more fields, then the need for our forces to be so evident in Asia might be greatly minimized.

The second part of our obligation, it seems to me, is that as a consequence of the liquidation of Western colonialism, as of the British empire, many of the new nations in Asia were not in position to pursue their aims and interests with the force and assurance that they might have done if they were going states for, let's say, a hundred years. Because they lack power fully to protect their own interests, they deserve help.

So, in a general sense, the West is lodged with some responsibility as the result of the long period when it controlled large numbers of peoples in Asia; I therefore regard this containment policy as one that should not depend only on the United States, but on all our associates in Europe who once controlled these areas as part of their imperial orders.

[pp. 217–218]

Sen. Church: Do you favor the American embargo on trade?

Dr. Lindbeck: It seems to me, looking at it not as an economist, but as a political scientist, that our current policy of embargoing trade with the mainland doesn't serve any major purpose.

Sen. Church: Does not?

Dr. Lindbeck: Does not.

Sen. Church: Does not serve our national interests.

Dr. Lindbeck: Does not on balance, as I see it. That is right. It is ineffective in putting pressures or constraints on China. In general, it seems to me that the notion, that both of us were trying to advance somewhat this morning, of involving China in more normal economic relations, as well as other types of relations, with the outside world is likely, in the long run, to be productive of political good.

Sen. Church: You would then favor an American policy that would permit our trade in nonstrategic items with China?

Dr. Lindbeck: Yes, without, however, immediately saying how this should be done or at what time, although I should favor sooner rather than later.

Sen. Church: In principle you favor it.

Dr. Lindbeck: In principle I favor it, right.

Sen. Church: Do you agree, Dr. Schwartz?

Dr. Schwartz: Yes, in principle I would favor it. [p. 232]

The Chairman: There is the question of what you and others mention about isolation which leads me to the next question. This word has been used on several occasions, and I wonder if it is useful to examine for a moment just what you mean by "containment." Is this military containment what you have primarily in mind or is it something which involves other kinds of containment? This has been used before by former witnesses. They favored containment, but not isolation. What does the word "containment" mean to you? I wondered what it meant to the other witness[es].

Dr. Schwartz: As I said this morning, the notion of containment as applied to Vietnam causes me no end of trouble. Personally, I am not sure of what it means, and whether it is even a helpful notion in finding solutions to the Vietnamese problem.

But I do think — well, to take the case of a country like India — now whether one wants to call what happened in India aggression or not, I do think that India, perhaps, is entitled to our support, as much support as we can give them, against further aggressions of the Chinese into India, and that is, I suppose, one meaning of "containment."

The Chairman: That is military.

Dr. Schwartz: That is military containment. Now, as far as containing subversion of the Chinese type is concerned, here, it seems, that if one takes a country like Thailand where it is said that the Chinese have now "turned on their strategy," if Thai society is strong enough to contain this strategy, we can help them contain it by various forms of technical aid.

I think the ultimate decisive factor here is the strength of the Thai government itself. That is the decisive factor. If it is strong, we can help it, it seems to me.

The Chairman: If it is not strong there is nothing that we could do to be of much use to them, is there?

Dr. Schwartz: Well, I am skeptical. . . .

The Chairman: The Secretary of State has made public statements about spheres of influence no longer being an acceptable idea. But how do we overcome the effect of proximity of smaller countries to a big country, whether it be Russia or China or the United States? I am not quite clear what he means by a sphere of influence. It has to do, I think, with containment. Do you wish to offer anything?

Dr. Schwartz: Well, I am not clear about the idea of sphere of influence either.

I think, in general, probably if China had a non-Communist government — if the government of China were a non-Communist government — it is quite conceivable that we might be willing to concede them some kind of sphere of influence in southeast Asia, although I must say that the argument usually put forth that the whole of southeast Asia was always within a Chinese sphere of influence is erroneous.

The only part of it that was, was Vietnam, and if India could exert its power in the world it could make just as legitimate a claim to having a sphere of influence in southeast Asia as the Chinese.

But, of course, it is complicated by the fact that China is Communist, and by the fear that their conception of a sphere of influence might mean that governments in such a sphere should adopt in toto the model of China in their internal organization. That is, I suppose, the fear. . . .

The Chairman: I was trying to clarify the real facts of life. The idea that we presume to contain China, let us say, a Communist country, is a kind of an unlimited undertaking; is it not? If containment goes beyond military containment, if we are going to say they shall not have influence, they shall not spread their ideas, this becomes quite a job to do, does it not? Do you think it is a feasible or intelligent one?

Dr. Schwartz: No. I certainly do not think we can prevent their influence from spreading. I really do not have such fear that their influence will have the hypnotic effect that some people think it will.

The Chairman: If that is true, is it proper to say that the word "containment" as previously used in these hearings meant overt military containment? Is that what you think is a proper interpretation of it? . . .

Dr. Schwartz: I think Mr. Barnett's statement included both military containment and containment of subversion, and it is on the latter that I would raise many questions. I would still maintain that we can only help a society to contain subversion, but that the society itself must do the major job.

The Chairman: Do you wish to comment on that?

Dr. Lindbeck: Well, I would go along with your suggestion, Mr. Chairman, that the real problem of containment seems to be a military problem. At the moment we want to make sure that military power is not projected across certain borders.

One of the complications here is the strong desire of Communist China's Asian allies, namely, the North Korean regime and the North Vietnamese regime, to unite their countries under their authority. This is what we are trying to prevent. There also is the problem of the extension of Chinese military forces across the Straits of Taiwan. So we have three points where military power is an important aspect of the situation, and we are involved in containing the extension of military forces, Chinese or not, beyond these borders.

However, I would add that there also are political consequences or implications in the use of military power. This works both ways, both for the Chinese and for ourselves. If American military forces were not at the three points of pressure, we almost certainly would hear a number of parties or groups in Asia say, "Well, if we cannot rely on American military power, let us see what kind of arrangements we can make with the Chinese in order to lessen the political pressures and influences the Chinese will try to exert in our region, on our country."

There are indirect ways in which we probably have been useful in helping, let us say, the Philippine government in restricting Chinese Communist influences. But this again is, as I suggested earlier, something very complex and very individual.

I would, then, agree with you that the main problem of containment, at least as I see it, is a military problem. [pp. 248–253]

Testimony of Morton H. Halperin
and Samuel B. Griffith

Dr. Halperin: [Prepared Statement] From the standpoint of our relations with China, and I would emphasize that there are a great many other factors involved, it is important for the United States to remain in Vietnam and to prevent a military victory by the Vietcong employing what the Chinese believe to be their model of revolutionary violence. . . .

Second, China's current stance suggests the importance of American assurances to China that we are not looking for an opportunity to attack Chinese nuclear installations or to launch an even larger attack on the Chinese mainland. I believe that an American declaration that was prepared to discuss with Peking the exchange of ambassadors would make an important contribution to this objective, as would American proposals — even though they would be deplored in Peking — to seat both China and Taiwan in the General Assembly of the United Nations.

Third, I think it is important for the United States to avoid the appearance of overreacting to very limited Chinese capabilities. The Chinese, I believe, are correctly amused by the credit we give them for every act of violence anywhere in the world. Such statements and our overreaction to the Chinese nuclear force, which six months ago we were deprecating, only serve to increase the belief in China and elsewhere in Asia that we are overly fearful of the Chinese and are likely to respond either by preventive war or by precipitous withdrawal.

Finally, I believe that we should avoid using China as a simple justification for our policies. The policy choices that we face in Vietnam and elsewhere in Asia are exceedingly complex. We are unlikely to make the right choices if we confine ourselves to an analysis of what will best contain a China which has a desire to control its neighbors, but only a very limited capability to do so. [pp. 287–288]

The Chairman: Would you agree with Dr. Halperin's statement that we should avoid the appearance of overreacting to limited Chinese capability?

Gen. Griffith: Yes, I would. I think we are doing the same thing now in respect to the Chinese that we did with respect to the Soviets in 1949, 1950, and 1951. I remember in those years it was fashionable to give the Soviets all sorts of capabilities which they couldn't conceivably have practiced. We were giving them the capability to overrun Europe and the capability to overrun Iran and the capability to intervene in Turkey. We were overreacting. We are doing the same thing now, I think, Senator, in respect to the Chinese. [p. 289]

Sen. Church: General Griffith, you have made several references to the Chinese view that southeast Asia falls within the traditional Chinese sphere of influence, and I would have to concede that history would tend to bear that out. But we hear from the State Department down in Foggy Bottom that spheres of influence are obsolete, that they are no longer a rational basis on which to fashion a modern foreign policy. Do you think that spheres of influence are obsolete and no longer existent?

Gen. Griffith: Well, Senator, I think as long as there are great powers in the world, with smaller countries contiguous to them, that spheres of influence are bound to exist. This is, it seems to me, an inescapable fact.

Sen. Church: Don't we regard the Western Hemisphere as within the American sphere of influence, and wasn't that the basis upon which the Monroe Doctrine was promulgated?

Gen. Griffith: Well, yes, indeed it was, Senator. And I think that this is borne out by our own actions over the past century and a half in South America. We hope to create a neighborhood of viable states. . . .

Sen. Church: Let us move to Europe, General. . . . Don't you think that implicitly we have acknowledged to the Russians a sphere of influence in Eastern Europe behind the Iron Curtain?

Gen. Griffith: Well, I do not know what answer you would get from the State Department on that, but in point of fact it seems to me that we have absolutely recognized it.

Sen. Church: I do not get that answer from the State Department, but I must agree with you, General, I think this is the fact. I wanted to make these points because it seems to me that, as a matter of reality, spheres of influence do exist. They exist in this hemisphere, they exist in Europe and, therefore, it strikes me as unrealistic when I hear the Secretary of State and others responsible for present American foreign policy contend that they do not exist in Asia.

Gen. Griffith: I was not aware that our Secretary of State had made that point, but I would be — perforce I would have to disagree with it. [pp. 307–308]

Sen. Church: Do you think, Professor Halperin, that we need to draw a distinction between whatever threat there may be of Chinese aggression in neighboring lands with the different threat of Communist expansion fostered by revolutionary wars?

Dr. Halperin: I think so. The first problem I consider a relatively trivial one, and one we can easily handle with our existing military force, probably with a good deal less.

I think the second problem, the threat of revolution, has to be dealt with by our policies toward the countries in which there may be revolutions. It seems to me you do not deal with the problem of revolution in Thailand or Brazil or whatever country by worrying about the Chinese. You deal with the problem by trying to bring about the necessary changes in the countries concerned.

Sen. Church: Don't you think that in dealing with this problem we really must rely, in the final analysis, upon the indigenous resistance of nationalist forces within the countries themselves?

Dr. Halperin: I think so. We have to try to give the people in the country a feeling we are supporting their efforts to bring about social and political change, and press them for that change where that pressure seems necessary, but, I think, waving the red flag of the Chinese does not do us any good and distorts our efforts.

Sen. Morse: It would do less if we waved the American flag at them.

Sen. Church: Well, let me say regardless of the outcome in Vietnam, don't you think we are going to continue to be faced with the problem of attempted Communist expansion through guerrilla warfare in many parts of Asia, Africa, and Latin America, and that this is not the kind of test case that is going to settle that problem one way or another?

Dr. Halperin: I think that is right. This is certainly not the definitive case that is going to settle the issue for all time. [p. 309]

Sen. Morse: . . . I want to take you to this morning's paper where we see by the news that Germany is going to sell a steel plant to Red China, and the second news story on it is that apparently France is going to work out some consortium with Germany and they are going to sell the steel plant together.

Let us assume they do. Would I be right in my conclusion that that steel plant would increase to a degree of its productivity the war-making potential of Red China?

Dr. Halperin: I would think only very marginally, Senator. My feeling would be that we should encourage this kind of trade and economic relations, and I was encouraged to see, according to the paper, that we did not object to this. I think our problem with China is not their military strength. As the General has indicated, they are going to be much weaker than us for a very long time.

I think the problem is to open up contacts and relations with them. The Chinese give first priority to their military forces, and they are going to have enough steel for their military force no matter how many steel plants they have, and the question is whether they are going to have steel for other purposes.

Sen. Morse: That leaves me to draw a line of distinction as to your view, if any, between noncombatant and combatant goods. It would seem to me as a novice in the matter of what is necessary for military preparation, that a steel plant is certainly directly connected with a military potential, whereas other goods that we might very well ship or join in shipping to Red China would not increase her military power. But I judge from your answer that you think I am wrong about that. The steel plant will not increase her military power.

Dr. Halperin: It depends on the kind of plant that it is. We do have a list of strategic items, and this particular plant apparently from today's press was not on that list, so it was not a strategic item. [pp. 319–320]

Testimony of Alexander Eckstein

Dr. Eckstein: [Prepared Statement] Since 1950, U.S. policy on trade with China has involved virtually a total embargo on all economic contacts between ourselves and the mainland and the maintenance of as stringent controls as possible on trade between our allies and the mainland. This policy was initiated as an emergency measure during the Korean war and was conceived within the context of economic warfare. It has been maintained since on the technical ground that the Korean war has never been formally terminated but ended only in an armistice.

To be more precise, U.S. policy and regulations concerning trade with China have remained unchanged since 1950, while those of our Allies have gradually and progressively been liberalized, more or less to our displeasure and in a number of cases despite our resistance. As a result, essentially all that is left of the elaborate structure of COCOM [Coordinating Committee for Export to Communist Areas] controls constructed in the early fifties is a continuing ban on the shipment of arms, weapons, military materiel of all kinds, fissionable materials, and some other clearly strategic goods. In addition, there is an agreement to limit credits to a term of five years.

Apart from its technical and legal basis rooted in the Korean war, what is the rationale of this trade policy vis-à-vis Communist China? U.S. policy toward China, in effect, is designed to isolate it and to contain it within its present boundaries, and trade controls are intended to support both these objectives. If adhered to by all major trading nations, such control would, of course, limit intercourse with China and therefore isolate her not only commercially but politically. At the same time, they would deprive her of modern weapons and other defense materials and thus tend to weaken her militarily. Finally, to the extent that they could deny China the wherewithal for modern industrial development, they would at least retard the country's economic growth and postpone the day when it would acquire a large enough industrial base to support a strong and more or less modern military posture. U.S. trade policy, thus, is designed to reduce Communist China's military potential in both the short and long run. . . .

Regardless of the merits of a policy designed to isolate China, are trade controls suitable and effective as one of the instruments for the implementation of this policy? A cutting off of all exports to China would undoubtedly have damaged her economy in several ways. . . . The Chinese economy, however, did not suffer these consequences because (a) no other major trading nation followed the U.S. policy of total embargo, and (b) up to 1960 China could obtain from other Communist countries virtually any commodities which Allied trade controls denied her. During the period of intimate Sino-Soviet economic relations (1950–1960), therefore, the practical consequences of the U.S. embargo and Allied trade controls were negligible. The Sino-Soviet trade relationships may possibly have increased the cost of China's imports, but the evidence on this matter is far from conclusive. Even if some costs did result, they were probably minimal.

The situation, however, changed after 1960. Sino-Soviet economic relations deteriorated markedly. As a result, China has had difficulty in obtaining imports of armaments and military goods, and she has been unable to obtain long-term credits. . . . From the mid-1950's on, however, Allied trade controls had gradually been eased. Therefore, Western countries were prepared and in a position to move into the breach left by the Soviets. While U.S. trade policy was formerly ineffective because China could obtain controlled and embargoed goods from the Communist countries, it is now ineffective because these same goods (except for military materiel) can be obtained from practically every country which exports them except the United States.

The only practical economic impediment to which China is still exposed under the controls lies in the field of credit. This fact raises two questions: how much damage do credit controls impose on the Chinese economy, and conversely, to what extent could credits be used to induce modifications of Chinese Communist policies?

The Chinese Communists do not seem to have any difficulties in obtaining all the short- and medium-term credits they can use or finance at present. Their international credit rating is good, and they have met their financial obligations without delay. In a practical sense, therefore, access to long-term credits would simply mean that China could either lighten her current annual debt burden by converting her present obligations or that she could service, at the current rate of yearly debt payments, a much larger credit.

Whether China could obtain sufficient economic benefits from this access to credits to induce her to pay a political price for it is difficult to forecast. On the basis of experience, it would seem rather doubtful unless, perhaps, the economic gain to be derived were indeed of major proportions. The history of Sino-Soviet relations, for example, would suggest that the Chinese were not prepared to sacrifice what they considered to be vital political objectives, even if they had to suffer the economic consequences of a break. In her relations with the West, therefore, China probably cannot be expected to give up or modify any of her important foreign policy objectives even though such decisions might benefit her economy. This judgment, however, does not necessarily mean that there may be no chance to obtain concessions in a mutual bargaining situation — at least concessions as to timing, relative priorities, and direction. For several years, for instance, the Chinese Communists maintained that they would not carry on trade with Japan unless the latter accorded them de facto recognition. Yet, since 1962, trade relations partly because of the Sino-Soviet split have been reactivated and broadened essentially on Japanese terms. . . .

Removal of the embargo may be peculiarly well suited to serve as the first step on the road to normalization between the United States and China. It can be initiated unilaterally without resort to negotiations, and it can be implemented without any economic cost. If the move is made, it should be carried out as a low-key measure and as a signal that other overtures might possibly follow if the Chinese repond to it.

Just as the embargo now stands as a symbol of our determination to isolate Communist China, its removal could symbolize a new policy posture on the part of the United States. At the maximum, such a move, possibly coupled with other similar measures, might widen our channels of communication with China and maybe even improve the general atmosphere of United States–China relations. At the minimum, a complete rebuff to our overtures would place the onus for implacable hostility at the door of Communist China.

In the same general vein, it may be worth considering more experimentation in the field of credit policy. A rigid policy of credit limitation ties the hands of our allies and deprives them of any bargaining power. On the other hand, a policy which would leave credit terms vague and unpublished would make it much easier to obtain a quid pro quo, not only in economic terms but perhaps in political terms as well. [pp. 334–337]

Sen. Morse: My last question, professor, because you have, as I have interpreted you, at least, suggested that we, at least, move toward a program of economic trade and economic intercourse with China: Do you think that that course of action might be helpful in restoring to the masses of the Chinese people over the period of a few years the friendship that existed for a long time between our two peoples and, therefore, might be an instrument for promoting peace?

Dr. Eckstein: I would not expect any miracles from restoration of trade. I think that there are some very deep-seated hostilities on both sides, China and the United States. I do not think these can be easily overcome.

There are some very deep-seated issues of difference between the two countries. I think all that one can visualize or hope for at the present time is to work toward some normalization of conditions between the two countries. I think the possibilities of friendship are rather remote under present and presently foreseeable circumstances.

Sen. Morse: Twenty-five years might make some difference.

Dr. Eckstein: Well, I would not venture a guess how long that might take, sir. I think there are many factors here. I think the very candid statement indicated they need the image of an external enemy, that is their view. That is one minor factor.

I think a much more important issue from their point of view than trade is Taiwan. This then also affects the United Nations issue. There are a whole host of other issues that have to be resolved over the next few years, and a lot of underbrush that needs to be cleared away before one can even think of this possibility.

Sen. Morse: Would you favor, as was suggested this morning, at least they are indicating we would be willing — I do not think she would be willing, I do not think she would have that good sense — that we would be willing to restore diplomatic relations, and we could work out some reasonable understandings, we would be willing to see her seated in the United Nations, and try to get ourselves in a position where we can at least carry on the same kind of international relations with her that we carried on with the Soviet Union? Do you think that would be a desirable foreign policy?

Dr. Eckstein: I think so. This fits in with my general view that it would be better to have China not isolated. But this does not mean that one should have any illusions about having a relationship of friendship with China. I think that is far off indeed. I do not think that Communist China is ready or willing to engage in any relations of friendship with the United States. [p. 365]

Testimony of Donald S. Zagoria and Harold C. Hinton

Dr. Zagoria: [Prepared Statement] I would like to endorse enthusiastically the changes in our policy toward China recommended to this committee by Professors Barnett and Fairbank. As I indicated, it seems to me likely that Peking's failures in foreign policy must inevitably lead the Chinese Communists to undertake a painful readjustment of their strategy and tactics that have brought them to the brink of international bankruptcy. If Mao were a British Prime Minister, he would by this time have been elevated to the House of Lords. There are credible reports that the Chinese leaders are increasingly divided on foreign policy, and when Mao dies, it is quite likely that we will witness as furious a succession struggle in China as we saw in the Soviet Union after the death of Stalin. I think it is now generally recognized that we missed the opportunity to strengthen the hand of the moderates in the Stalin succession struggle and we should not repeat the same mistake in our policy toward China. A change in our policy toward China now could provide an alternative to those Chinese leaders who believe that Mao's policy has been too rigid.

It might be countered by some that if China is in such serious difficulty, why is there any need for a change in our policy? I believe such a change is necessary at some point if we are ever to achieve stability in Asia and to solve a host of international questions that cannot be resolved without Chinese participation, including arms control and disarmament. In the past, objections have been raised to a change in U.S. policy on the grounds that it would be interpreted as weakness by the other side. But if this is the case, what better time is there for such a change when it is quite clear that we are not leading from weakness?

Moreover, there are many countries and people, particularly in Asia, who believe that Chinese intransigence and militance is largely the result of isolation by the United States. We can prove that they are wrong only by ending our policy of isolation. If the Chinese continue, as they have done in the past to isolate themselves by their own inept policies, at least the onus will be on them.

Finally, and not least important, our only hope to achieve a stable and tolerable relationship with China is to do all we can to promote not a change of the system — which can be done only by war — but a change within the system. The kind of evolution that is already transforming Russia and the East European Communist countries will have to come one day in China too. We can help to hasten its growth. [pp. 375–376]

Dr. Hinton: [Prepared Statement] There is no compelling reason to assume that American persistence in containment of Communist China — notably, by giving it reason to stay out of Vietnam even if the military situation there continues on balance to develop adversely to the Communist side — will put the United States on some sort of collision course with China. Nor is there any reason to think that the possession of more than token nuclear power, which will accrue not to the present Chinese leadership but to its successors, will pose a mortal threat to peace in the absence of formal disarmament. In the nuclear age, power confers vulnerability as well, and, therefore, tends to lead to responsibility and the acceptance of at least tacit arms control agreements.

It is still less likely that Communist China will ever be able to equal or surpass the United States or the Soviet Union in strategic military power. Communist China will remain a problem and at times perhaps a threat, but not an unmanageable one so long as the United States is willing to do what may be necessary to keep it manageable.

Mr. Chairman, if I may add a few words to my prepared statement, I should conclude that just as the maintenance of a military balance with respect to the Soviet Union requires an American military presence on the European continent, so the maintenance of a military balance with respect to China requires an American military presence in continental East Asia. This presence should, of course, be used to contain Chinese power, political as well as military, not to attack it on its home ground. It will be recalled that Abraham Lincoln's policy, whose rejection by extremists on both sides brought on the Civil War, was to contain slavery within its existing borders rather than abolish it outright, on the theory that in time it would mellow or break up. It seems to me that this is one dogma of the past that is adequate to the stormy present. [pp. 380–381]

Sen. Sparkman: Do I understand correctly that both of you gentlemen suggest that it would be well for the United States to establish diplomatic relations with Communist China?

Dr. Zagoria: Well, speaking for myself, yes; I think it would be well to establish diplomatic relations with Communist China. I note that approximately the same period of time elapsed between the Bolshevik revolution in the Soviet Union and the time when the United States came to recognize the Soviet Union, and the amount of time that has elapsed between the Communist revolution in China and the present year. Just as was the case with the Soviet Union, it seems to me that by now most people have come to the conclusion that the Communist regime in China is not just a passing phenomenon: that it is here to stay. There is very little chance, I think most experts would say, that the regime is going to be overthrown from within or that there is a reasonable chance of overthrowing it from without, without taking the kind of risk that we wouldn't want to take.

Therefore, it seems to me that eventually, if we want to solve the many problems in the world and in Asia that cannot be solved without a dialog between us and the Chinese Communists, eventually we have to have such a dialog, and I don't think the corridors of Warsaw are the place to have such important conversations.

I don't think if the United States announced tomorrow night its willingness to exchange diplomatic representation with Communist China, I don't think they would accept. I am quite confident they would denounce it as a trick by the American imperialists because to a large extent they need an American enemy at the present time, and they are making unreasonable demands on the United States.

But it really does not concern me what their immediate reaction would be. I think in time their position would change. I think our position needs to be changed, not out of any expectation of their grasping our offer of friendship, but largely because it would put our policy more in harmony with many of our friends and allies, it would make it easier to justify our policy to many of our friends and allies and many people in Asia. . . .

Sen. Sparkman: Do you think it would be worthwhile for us to make such an offer, if we knew that China were going to reject it?

Dr. Zagoria: Yes, sir; I do. I think so for the reasons stated. I think that it would immediately clear the air if we were to make such an offer and if it were rejected by Communist China; I think it would clear the air in many parts of the world where peoples and nations think that the United States is to blame for Communist China's militancy.

Sen. Sparkman: Suppose Communist China accepted the proposal and then gave us the same treatment she has given Great Britain. Do you still think it would be worthwhile?

Dr. Zagoria: Well, I know, although the British have not made very great progress in their relationship with Communist China, I know of very few British diplomats who do not think it was worthwhile for Great Britain to recognize Communist China, and indeed the British government would like to see us recognize Communist China.

Sen. Sparkman: Like to see us recognize Red China?

Dr. Zagoria: Yes.

Sen. Sparkman: I think you are right. Mr. Hinton, do you concur?

Dr. Hinton: No, sir, I do not. I think it is neither necessary nor desirable nor feasible for the United States to recognize Communist China. Our China problem is not the same as that of any other country, since no other country has either the ability or any real incentive to perform this containing role more or less around the Chinese periphery, and I do not think therefore that our policy need be the same as other countries'.

Those countries that have established diplomatic relations have really no useful dialog with the Chinese unless they are on very friendly political terms. . . .

Finally, it takes two to tango, and it is quite clear that the Chinese are not interested in any such relationship. . . . [pp. 385–387]

Sen. Church: Dr. Hinton . . . I took it that you would favor the lifting of the American trade embargo, is that correct, insofar as non-strategic items go? . . .

Dr. Hinton: I see no objection to reducing our controls against mainland China to the same level as those against the Soviet Union. . . .

Sen. Church: Aside from possible changes in our trade policy, have you any other recommendations to make that would alter present American policy toward China?

Dr. Hinton: Well, actually, American policy has been moderating, at least marginally, over the last several years, and a rather good indication of that was given in a recent speech by Assistant Secretary [of State] Bundy in February, a relaxation of passport controls, and of travel restrictions in general.

This, I think, is entirely desirable, although I doubt very much if anything very significant will come of it, but I feel very strongly, as Senator Hickenlooper suggested earlier, that we really do need some sign from the other side. We have at least given a few signs of a willingness to establish some kind of a more civilized relationship. The other side has given effectively none, and to revert to the old saw, it does take two to tango. [pp. 394–395]

Testimony of Walter H. Judd
and George E. Taylor

Dr. Judd: [Prepared Statement] From what I have seen in the press, most of the changes in American policy toward Communist China proposed by various witnesses before this committee appear to be based on certain assumptions which do not seem to me to be justified:

1. That the Communist regime now in control of the China mainland is here to stay. But the same was said of Hitler, of Khrushchev, of Sukarno, of Nkrumah. People are not so sure now that Castro will last forever. Despots generally appear invincible — "until the last five minutes."

2. That the United States is stubbornly keeping Red China isolated and therefore we are responsible for its hostility and belligerence. The re-

verse is the truth; it is Red China's hostility and belligerence in its international attitudes and actions that are responsible for its isolation. . . .

The cause of Red China's hostility is not its isolation, but the Communist doctrine of the necessity for use of armed force to achieve world revolution. To remove China's isolation now would prove that the doctrine is correct and should be adhered to by them even more tenaciously.

3. That there is a better hope of getting Red China to change its attitudes and activities by giving in to it on matters like diplomatic recognition, trade, and admission to the United Nations than by resolute continuance of the policy of containment as long as Red China refuses to act like a responsible member of civilized society.

4. That changing our policy vis-à-vis Red China just might start an evolutionary process there. But, of course, it might just as easily reduce the chances of such an evolutionary process. Everybody desires and hopes for "evolution" in Red China. The debate should be over what measures are most likely to produce it.

For example: (a) giving Red China greater prestige, influence, entree; that is, making it stronger? Or keeping it as weak and isolated as possible?

(b) Concessions from its intended victims — like the United States? Or pressures from its present victims — the Chinese within Red China, those on Taiwan and in southeast Asia, Muslims in Indonesia and Malaysia, et cetera?

(c) Providing that Red China's truculence and stubborn defiance of the world succeeds? Or showing that it will fail?

(d) Taking the mountain — United Nations — to Mao? Or patiently and nonbelligerently insisting that Mao come to the mountain of better international conduct if he wants the benefits to Red China of membership in the international community?

What has caused the reported mellowing and evolution inside Yugoslavia, Rumania, the Soviet Union? Influences from without? Or their failures within?

If economic and other pressures from within and without are compelling some Communist governments to moderate their policies, at least toward their own people, shouldn't we keep the pressures up rather than reduce them by helping those governments to solve their problems? . . .

In contrast, there is no uncertainty as to the losses that would result from the suggested weakening of American policy. Here are some:

1. It would pull the rug out from under our loyal allies on Taiwan. The Chinese are a realistic, even fatalistic, people. With no hope for reunion in freedom with their brethren on the China mainland, they would have little or no choice but to prepare for the inevitable.

Americans who advocate admitting Red China and then add glibly, "Of course we would support the defense of Taiwan," may be salving their own consciences, but I think no Asians will be deceived. Twelve million Chinese could hardly maintain indefinitely the will or the capacity to resist 700 million, with the world organization for peace itself rejecting the 12 million and accepting the 700 million. . . .

2. With weakening or loss of Taiwan our Pacific island chain of defenses would be breached. It is doubtful that the Philippines could long resist Communist pressures and blandishments. Filipinos remember that it was from Taiwan that their country was invaded by the Japanese. It would take vast intervention with American forces to save that new nation for which we certainly have a special responsibility in the Pacific. I have not found any responsible Filipino leaders who favor recognition of Communist China, or its admission to the U.N.

3. The 15 million or so Chinese living in southeast Asia would be shaken. They occupy key positions of power and influence in Vietnam, Malaya, Thailand, Burma, Indonesia, the Philippines. The governments of those countries could not refuse to recognize Communist China once we did. That would mean every Chinese embassy and consulate in southeast Asia, and in the world for that matter, would become a protected center of Communist espionage, propaganda, sabotage and subversion of the host government — as recently exposed in Indonesia and Ghana. Through these embassies and consulates, the Chinese minorities would be under direct and almost irresistible pressure to support the aggressive policies of the Mao regime. The stability of the strategic countries of southeast Asia would inevitably be weakened.

4. If the United States were to show that it is not a dependable ally in Asia, our allies elsewhere, including those in Europe, would know they cannot count on us either. What would happen to the whole system of collective security we have been building at such cost and effort, and which this committee has taken such effective leadership in developing, and which is absolutely indispensable to our own survival as a free nation? Why should any country anywhere stand by us if it is not sure we will stand by it?

5. It would tell the neutrals and "uncommitted" nations that they were right all along and that they might as well give in to the winning side at once.

6. Perhaps worst of all, it would tell the 700 million people on the China mainland that we are accepting their subjugation, that we think there is more hope for peace for ourselves in deals with their oppressors than in standing steadfastly with them, the oppressed.

During the war and postwar years the United States relaxed under the skillfully built-up illusions that the Soviet Union was a "peace-loving democracy," eager and willing to cooperate to build a world of order and peace, and that the Chinese Communists were just agrarian reformers. Now they are strong and able boldly to threaten us. Perhaps our best hope of getting out of our present predicament and peril without a nuclear holocaust lies in the urge to be free that lives in the hearts of a billion human beings behind the Communist curtains. Unless these peoples are able from within to force their Communist regimes to change and eventually to abandon Communist world objectives, there is little hope of our avoiding an ultimate all-out clash. Is it intelligent or realistic to adopt a foreign policy that can cause those millions behind the curtains to abandon hope? If the strong accept the Communist overlords, how long can the weak continue to resist them? [pp. 438–442]

Dr. Taylor: [Prepared Statement] How far should containment go? Clearly, far enough to prevent the exploitation of wars of national liberation. What is the ultimate purpose? I have argued that it is naive to expect containment to reform a Communist country. We must obviously make it clear to Peking that we welcome and are always ready to accept any overtures directed toward improvement of relations. But the real problem is the future of the National government of the Republic of China. We are the only great power involved in the Chinese civil war. But there are other civil wars in the world today which have been created or intensified by Communist action — two Germanies, Koreas, Mongolias, Vietnams — that are of equal, if not greater, urgency and magnitude. They also raise problems of representation. The difference is that one of the Chinas has a permanent seat on the Security Council and the other China has, in effect, been at war with the U.N. since 1950. If the civil conflict cannot be resolved, the problem of policy comes down to the question of what sort of international status we are willing to accord to the National government and to the People's Democratic Republic. The United States will not allow the Communists to take Taiwan by force or assist the Nationalists in returning to the mainland unless we are at war with Peking, so the status quo is what we have to live with, as do the Koreans, Germans, Mongols, and Vietnamese, to say nothing of the Irish. Someday, sometime, the international status of the two parts of China must correspond to the facts of power, but there is no hurry. At the present time there is no advantage to the United States in talking about recognition or admission to the U.N., and there are a great many disadvantages. Why help the Peking regime when it is in trouble? What conceivable interest do we have in assisting this regime to become a great power?

It is said that we should not isolate Peking. It is Peking that is trying to isolate us. Communist China is far from being isolated; she has diplomatic relations of a sort with about forty countries and is trading with many she does not recognize, such as Japan and Canada. She is very much in the international community where it counts, in fact much too much. The terms she has announced for taking a seat in the U.N. are so outrageous that they must have been designed to show her contempt for that organization. Her terms for accepting recognition are humiliating in the extreme, although she would be delighted to have us help her finish off the civil war by reducing or eliminating the international status of the National government. If the Chinese Communists really want to live in peace with the world they are quite capable of making a move in that direction.

In the meantime, it should not be beyond the wit of man to devise ways and means of putting the burden of proof, as far as peaceful intentions are concerned, on the Peking regime, so long as nothing is done to damage American credit in Asia and our willingness to stand by our friends and our principles. [pp. 458–459]

The Chairman: Dr. Judd, you were in China a good while. What is your estimate of the Chinese people? Do you feel they are people without many good qualities?

Dr. Judd: No, indeed. . . .

My concern about China has been concern for my own country and for world peace. But I also have a great respect and affection for the Chinese people because they are a highly civilized people. They have good manners, they are mature, and have a rich, mellow culture. They have been trained that way for centuries. But you know, as a college president, that people are what they are taught to be, and the Communists are perfectly sure that, given time, they can change these qualities of the Chinese. . . .

So my concern about the Chinese is primarily for our own country. If the Chinese are free and friendly, as they would be if they were free, there is no insoluble problem in Asia. . . .

The Chairman: That would seem to lead to the conclusion that we ought to use force to throw out the Communist government in China.

Dr. Judd: If we were perfectly logical and had IBM machines for minds, and had no moral restraints and ethical values, that is what we would do. But we don't have IBM machines for minds. We do have moral and ethical restraints, so I think it is idle to speculate about that. We won't start a preventive war, we won't take such action. [pp. 462–463]

Sen. Mundt: The hearings have given rise thus far to a phrase which is used by the press, discussed editorially and discussed around the corridors and on the floor of the Senate and the House, which is that our policy toward China should be one of "containment but not isolation." I am not just sure about everything entailed in that phrase or what it means or where it would lead. It would seem to me that to have containment, you can have containment with increasing pressures to make the containment more effective, but that when you have containment without isolationism, you imply that there are going to be some leaks in this containment process.

But I wish that each of you would comment on what that means to you when you see the phrase "containment, not isolationism." Wherein lie its elements of validity, if there are elements of validity, and what is wrong with it if there is something wrong with it? . . .

Dr. Taylor: I assume, as I tried to suggest in my paper, that the use of the phrase "containment but not isolation" is a way of trying to loosen up the situation, as it were, by men who feel that our China policy is static, rigid, and even reactionary. I think the same people who say we would continue to contain do support our stand in Vietnam, but they do seem to suggest that apart from that there is not much else to contain, that wars of national liberation are not for export, that they haven't succeeded anywhere except possibly in Vietnam, and that China is not a great military power. This seems to me to miss the point, of course. I feel that the danger from China is not her formal military power, but her genius at coup d'etat [*sic*], subversion, and wars of national liberation. . . .

Containment without isolation, comes I think, from a very genuine and thoughtful effort for us to recover the diplomatic initiative. I think this is the general aim. The feeling is that the Chinese would not come into the United Nations if we invited them. They wouldn't recognize us if we offered recognition, so what do we have to lose by offering to do so? It is a part of a diplomatic game. But it is also part of a move to try to get the Chinese into a discussion of our mutual relations in the hope that eventually Taiwan and Peking will agree to some sort of modus vivendi that will permit us to have some sort of diplomatic recognition of Communist China, and for Communist China to have some sort of position in the United Nations.

If that could be done without damaging our present position and our interests in the present stage of the civil war between the Nationalists and the Communists in China, I personally would be in favor of anything that could be done to establish normal relationships as far as the U.N. is concerned; since 1956 when we accepted the package deals, membership in the U.N. is certainly not limited to the peace-loving types. Everybody is in there now. But my feeling is that this is completely unrealistic. We are talking the problem away instead of facing it.

Sen. Mundt: The question is can it be done under those terms and with those repercussions.

Dr. Taylor: I don't think so. I am all in favor of any devices that could put the Chinese Communists on the defensive so that the American public wouldn't have the picture of our government refusing, as they think, to have anything to do with Communist China; I hope it can be done, but I think it would be quite a neat trick to do it.

At the present time I think the phrase "containment without isolation" is merely a neat formula to conceal a move to de-emphasize our relations with Taiwan, to get away from, eventually, from our commitments there, and to bring the Chinese Communists into closer relations with the great world institutions in the hope that we can have some influence on them.

I think I have made it clear, I am against it.

Sen. Mundt: Dr. Judd.

Dr. Judd: I agree completely with what Dr. Taylor said. It is a phrase that has a new sound to it but when you examine it, I don't see any possibility of its being fruitful.

In part of my written statement that I omitted in reading, I said we must always keep the door open to any genuine change on their part as proved by deeds. We must keep the door resolutely closed to Communists [*sic*] threats, tricks, or promises not supported by performance. . . .

There is always the temptation for us to make another little concession or two. This is a standard tactic they use. They want us to make little concessions, but they don't make any. The Soviets have won their victories mostly by the use of one word, *Nyet*. We make a proposal and they say "*Nyet.*" We make another one; they say "*Nyet.*" We say this is our last offer. They say "*Nyet.*" And then we make another offer. . . .

Our door always is open to genuine cooperation. We need constantly to give them assurance. I wish they would let outside doctors come back in to work, American doctors. I would be tempted to go back myself. I would love to have a chance to work again with the Chinese people. But they won't. . . .

Dr. Taylor: . . . I would personally be in favor of cultural exchanges as I was in the case of the Soviet Union. I am in favor of all sorts of intellectual and cultural contacts with Communist China. I would feel that we have much more to gain from them than they have. There is more chance that they might like our ideas than that we are going to like theirs.

So I personally, perhaps Mr. Judd doesn't agree with me, would be in favor of cultural relations with Communist China, and exchange of scholars and journalists, if we include journalists in culture, and of as many other professions as possible.

Sen. Mundt: Dr. Judd, will you address yourself to it?

Dr. Judd: Well, I helped get the cultural exchange program with the Soviet Union started. It hasn't been as successful as I hoped, for one main reason. We are inclined to assume that if we just send over any American who wants to go and has the money, automatically he and his contact behavior, and so on, will impress them and he will be more successful in changing them than the ones they send over will be successful in changing our thinking.

The difference is that we too often send over unprepared citizens, whereas they send over trained agents. If they were to let anybody come who wants to come and has the money, there would be a million of them on the way the following morning. They screen their people carefully, and our folks are often amateurs. They know inside that our system is better but they haven't studied how to explain it convincingly. We send over genuine farmers; they send over persons that look like farmers but are agents, or are supposed to be professors but are agents, or businessmen but are agents.

Amateurs have difficulty defeating pros in any kind of contest. Therefore, my answer is, we should be more selective in making sure that our people who go abroad in cultural exchange are experts too, who can hold their own, who can explain why our system is better than theirs and why it would be to their advantage to work as best they can to change their system. [pp. 474–478]

Sen. Mundt: Among the more glaring breakdowns of the Communist system in Russia has been their agrarian system, in agriculture, an inability to produce, a reluctance of the peasant to go along. . . .

The question is, therefore, had we yielded to the temptation to move in with great amounts of surplus American farm commodities to alleviate the pains of their agricultural failure, would we have encouraged or retarded the change within Russia? . . .

Dr. Judd: I think we would have retarded the changes. . . .

America's great resources ought to be used on the side of the oppressed, not on the side of the oppressors. If they refuse that reasonable condition of observation, then they would have to take the responsibility for whatever hardship resulted.

This is one of the major reasons why the changes in policy toward Red China being proposed to this committee seem to me so untimely, as a minimum. Communism is in trouble. They have had it in Russia almost forty-nine years. They are not short of land, they are not short of resources, they are not short of strong, competent, brilliant industrious people. Yet they have shortages, there is something wrong with their system. It does not work. . . .

Sen. Mundt: You apparently share the same position as Dr. Taylor [Dr. Judd?], judging by the rhetorical question you ask on page 10 where you ask what conceivable interest would we have in assisting this regime to become a great power. You were alluding to China at the time because included in the policy of containment without isolation is the theory that we should go over there and build up China's shortages, agriculture products, machine tools, and thereby endeavoring to influence a change which would be beneficial to us.

I would gather you would feel also in our relations with China if we did that we would tend to retard the pressures from within for a change instead of an acceleration. . . .

Dr. Taylor: While China is behaving the way she is now I certainly feel that we should do nothing whatsoever to give her any assistance. As far as bringing about changes in Communist China are [*sic*] concerned, I think we could do a great deal to bring about changes in her economic condition but almost nothing to change the basic political situation, and this is the thing that is the basis for her attitude toward the rest of the world. [pp. 493–494]

Testimony of David N. Rowe

Dr. Rowe: [Prepared Statement] What are the main themes now being pushed by the pro-Communist China and anti–anti-Communist elements along this line [i.e., to soften the U.S. approach to Communist China]?

A. (Theme: The historical causation line.) The Communist Chinese foreign policies are merely a logical result of China's frustrations and suffering at the hands of the outside world for the last century or more.

Question: Why are these frustrations and hostile reactions focused on the United States, the one nation with the longest and best record of pro-Chinese aims and actions for 125 years?

Answer: Because our past pro-Chinese policy and our present anti-Communist policies are identical. Both involve . . . the defense of the territorial integrity and sovereignty of small and/or weak countries in Asia. The Chinese Communists today are the chief declared opponents of this policy of ours, as Japan was previously. . . .

B. (Theme: The "inevitable softening of the Communist Chinese.") This line is pushed hard by all the pro-Communist China and anti–anti-Communist elements. . . .

Question: Was Khrushchev better than Stalin, and is the present leadership of the U.S.S.R. better than Khrushchev?

Answer: No.

C. (Theme: The "two Chinas" line.) This is tantamount to saying we can play with enemies without alienating friends. Whatever the distant future holds we cannot know. But for the responsible policymaking future there can be no two-Chinas policy for the United States or anyone else. For example, the United Kingdom has tried to adopt a two-Chinas policy: recognition of Peiping and trying to do business with Taipei. Result: it has neither China. . . . By contrast, the United States without recognition of Peiping, has much higher level diplomatic contacts with the Chinese Communists than Britain, and is the main ally and collaborator with the Republic of China on Taiwan.

Question: Should anyone believe there can be any formal United States–Communist China diplomatic relationship without U.S. abandonment of the Republic of China?

Answer: No.

Question: Can any U.S. administration advocate abandonment of the Republic of China without committing political suicide?

Answer: This is what two-Chinas policy advocates really are urging the administration toward, some knowingly and others unwittingly. That is, the two-Chinas policy means, to start, full diplomatic and other relations with Communist China, and with a trend toward this once set in motion we can more easily abandon the Republic of China on Taiwan, particularly since it would break relations with us if we recognized Communist China.

D. (Theme: The "they don't mean what they say" line.) Anyone who believes in drawing the lessons of history should not object if we say the world would have been better off if more people had taken seriously such historical documents as the Marxist manifesto, Hitler's *Mein Kampf*, or the pre-World War II utterances of the Japanese imperialists. The current utterances of the Communist Chinese leadership seems [sic] just as dangerously unrealistic today as the previously cited ones did then. They are therefore hard to give credence to. . . .

Question: When men talk madness — as the Communist Chinese do — would it not be wise to assume they mean it until and unless they prove otherwise by their acts? Yes. Are the Communist Chinese proving otherwise by their acts? No — they do just the opposite. Witness: Korea, the Taiwan Straits, the Indian frontier, Laos, and Thailand, as well as Vietnam.

E. (Theme: The "simultaneous hard and soft" line.) "Containment but not isolation." The friends of Communist China and the anti–anti-Communists are constantly describing our post-World War II policy toward the U.S.S.R. as combining these two features and advocating that we adopt such a policy toward Communist China.

What is the truth?

1. Our immediate postwar policy toward the U.S.S.R. was not one of containment but of surrender. Eastern Europe and Outer Mongolia were surrendered to the U.S.S.R. with the connivance of the United States and even with highest pressures being brought to bear by the United States on our Allies to surrender to the U.S.S.R. land-grabs, as in the case of Nationalist China and of Mongolia. This was an effort to appease Stalin and get him to accept this as his price for cooperating with us. He took the price, but did not cooperate.

2. The containment policy was then resorted to and it has prevented further territorial takeover. However, this whole policy is now threatened by French action in re NATO, and the chief deterrent to armed action by the U.S.S.R. in Europe is now the mutual thermonuclear threat.

3. Accordingly, we have generally not applied the policy of surrender of territory to Communist China, and in every case but one, have resisted Communist Chinese efforts to push outward. This case was Laos in 1961–1962, and much of our trouble in Vietnam stems from the application to Laos of the formula of appeasement and surrender through the device we tried to use in China [in] 1946–1947 to prevent a Communist Chinese takeover pure and simple; that is, the coalition government with Communists in it. . . .

4. As far as Communist China is concerned, containment means isola-

tion: the two are one and inseparable and the crux of this problem is Taiwan. The Communist Chinese price for non-isolation — which is a two-sided matter, not solely under our control — is the handing over of Taiwan to them; that is, destruction of containment. Any U.S. administration which would even suggest any such thing would commit political suicide by producing a major catastrophe in Asian affairs. . . .

F. (Theme: The line "we have no support among our Allies" for our southeast Asian policy.) . . .

The Japanese people will respect and honor success on our part in Vietnam. Like others, they view with apprehension any irresolution, lack of determination, or willingness to pull out and surrender, on our part. This is generally true of all Asians, from Japan clear around through Korea, Taiwan, the Philippines, southeast Asia, and south Asia. This is one of the many reasons why we cannot and must not fail in Vietnam. . . .

G. (Theme: The line "if we can get to know enough about China and the Chinese people we can promote better relationships with the Chinese Communists.")

This, in my opinion, is the exact opposite of the truth. Actually, the more we study Chinese history and culture the more we can see that the Chinese Communists are revisionists who have chosen to reemphasize the worst that can be found in the Chinese tradition instead of the best. What are some of these things? Totalitarianism, authoritarianism and autocracy, conspiratorial politics, dogmatic subjectivity, the perversion of education into sheer indoctrination, the exaltation of political dogma, and the corresponding debasement of technology, true science, and scientific expertise. They have chosen these emphases, and allied them with the religious subjectivism of Marxism, which appeals to them because it demands so little in the way of abandonment of those reprehensible features of the Chinese tradition that they have seized upon in their fanatical desperation and urgency to change China and the Chinese overnight. This latter characteristic they assert over and over again in such terms as "the Great Leap forward," "socialism within five years," "do twenty years' work in two," and so forth. . . .

Indeed, the notion that to know the Chinese Communists better will make it easier for us to tolerate them is no more true than if we were to say that to know Italy better would make it easier for us to tolerate the Mafia. The fact is we already know enough about both the Mafia and the Chinese Communists to know one thing, and that is that we do not need to know any more in order to justify our policies of opposition and hostility. Of course, we can always use more knowledge on what can be described as a tactical level, such, for example, as is being supplied by U-2 overflights from Taiwan. But we are not likely to learn much from proposals to allow our scholars and students of China to visit Communist China, and for two reasons:

1. The Chinese Communists are not going to allow anyone to come

there unless they are convinced that he is a dependable friend of communism, and of Chinese communism in particular. They have been following this policy for years.

2. Under these circumstances what knowledge is brought back is likely to be either superficial or biased along pro-Chinese Communist lines. [pp. 497–502]

Sen. Symington: Dr. Rowe, I have listened to your statement with great interest, and some of it I agree with. I would ask this question, however. Let us assume that the Chinese situation, from the standpoint of improved relationship, is as hopeless as apparently you believe it is. What are we going to do, say in ten years, certainly in fifteen, when the Chinese have nuclear weapons plus the capacity of delivering them on the United States?

Following that up, in this nuclear age, with all this telescoping of time and space putting all countries now in effect in the same orbit, can any nation afford to turn its back on a country which demonstrates currently that it is so anxious to stab us in the back if it gets the chance? What is your philosophy with respect to that problem, from the standpoint of our children?

Dr. Rowe: If the situation and all other aspects remain the same as it is today — namely, that the Chinese Communists do not get out, are not allowed to expand outward, if they are contained and restrained within their present boundaries during the period in question — then, by that time, you would have the same kind of a thermonuclear confrontation between ourselves and the Chinese Communists as you now have between the United States and the Soviet Union.

It is a seemingly anomalous and contradictory fact, but I think it is a fact, that the closer they get to a real potentiality to attack us with thermonuclear weapons, the more obvious it is that they have to be restrained, they have to restrain themselves. . . .

The problem in restraining China today and keeping it back, and possibly allowing the situation to develop that I have sketched out, is that although we have an effective thermonuclear deterrent vis-à-vis the Soviet Union, and they have vis-à-vis us, we do not have any such thing in the realm of the kind of warfare which the Chinese Communists are practicing. We do not have it, we may develop it before we are through with the Vietnam war. If we do not, we had better watch out, we will be in a very dangerous situation and, possibly be defeated. . . .

I do not think that the answer there, and I am not a military specialist, but I do not feel the answer there lies in an attempt to counteract the so-called peoples' war by another peoples' war.

The avenues that are open to us there, seems to me, have to involve the careful application of the closest possible study — and if you want to study China, here is a place to do it — of the real vulnerabilities that the Chinese and the peoples of southeast Asia, the nonindustrialized, underdeveloped countries have.

Their vulnerabilities are not ours, and ours are not theirs, but as far as I know, very little effort has been made to study the culture of China from this point of view. [pp. 505–506]

Sen. Symington: Then, am I to understand that you believe the more we isolate the Red Chinese from the rest of the human family on this planet, the better off will be the other people living on the planet?

Dr. Rowe: The more you isolate, the better off? I do not think this is necessarily true.

Sen. Symington: Yes.

Dr. Rowe: But I certainly would not decrease the amount of isolation of Communist China below the level that has been embodied in the policy not only of this administration but of the Kennedy, Eisenhower, and Truman administrations that have been discussed today. . . .

Sen. Symington: Don't you think it might be mutually advantageous for us to have, say, fifteen good American newspapermen go to Red China and fifteen Red Chinese newspapermen come here?

Dr. Rowe: Senator, this seems to be at present an unfeasible policy because we have repeated[ly] tried to send newspapermen over there and invited newspapermen here, but nothing happens.

Sen. Symington: I know we have; in fact we have done it on a unilateral basis. But don't you think, from the standpoint of the way the world is today in this nuclear space age, that it would be a net plus if they came over here and saw this country and then were willing to let us go over there and see theirs?

Dr. Rowe: It might not be 100 percent profit, but it still might be worth doing. . . .

Sen. Symington: Well, again then, for the record, you approve of less isolation if you could find some way to obtain less isolation, is that correct?

Dr. Rowe: I think that is a reasonable statement of it, because what this implies is, it does not imply anything about the feasibility of the policy. It does not imply, for instance, that the Department of State and the administration should talk any other way than in a realistic way, namely, that the policy of decreasing our isolation from Communist China and theirs from us in reverse is today impossible.

Sen. Symington: . . . If you are just going to isolate them, turn your back on them, I am not in agreement. I do not see how you can expect anything ultimately but some very serious trouble, because you would not know what they were going to do until they have done it.

Dr. Rowe: Well, I should doubt if the degree of isolation can ever be quite that. I should doubt, for instance, that we do not know a great deal more about Communist China than would be involved in any such situation. [pp. 533–535]

Testimony of Hans J. Morgenthau
and Robert A. Scalapino

Dr. Morgenthau: [Summary of Prepared Statement] We have pursued in the past two policies vis-à-vis China: the policy of isolation and the policy of peripheral military containment.

We have tried to isolate China diplomatically, commercially, and politically in order to impair the legitimacy of her Communist government. That is to say, our policy of isolation is intimately connected with our recognition of the Chiang Kai-shek government as the legitimate government of all of China. We thought that by withholding recognition and by being able to persuade most nations of the world to withhold recognition as well, we could impair the legitimacy of the Communist government of China and bring it down. . . .

It is obvious that the policy of isolation has been a complete failure. As far as the admission of China to normal diplomatic, political, and commercial relations is concerned, it is the United States which is isolated, and not China. Insofar as China is isolated, as she actually is in relation to the other Communist nations, it is her doing and not ours. . . .

I should also say that to give up the policy of isolation, as has been suggested to this committee, may be wise or unwise, but it is not decisive. This suggestion misses the decisive point of our relations with China, which is the problem of containment. That is to say, even if we were able to send professors and journalists and doctors to China and vice versa, and even if the Communist government of China were admitted to the United Nations, the basic issue, the basic conflict of interests between ourselves and China would be unaffected by such moves, however much they might improve the international climate of opinion. The decisive, crucial issue is the issue of containment.

We have been trying to contain China at its periphery through isolated military strong points, especially that the policy of military containment, which was so successful vis-à-vis the Soviet Union in Europe in the forties and fifties, could be successful in Asia. But I think this is a fundamental mistake, and I should say right away it is the fundamental mistake of our policy vis-à-vis China. For the threat which we were facing in Europe in the form of the Soviet Union was primarily of a military nature. The Red Army stood in the center of Europe, and the nations of Western Europe were under threat of Communist revolution and subversion. . . .

Furthermore, the policy of containment was an eminent success, not because of the six divisions we stationed beyond the Rhine in opposition to the Red Army, but because those six divisions were a token of our determination to use our retaliatory nuclear power if a Russian soldier should step over the line of military demarcation of 1945.

This character of our European policy of containment and the reasons for its success are very relevant for an understanding of the weakness of our policy of containment vis-à-vis China. First of all, the threat which China constitutes to Asia is not primarily of a military nature. . . . It is rather the natural, and in a sense inevitable, attraction which this enormous empire and this imposing culture have always exerted, and have started to exert again, upon the mainland of Asia. I remember very vividly when I traveled in Asia for the first time in 1955 how impressed I was with this psychological impact which the renascence of China has had upon its neighbors, from Japan to Pakistan.

The primary threat China presents is cultural and political. Such a threat cannot be contained by local military means in Taiwan or Vietnam or Korea or Thailand or elsewhere, because the Chinese have simply jumped over those so-called military barriers and have exerted at times very considerable influence in Indonesia, in Tanzania, in Mali, in the Republic of the Congo (Brazzaville), and elsewhere. . . .

Thus the policy of peripheral military containment is bound to be ineffective. It has been effective for the time being only by virtue of the temporary military weakness of China. If we are convinced that the cultural and political influence which China is bound to exert upon Asia is not compatible with the vital interests of the United States, it will not be sufficient to try to contain China at the periphery of its empire by military means. We have to strike at the power of China itself. We have to destroy China. We have to go to war with China. I think this is the inevitable logical conclusion to be drawn from the assumption that the paramountcy of the Chinese power on the Asian mainland is incompatible with the interests of the United States.

Yet considering the policy we are actually pursuing, we are trying to achieve an end which cannot be achieved with the means which we are willing to employ; we cannot contain the political influence of China without going to war with her. Thus we have to make up our mind as to whether we want to achieve that end with the drastic means appropriate to it — that is to say, through war against China — or whether we want to cut down our aims in order to bring them into harmony with the means which we are willing to employ. [pp. 553–555]

Dr. Scalapino: [Prepared Statement] . . . Nearly six years ago, Mr. Chairman, I had the privilege of writing the northeast Asia section of a report on U.S. foreign policy in Asia which was submitted to this committee. At that time, I defined our current policy as one of attempted containment by isolation, and I suggested a variety of reasons why, in my opinion, we should move away from such a negative, inflexible approach to an admittedly complex, difficult problem.

Naturally, I am gratified to note that in recent months and weeks, there have been increasing signs that our government is seeking a more broadly gauged policy. Some of the steps which I advocated in 1959 are now being initiated or at least actively contemplated. These include a willingness to allow American scholars, scientists, journalists, and certain other citizens to travel to China; positive steps to seek the involvement of China in international negotiations on such problems as disarmament, nuclear weapon control, and similar issues of world importance; and the establishment of terms under which mainland China might come into the United Nations.

Because these steps, and others which should follow will be strongly debated, I should like to reiterate the reasons why I believe such actions, on balance, are highly desirable. A policy of containment by isolation robbed the United States of initiative or leverage, and tended to posit our rigidity against that of Peking. This in turn served to separate us from our allies and the neutrals, making collective thinking and action with respect to China vastly more difficult. It also rendered far less effective the type of multiple external pressures that are essential if the element of extremism in Chinese foreign policy is to be effectively curbed or countered.

Our past policy has been insufficient in certain other respects. To foster isolation is to foster fanaticism. Isolation, indeed, is one of the major weapons of a police state, and there is no reason as to why we should be a party to its support. On the contrary, a truly sophisticated American foreign policy will always aim at complicating the decisionmaking processes of a totalitarian state. To be able to engage in selective diplomacy and to bear negligible responsibilities in the world community represent significant tactical advantages which we should not bestow lightly. Such a situation also encourages a purist, uncompromising, and irrational attitude, an air of complete unrealism.

A policy of containment by isolation, in short, not only provides an inadequate approach from the standpoint of international political realities, but it is also highly unsatisfactory from the standpoint of its impact upon the Chinese nation itself. In immediate terms, therefore, we must move from such a policy toward one that heightens the element of choice for the Chinese political elite by providing additional incentives for moderation and firm, explicit deterrents to extremism. We must find a way of making peaceful coexistence the only conceivable path for the next generation of Chinese leaders and we must do this without abandoning any of the basic rights or requirements of the non-Communist world.

I do not claim that this will be easy or that it can be done quickly. . . . The time may not be too long . . . before China's military capacities come closer to matching her political visions. We must prepare for that eventuality now.

There are a few individuals who would argue that we should forcefully remove the Chinese military threat before it becomes serious. But preventive war, in my opinion, is politically impossible even if one were to waive all questions of morality. We are a democratic society, and neither our people nor our officials would sanction such a policy. Moreover, preventive war by its very nature would fail because it ignores the response of the world community as well as of the people most immediately affected, and provides therefore no basis for erecting a meaningful world order.

The only realistic approach in my opinion is the complex one of creating an elaborate structure of opportunities and deterrents, and in this task we must have the cooperation of other nations, particularly those of non-Communist Asia. Our first steps seem clear enough. Progressively, we must make it clear by concrete actions that if China is isolated, the initiative lies with her, that we are prepared to enter into cultural relations with her, engage in trade on the same basis as with other Communist nations, and negotiate with her on all matters of international importance. At the same time, we should accept in principle the desirability of universal membership in the United Nations, a principle which among other things would make natural the acceptance of both China and Taiwan as de facto states deserving international representation. Bilateral recognition between the United States and China is not, in my opinion, a first priority item under present circumstances. Once again, however, I believe that we should move toward the establishment of a general principle, namely, the complete divorcement of recognition from the question of moral or political approval. . . .

Thus far, however, I have advanced and defended only one side of the policy proposed earlier. But it is my firm belief that moderation will be encouraged only if the risks of extremism are made both credible and clear. . . .

At this point, for example, we should make it absolutely clear that any attempt to change the status of Taiwan or South Korea by means of the use of externally directed or assisted force will be resolutely countered by the application of American force. We should also continue to make it unmistakably clear that we do not intend to allow these tactics to succeed in South Vietnam. In my opinion, nothing would be more calculated to pump life into the extremist movement within China and within the Communist world than a Maoist victory in Vietnam — and nothing would lead us more quickly into the awful choice between precipitous retreat everywhere and World War III. The Chinese have repeatedly emphasized the fact that Vietnam is a supreme test of Maoist principles in statements to their own people, to other Asians, and to fellow Communists. We can be certain that the path toward moderation and peace will be infinitely longer and more painful if extremism pays in this crucial test. [pp. 570–572]

Sen. Hickenlooper: But the confusion in my mind in trying to understand your approaches here is that we adopted policies of deterrence, so far as the Soviet were concerned, by building up NATO. Now, was that directed at isolating the Soviets or was it aimed at inhibiting expansion? . . .

Dr. Scalapino: Had we done toward the Soviet Union in 1945 what we began to do toward China in 1950, namely, prohibit all trade — impose a total trade embargo — operate in such a fashion as to keep the Soviet Union out of the world stream, or at least not encourage the Soviet Union to enter into international organizations, had we taken positions with respect to travel and cultural contact that represented a total freeze in our mutual relations, then I would have said we were isolating the Soviet Union or seeking its isolation. Our policy of developing a set of deterrents, both military and political, to Soviet expansionism was quite a different policy.

Sen. Hickenlooper: Wouldn't you agree that the twilight zone between inhibiting aggression by certain action and trying to isolate them is a pretty thin line?

Dr. Scalapino: It may be a thin line but I also regard it as a crucial one, and this ties in with what I have suggested earlier. I think that our policy toward China has been one of those 100-percent or zero policies, and I think that what is critical is to build in these elements of sophistication that make more possible an alternative choice for the Chinese leadership, make it much more difficult for them to be extremist than we have done in the past. This, it seems to me, is going to be a critical test of our policy. . . .

Sen. Hickenlooper: . . . There comes a time when there should be some willingness on the other side to give some indication that they are really desirous of edging a little bit more into the community of nations as the world. French and British recognition of the Red Chinese and actions by other nations who have at least tried to keep the door open don't seem to have broken the ice very much. . . .

Dr. Scalapino: May I just make one final point on this matter? I don't think that a change in our China policy would be of great advantage to Communist China. Therefore, I don't believe as I said earlier, that they would really welcome this change. I am trying to think in broader and longer range terms of our capacity to develop a policy that will have greater world support, be more realistic, and put more meaningful pressures upon China — pressures upon China that will cause her leaders to consider moderate as well as extremist approaches. With respect to Asia, I would say that perhaps we should not be too discouraged about Asian attitudes toward the United States. This is a time, it seems to me, when it is wise to distinguish between surface and subsurface trends. . . .

Sen. Church: [Do] you think if the changes you have recommended were placed in effect, this would be of any immediate value in securing for the United States greater measure of Asian support and understanding for our position and objectives there?

Dr. Scalapino: I do. . . .

I am prepared to suggest that in the case of relations between the United States, China, and the world, sincere overtures on our part pertaining to cultural relations, trade, and peaceful coexistence with China, reiterated over time could not help but influence not only Asia but all of the states who have a natural interest in world peace. Thereby the cumulative pressures would be built up around China which in the final analysis are going to be the only meaningful pressures. No one state is going to be able to move the Chinese glacier. It has got to be a collective process, and this is, I think, the most important fact of all, that that collective process has got to ultimately work its way inside the Chinese policy itself. There has [*sic*] got to be more debates within top Chinese political circles about the price of isolation and extremism, and the possible gains of moderation. The sooner that debate begins to take place and the broader the scale upon which it takes place, the better it will be for all of us.

Thus, I do not think it is germane to say that because China rejects a policy, it is bad. On the contrary, we have only begun and it is going to be a long, hard road, but these cumulative pressures are the critical elements.

Sen. Church: I think there is much sense to what you have said. . . . But politically this is very difficult to do, because any change in American policy that isn't immediately met by some reciprocal change in Chinese policy will at once be condemned in this country as foolish appeasement that has produced no fruit. Therefore, it seems to me, that the kind of sophistication you have called for lies at the heart of the issue, and one can seriously question whether we yet possess it.

Dr. Scalapino: I am optimistic. I think that if our leadership at all levels — in public life and in scholarly life — not only on this issue but upon others, will point out the enormous importance of avoiding what I have called the zero or the 100-percent approach, the great value of gradations of policy, and playing for long-range results, our people will understand these points. I don't think it has been presented to them yet. [pp. 582–586]

The Chairman: Dr. Morgenthau, you stated a moment ago that there needs to be a change in our attitude toward Communism, didn't you? Do you see any tendency whatever that such a change is taking place in this country?

Dr. Morgenthau: I see it in Europe. We are dealing with Russia on its own terms. We are dealing with Yugoslavia and with Poland on their own terms. But I don't see it in Asia. Strangely enough, there is a gap between our rational recognition that the monolithic character of communism has been replaced by polycentrism, on the one hand, and an almost mechanical application of obsolescent modes of thought and action to the situation in Asia. I find this interesting from a psychological point of view, but it is also rather disturbing, in political terms. . . .

Sen. Case: Many of your colleagues have been urging containment yes, but isolation no, as a means of trying to lift this rigidity. Aren't you going to counter to this worthy effort? . . .

Dr. Morgenthau: This idea of abandoning isolation but maintaining unchanged containment, and of simply applying to Asia the principles of the containment of the Soviet Union without taking into account what it is we are trying to contain — this idea is an attempt to evade the issue.

The policy of isolation is essentially irrelevant to the central issue, and the policy of abolishing isolation is equally irrelevant to the central issue. It is an attempt to have it both ways, to look flexible, enlightened, and benevolent, on the one hand, and at the same time to continue the status quo where it really counts. This policy will not succeed. . . .

Dr. Scalapino: May I make two comments at this point which will place me in some opposition to Professor Morgenthau?

In this first place, it seems to me whenever you post these things as absolutes you get into both factual and logical trouble. Questions of hardness and flexibility are never absolutes. They are matters of degree, and one opens up new avenues of growth, as one makes policy overtures and changes. I think the most fundamental difference, perhaps, between Professor Morgenthau and myself lies in the whole philosophy with which we approach foreign policy.

. . . We do not need to choose between surrender and war, the two extremes. . . . If we ever take the position that relations between states are totally dependent upon one or two issues — that these are the only keys to any improvement — then we will get ourselves into positions of rigidity and unrealism. One can sometimes make significant gains by working at the edges, when central problems will not submit to any immediate solution, and allowing time to introduce new elements into the equation.

With respect to our attitude toward European communism and Asian communism, I think there has been a difference. This question, however, needs to be analyzed not only from the standpoint of American psychology but also from the standpoint of the objective conditions in the two areas.

. . . any close analysis of the nature of the Asian Communist states and parties suggests that they have been less amenable to accommodation with us for a variety of reasons. Quite naturally, perhaps, they have been more militant, more committed to a program of frontal assault on the status quo and on what they call "the world imperialist camp headed by the United States." And China has been a leader in this respect.

[pp. 594–597]

9 CHINESE REPRESENTATION IN THE UNITED NATIONS

Testimony of A. Doak Barnett

Mr. Barnett: [Prepared Statement] The China issue in the United Nations is in many respects an urgent question, since unless we can soon evolve a new and sounder position on this issue, we are likely to be defeated in the General Assembly, and then our entire policy of isolation of Peking will begin to unravel as a result of a major political defeat, even before we can, on our own initiative, attempt to redefine our posture.

Last fall we were barely able to get enough votes to sustain our position. Conceivably we might do so once or twice again; but it is equally conceivable that next fall the General Assembly might, despite our opposition, vote to seat Peking in the present China seat occupied by the Chinese Nationalist regime. If this takes place, there is little likelihood that the Nationalists could later be brought back into the United Nations since this would then be a question of admitting a new member, which is subject to the veto.

It would be to our interest, therefore, to take the initiative in the General Assembly in promoting a solution in which the Assembly would declare that there are now two successor states ruling the territory of the original China which joined the United Nations when it was formed in 1945, and that both should have seats in the Assembly. Neither the Chinese Communists nor the Chinese Nationalists are presently willing to accept such a solution, and conceivably both might boycott the United Nations for a period of time, if such a solution were adopted. Nevertheless, it is a realistic and reasonable position for the international community as a whole to adopt, and I believe that if it were adopted, there would be numerous pressures operating over time to induce Peking and Taipei eventually to reexamine their positions and consider accepting seats even under these conditions.

If and when Communist China does assume a seat in the United Nations, its initial impact is likely to be disruptive, but I firmly believe that over the long run it is nonetheless desirable to involve Peking in this complicated political arena where it will have to deal on a day-to-day basis with such a wide variety of countries and issues. It will soon learn, I think, that dogmatic arrogance will result only in self-isolation and that

169

even a major nation must make compromises to operate with any success in the present world community.

A shift of American policy in the United Nations issue — and, in fact, any significant change in our posture toward Peking — will inevitably require some modification of our policy toward the Nationalist regime on Taiwan. For many reasons — political, strategic, and moral — we should continue defending Taiwan against attack and should firmly support the principle of self-determination in regard to the 13 million inhabitants of the island. But we will not be able to continue sustaining the fiction that the Nationalist regime is the government of mainland China.

Our view of the Nationalist regime should be one in which we recognize it as the legal government of the territories it now occupies, essentially Taiwan and the Pescadores, rather than as the government of all China; this, one might note, is essentially the position which the Japanese government already maintains in regard to the Nationalists. We should do all we can to obtain representation for the Taipei regime in the United Nations and to urge the international community to accept and support it as the government of its present population and territory. But we cannot indefinitely sustain the fiction that it is the government of all China. [pp. 14–15]

Sen. Sparkman: Do you believe that Communist China sees any particular advantage to her in having membership in the United Nations?

Mr. Barnett: I think that from the Chinese Communist point of view this is an extremely low priority objective. As a matter of fact, one can even argue that statements made last fall almost indicate that right at the moment they do not want to get into the United Nations, because they set such extreme conditions.

My own feeling would be that the Chinese Communists have felt in the recent period that this is not an important enough objective for them to make significant concessions to achieve. I think they probably have also felt, however, that with the U.N.–China issue unresolved, and coming up every year, with the future decision being unclear as to whether there would be a simple replacement of the Nationalist regime by the Communist regime or whether some alternative type of proposal would be accepted, that tactically Peking has felt it was a wise thing to take the most adamant kind of position upon this issue, to try to say that "You have to accept our point of view fully or don't count us in."

So, this has been the situation and remains the situation today. The situation today is that the Chinese Communists say that not only does there have to be a total switch from Nationalist to Communist representation, but the U.N. has to retract resolutions taken during the Korean war, and so on — things that are not likely at all to happen.

My own feeling, however, is that if there were a change in the situation in the U.N., if there were, let's say, what I have suggested, a decision that two seats exist, take them or leave them, I am inclined to think that over a period of time Peking would reevaluate its situation. It would be less able to exert, by whatever posture it takes, some influence on what will happen in the U.N., since a decision would simply be whether they took a seat or didn't take it.

I would think that it would be very possible, and I am inclined to think even likely, over time, although I don't know over how long, that eventually Peking would think it is to its advantage to come in. [pp. 24–25]

Sen. Symington: As I understand it, Chinese leaders have laid down the condition that they will not join the U.N. unless the Republic of China is expelled from the U.N. and all its organs. I have read your statement and it is clear. But I wish you would comment a bit more for the edification of the rest of us.

Mr. Barnett: Well, that is their position, and it has become stronger in the last year or two than it was before, and I think they mean it now, in a sense, as well as feeling that it is tactically desirable to hold this position. So they will resist the kind of thing that I am proposing.

But in my estimate, looking at the past seventeen years, when there is some maneuver in a position, they are able to take a certain stand for tactical reasons. But when there is no maneuver in a position, and it is against their interests to hold their present position, they very often reevaluate their position.

So I genuinely believe that the pressures operating in the long run, if there were a seat there, would be for them to reevaluate their position and decide eventually, on balance, that it would be better to be in than to be out. This is an estimate that one cannot prove. It is speculative, but it would be my estimate.

Sen. Symington: As you point out, originally we could be subject to a great deal of abuse but there was some shoe-banging, at the time, even with a now more friendly Communist power.

Mr. Barnett: I think for a period of time after they come in, if they do, we would be faced with something quite comparable to the Soviet role in the U.N. at the height of the Soviet intransigence, and it is not something that one looks forward to with anticipation, but it is something that the U.N. survived before, and I think it can again. And, as I say again, I am convinced, myself, that trying to play that role for any extended period of time, the Chinese would learn that in terms of their own goals and interests this may be a counter-productive way to go about it.

My understanding of the U.N. leads me to feel that it is a most complicated political arena where everybody has to make compromises on certain things to move in certain other directions.

Sen. Symington: Certainly, it would be better to put up with a little abuse now as against ten to fifteen years from now, facing an isolated China which might be a complete nuclear power.

Mr. Barnett: I agree, and I think that whether or not we can moderate the atmosphere of relations between ourselves and China, and the general atmosphere in which China operates on the international scene, in the next ten to fifteen years will have a lot to do with how much of a threat China is ten to fifteen years from now. [pp. 41–42]

Sen. Symington: Let me proceed in my next question. Suppose we agreed to let the Red Chinese come in on terms that would have to be worked out but, at the same time, the Taiwanese stayed in only as members of the General Assembly. Do you think the Red Chinese would agree to that?

Mr. Barnett: It is my estimate that over time they would come around to accepting it, although it would take time.

Sen. Symington: Well, not to labor it, but to be sure I understand, they would have to agree to it in the beginning, would they not? In other words, if they objected at all they would object in the beginning; and that would mean they would say, "We will not come in unless you get them all the way out."

Mr. Barnett: I would say it is conceivable that the General Assembly itself could take action in which it could declare that there are two successor seats and, therefore, two seats available.

Sen. Symington: I see.

Mr. Barnett: There are many kinds of legalistic and diplomatic complications involved in this. But this is what I think is conceivable; it could happen.

If this is not conceivable, I mean, if immediate agreement on the part of either or both of the parties concerned was required, then I could not see a solution, and I think what is most likely to happen is that in the next year or two Communist China will be seated in the place of Nationalist China which, I think, is not the most desirable outcome from my point of view. . . .

Sen. Symington: The next question, Do you think the people of Taiwan would agree to stay in on any basis if the Red Chinese came into the General Assembly?

Mr. Barnett: I think over time.

Sen. Symington: Over time.

Mr. Barnett: They might well agree to this, but not immediately.

Sen. Symington: Wouldn't that be something they should have to decide in the beginning?

Mr. Barnett: Well, I do not believe so. I think that it is possible that the Assembly could act, as I say, and that then two seats would be there. Then both regimes would have to consider over time whether to occupy them or not.

As I say, if this is not possible, then I think that the prospects that we must accept are that in the foreseeable future Communist China will be in and Nationalist China will be out. So that I certainly think we must explore the possibilities. There are many kinds of unanswered questions because there really has been no active exploration of the possibilities.

Sen. Symington: Isn't there a strange dichotomy between the American position, namely, that the United Nations is the last great hope of the world — which may well be true — but at the same time we consistently refuse to let in 25 percent of the people of the world even to discuss matters, this while we are facing up to the vital problems of proliferation?

Mr. Barnett: Yes; I do believe it is inconsistent. In the early 1950's it was based on a presumption, on the part of the U.S. government that, perhaps, the Chinese Communist regime would not be a long-lived regime. I think this has not been the case in recent years; the U.S. government has implicitly accepted the fact the Chinese Communist regime is a regime that is going to exist for a long time, and that we are going to have to deal with it. I think there is an inconsistency. [pp. 92–93]

Testimony of John K. Fairbank

Sen. McCarthy: Dr. Fairbank, on February 12 Mr. William P. Bundy spoke in Pomona, Calif. During the course of that speech he came out strongly against having the Chinese Communist nation represented at the United Nations He raised some technical difficulties which I think we understand.

But he included among the reasons he gave for opposition one evidence of Communist China's intent to disrupt any peacemaking effort the United Nations might undertake. Do you feel that would be a serious objection to their being admitted to the United Nations?

Dr. Fairbank: No, not on balance. I would favor their admission even if they are claiming they are going to dynamite the place as soon as they get in. Because I think on balance it is more constructive to have them in, and let them wear themselves out antagonizing everybody if they want to be obnoxious.

Sen. McCarthy: Do you think they would really attempt to disrupt any peacemaking efforts?

Dr. Fairbank: I think they might well, in many cases, be very disruptive. I don't think there is any happy future between us and China. There are going to be lots of disruptive efforts on their part if they come into the U.N. or any contact with us. They will be extremely annoying. They have a tremendous capacity to annoy us.

Sen. McCarthy: That would not make them unique in the United Nations, would it?

Dr. Fairbank: No. There is good precedent.

Sen. McCarthy: It is said the psychological effect on the leaders of

Communist China and these nations resisting Chinese pressures would be very serious. Would you consider that to be an objection worthy of consideration? . . .

Dr. Fairbank: In the end — my whole point this morning has been that in the end if you want the Chinese Communists to stop trying to stir up the underdeveloped world as their main claim to fame, your real alternative is to get them into international contact. The most obvious place is the U.N. So I think that it has a great psychological curative value for them in the long run because I think they are very prestige conscious.

Sen. McCarthy: What about the other nations resisting Chinese pressures, do you think they would be very much upset, psychologically disturbed, if we were to accept the admission of Red China to the United Nations?

Dr. Fairbank: That is what I was referring to a moment ago, that is a very valid point, they would be upset.

Sen. McCarthy: All of them?

Dr. Fairbank: And consequently you have to work toward a complex and combined policy in which you are not just giving in to Peking. You are doing something constructive, you are not letting go of your alliances, you are not selling out the other countries that feel threatened by China. You have to hold up both sides. In other words, build the international order with Peking's participation at the same time that you have a certain amount of containment of Peking's expansionism, if it occurs in these other places on this subversive revolutionary model. [pp. 131–132]

The Chairman: Well, lastly . . . you wrote a very interesting article recently about Taiwan. Could you in a moment just for this record tell us what you think our attitude should be toward Taiwan, the problem of Taiwan and China?

Dr. Fairbank: I have been concerned for a long time about the future of Taiwan because it seems to me it deserves to be an independent country in its own right. It has its own resources and native life now. It is, in fact, a country bigger than about two-thirds of the U.N. members, 12 million, 13 million people.

When one mentions the idea of an independent Taiwan, one is known as a capitalist spy in Peking, and a Communist traitor in Taipei, and I can show you clippings on both of those. Because, curiously enough, both sides in this Chinese civil war, which still goes on in their mind, have the same view that China is a unit, an entity. They have this really tremendous sense of Chinese history behind them, and they are not going to break that.

They both want the whole thing, and in this situation for us from the outside to tell them what to do is not easy, and even our friends in Taipei, you do not tell them what to do very easily, and so it has occurred to me that, perhaps, the thing for us to do is to relax and not try to settle this for them.

They do not like the kind of things that seem logical to us, that this country would go along with an independent Taiwan, a country, there it is, and it exists, and it makes sense to us. But if they do not like that, let them work it out, let the U.N. work it out.

Why should we take on the burden on deciding this question which is a Chinese political question? So if we come to a vote in the U.N., if we have a relaxed attitude and are not trying to twist everybody's arm, perhaps there would be some move to get Peking in, at that point it would be very desirable if Taipei could be kept in, too.

Now, if we try that, it might not be any more effective than if we left other U.N. country members to try it and work it out from their side, because any U.N. country can see that Taipei is a pretty good country. Taiwan is an active, well-organized place compared to many developing countries, and it ought to be in the U.N. So there are many ways in which this might be worked out. [p. 177]

Testimony of John M. H. Lindbeck
and Benjamin I. Schwartz

Sen. Case: I wonder if any of you would comment on this question. You are in general agreement, I take it, with the broad thesis that both Mr. Barnett and Dr. Fairbank presented to us. Now, have you any suggestions as to how specifically our course in regard to the United Nations might be guided in the next, say, six months to a year in relation to such suggestions as that which has been raised from a two-Chinas policy? . . .

Dr. Lindbeck: My own feeling is that we have certain obligations toward the Chinese on Taiwan. For a variety of reasons . . . we can't disregard these obligations which we have assumed. I think that, on the other hand, we ought to move toward normality in our relations with the Chinese on the mainland. I agree with Mr. Schwartz that they are unlikely to respond at present to our overtures. . . .

Nonetheless, we have seen the Chinese Communists do some very curious things. They have been dealing with regimes, or governments, which are obviously hostile to communism. Yet they have felt that it was in their practical interest, to their benefit, to deal with these countries. Who can tell at what point they will see a genuine, practical interest for themselves in working with the United Nations? . . .

Dr. Schwartz: . . . I do think the real problem for us, assuming that we are willing to reconcile ourselves to the entry of mainland China into the United Nations, is how we preserve a place for the government on

Taiwan, perhaps in the General Assembly, and I think — I don't know the technicalities of this — this is an area where we should be concentrating.

As far as the desire or lack of desire of the mainland government to come into the United Nations, I think that some people have exaggerated their indifference to the United Nations. That is, of course, so long as they are not in it, it is to their interest to downgrade it as much as possible. I have no doubt that as part of their optimum vision they would certainly prefer the plan which was put forth by Sukarno and themselves a few years ago of a new United Nations of the newly emerging countries.

At the same time I noted editorials in their press, after the last meeting, at which — in which they took great comfort from the fact that the forces within the United Nations which are opposed to the U.S. position are growing, and they frequently do allude to their legitimate seat in the United Nations.

Thus, while it may not be the matter of topmost priority to them, I think to say they are absolutely indifferent to it is also wrong. [pp. 215–217]

Testimony of Donald S. Zagoria

Sen. Hickenlooper: [We] hear repeatedly day after day people who write on one side or the other of this thing say, "I think we ought to be doing more." We ought to be doing this, that, or the other thing in generalities but it seems to me most of these things we have done repeatedly and nothing has happened.

Dr. Zagoria: Well, Senator, I can only repeat some specific proposals that I think go beyond the realm of generality, and that do represent things that we have not done, and it seems to me do not intend to do in the near future. One is [to] stop our opposition to Chinese entry into the United Nations. I don't think necessarily we ought to support such entry, but it does seem to me that we ought to stop opposing it because the majority of the countries at the United Nations, the majority of the international community, I think, would like to see both Communist China and Taiwan represented in the United Nations. . . .

There are many Asian problems that have come up in the past and are likely to come up in the future. The Chinese-Indian border dispute, the problem of Vietnam, these and other problems are problems in which Communist China, as a potentially great Asian power is indirectly or directly interested in and involved in, and it seems to me to be unrealistic to think that such problems can in the long run be fully resolved without Chinese Communist participation in their resolution. . . .

Sen. Hickenlooper: Along that line would it then follow that we ought to take a blue pencil or a red pencil and cross out the principles of the United Nations, that is, peace and nonaggression and peaceful settlement of disputes? Can we just pencil that out of the United Nations? . . .

Dr. Zagoria: There are two approaches, two points of view on how to interpret the Charter of the United Nations and the purposes of the United Nations. One point of view is that the United Nations is a peace-keeping organization or an organization of only peace-loving countries in which aggressors, and so on, should be kept out.

Another point of view is that the United Nations is intended as an international organization to try to conciliate differences between nations, and this assumes that at some point in time one nation may be an aggressor or some nations may think that they have been the victims of aggression, and therefore that the United Nations is a forum for resolving international conflict and dispute and therefore should be a universal organization.

My point of view would lean toward the latter, that we must, of course, recognize that the Chinese Communists have done a lot of things in the past that we do not approve of, but so have other Communist countries who are presently represented in the United Nations, and we are not urging on the ground of principle to throw out the Russians or the Yugoslavs who shot down American airplanes in 1947 or 1948, so I would stand on the ground that the United Nations is an organ for trying to resolve, conciliate disputes, and that although Communist China may not be a peace-loving nation in the sense that we would like it to be, that is all the more reason for it to be in the United Nations in order for us to be able to exercise international pressures and leverage on it and to discuss with it its grievances.

Sen. Hickenlooper: You mean on the theory that the greater the sinner, the greater the rejoicing if you can get him to repent a little bit?

Dr. Zagoria: I don't think it will be an easy problem, I don't think we are going to be very successful in getting Communist China to recant. I think these people are very convinced, dedicated Communist and nationalist revolutionaries with a great sense of national pride, with a great sense of humiliation at the hands of the West, as has been pointed out here before.

Herman Kahn once said that the United States and the Soviet Union were two powers that could be compared to two people who had won a lot of money at a poker game and wanted to go home. Most of the rest of the countries, to follow this analogy, are people who hadn't won so much money at this poker game and are interested in it to go on for quite a bit longer.

I would suggest to you that the Chinese Communists are one of the many countries in the world who are profoundly dissatisfied with the status quo and that that is, has been, and is going to continue to be a source of great tension between the United States and the Soviet Union on the one hand, and China on the other.

So I don't have any illusions about getting them to recant. But I would like to see a forum in which we could try to resolve and bring other powers to help us try to resolve China's legitimate grievances, and to discuss all their demands even though I don't think we should by any means be prepared to give in to all their demands.

Sen. Hickenlooper: Shouldn't they be expected, if they act in good faith, to show some willingness to make some concessions, just as we have shown willingness to make many concessions to many countries in the past?

Dr. Zagoria: Yes.

Sen. Hickenlooper: As far as I know they have shown no willingness to do anything that would bring them closer to the possibility of social acceptance by the other countries. . . . But, so far as I know, the mainland Chinese have done nothing to really create the idea that they want to become a part of the family of nations even though they may be in disagreement on many, many things. I think it is high time that they did something of that kind if they are really in good faith.

Dr. Zagoria: Yes. Well, I must say that I agree with you that there have been few signs from them that they are willing to change their policies. The line of reasoning that I am suggesting is that as a result of that they are becoming increasingly isolated in the world today, they are running into a stone wall. Their policies are increasingly discredited, and I would anticipate changes in that policy, and I would like to see us place ourselves in a position where we could be alert to those changes when and if they are signaled.

Sen. Hickenlooper: Well now, just one question about Taiwan. I have the impression Taiwan is one of the two highly developed and viable economies in all of Asia, the other being Japan. I think there has been a remarkable job done there on Taiwan, and it has been done, I believe, under the expansion of policies of what we would call increasing freedom and increasing self-determination. Yet there are those who would throw Taiwan down the drain and embrace the Communist world on the mainland — in other words, destroy it. . . .

Dr. Zagoria: Yes. I think that the only ultimate solution for Taiwan that makes any sense at all is, eventually, autonomy in which the five-sixths or more of the population on the island of Taiwan who do not come from mainland China, and who do wish to be independent of both the mainland Chinese regime and the present Nationalist government, that that seems to me the most logical solution, that there will be a government led by Taiwanese.

Now, it is a very difficult question as to how we get from where we are now to that point, and I have no particular solutions for that. I do think we are committed and should remain committed to the defense of

Taiwan against Communist Chinese or any other outside aggression, and at the same time I think we ought to be committed to the principle of self-determination for the people of Taiwan, and I think that, as I say, any self-determination would show a desire to be independent of both the Nationalists and Communist China. [pp. 390–392]

Testimony of Walter H. Judd

Dr. Judd: [Prepared Statement] What would be the result of admitting Communist China to the United Nations? I cannot see any important benefits for us or for the United Nations, but the benefits for the Communists would be enormous. . . .

Some say, "But Communist China is a fact. We must be realistic. We cannot hide our heads in the sand and ignore it or pretend it is not there." But that is not a description of our policy. On the contrary, it is just because we recognize that Red China is indeed a fact, and such a powerful and dangerous fact, that intelligent concern for our own and the world's future requires its exclusion from the United Nations until it is willing to meet the qualifications for membership. To admit it prior to that time would only make it more powerful and more dangerous.

The Communist regime in China avowedly is dedicated to the isolation and destruction of the United States. Should Americans help it get into a better position to work for that objective? It is a complete non sequitur to say that because "Red China is there," therefore it ought to be admitted to the U.N. There are gangsters in some of our cities. We do not argue that therefore the city councils, courts, and police force should take the gangsters in. Rather we demand that lawless elements be kept out of the forces responsible for maintaining law and order, or "peace and security" — which the U.N. Charter states is the purpose for which that organization was established.

It is said that the 700 million Chinese are entitled to be represented in the U.N. Certainly. But the Peking regime does not represent the Chinese people any more than the Quisling regime in Norway represented the Norwegian people. Mao has got to destroy the Chinese culture and its values — moderation, gentlemanliness, primary loyalty to the family, reasonableness, the middle of the road, good manners, which are the essentials of that culture; or he knows it will transform and absorb communism. Mao and the Communists are wholly un-Chinese. How can they represent the Chinese people? Whenever the Chinese people have opportunity to choose their own representatives in free elections, those representatives will undoubtedly be admitted promptly to the United Nations. Incidentally, is it not strange that free elections are demanded in

Vietnam "to determine the people's wishes," even during a cruel internal war, but such elections are not demanded in mainland China?

To keep Red China isolated and weaker than it would otherwise be is not denying or ignoring its existence: It is the realistic way to deal with its existence.

It is said that the United Nations ought to be a universal organization with all existing governments in it. But the charter makes perfectly clear that the U.N. was never intended to be a universal organization. That concept was discussed at San Francisco — and rejected. Why would the Charter have Article 6 which provides for expelling a member which has consistently violated the principles contained in the present Charter, if the organization was supposed to be universal? . . .

Perhaps it might be useful to establish a new universal organization — a league of all existing governments, lawless as well as law-abiding.

But the United Nations is not such an organization. Let us not destroy its character as a union of peace-loving states pooling their strength against lawlessness and aggression from whatever source.

It is hard to understand how some can advocate world peace through world law and at the same time advocate brazen violation of the nearest to world law that we have, the Charter of the United Nations. One would expect that those genuinely wanting to build respect for international law and order would advocate amending the Charter according to its own provisions, rather than cynical nullification of it.

If some members of an organization break its rules and standards, that is not fatal to the organization. But if the organization itself votes to scrap its own rules and standards in a vain effort to appease some lawless members, that is starting down the road to its own destruction. I do not want to see the United Nations destroyed, as was the League of Nations, by its own action in violating its own principles.

It is suggested that if we recognize Communist China and admit it to the United Nations, it might improve the functioning of that and related international organizations. There is far more evidence that it would hamper their functioning. The only time the United Nations has ever been able to operate as it was intended to on a matter as serious as aggression was in 1950 when the Soviet Union was absenting itself from the Security Council in an effort to pressure the United Nations into admission of Red China — and thus was unable to veto U.N. action against the Communist aggression in Korea. . . .

It is contended that it is necessary to have Communist China in the United Nations because no agreement on disarmament can be effective without its participation. But until there is some prospect of an agreement with the Soviet Union which already has deliverable nuclear weapons, what point is there in including Red China which most experts believe cannot have the capacity to deliver powerful nuclear weapons in a decade or more? If and when the day comes, and I hope and pray it may, that the

Soviet Union will agree to effective disarmament proposals — which means with inspection — there will be some point in negotiation with Red China on this subject. But it is not necessary to have Red China in the U.N. in order to negotiate with her, on this or any other matter. We have had over 130 negotiations in the last eleven years — almost one a month — far more than any other non-Communist government has had.

It has been said that the Chinese Communist regime should be accepted because the Chinese people under it are "better off" economically. Such is not the case, as compared with Chinese in Free China. But even if it were true, it would not prove the point. People were better off economically under Hitler than in any other nation in Europe. Did the groups who now urge acceptance of Red China advocate acceptance of Hitler on that ground?

Then there is the old diversionary argument, "What about Chiang Kai-shek?" Well, what about him? History will decide his proper place, and I predict it will be a high one. But our policy is not and has not been based on Chiang; if he were gone tomorrow, America's interests would be precisely the same. We are trying to help free peoples remain free; therefore, it is to our interest to support all peoples who will make determined efforts in that direction. The free Chinese on Taiwan certainly are making such efforts — and succeeding. They are now ahead economically of every other country in Asia except Japan. We were able to stop our economic assistance to Free China last July.

So, if one examines the results of the proposed changes in American policy toward China, it is apparent that the benefits would be minimal, if any. The dangers to the countries still free in China [Asia?], to the United Nations itself, and to our own security and peace, would be certain and serious indeed. [pp. 443–447]

Testimony of David N. Rowe

Sen. Hickenlooper: This is hypothetical anyway: Suppose the Red Chinese do not or would not change their basic orientation and basic political attitude, and came into the U.N. Considering that they would keep right on with their present philosophy, do you think that the likelihood of their refraining from the use of nuclear weapons would be any greater than if they were outside the U.N.?

Dr. Rowe: No, I do not. I do not think this would have any influence on it whatever.

Sen. Hickenlooper: In other words, they would use it whenever they would feel it was to their convenience to use it, and the threat ——

Dr. Rowe: Their presence in the United Nations would certainly not constitute any inhibition over them whatever as far as the use of nuclear weapons is concerned. . . .

Sen. Church: Professor Rowe, proceeding along the same line of inquiry with respect to the United Nations, I am not sure that I completely understood your answers.

You said, for example, that Japan and Germany [*sic*] have now been admitted into the United Nations, although there was a time, at Pearl Harbor, for example, when it would have been hard for us to have envisioned a Japanese membership in any United Nations. Of course, that is true. . . .

Do you mean to imply in your answer that China may also have to be defeated first, and the same kind of transformation be imposed, before China becomes a member?

Dr. Rowe: I certainly would not want to give the impression that I think it is worth a war and the destruction of Communist China's present government to get them into the United Nations. No, I would not say that. But I would say that the Chinese Communist regime, as it is constituted today and as it acts today, is incompatible with the United Nations. If it changes and when it changes, the situation will be completely different, and we can hope that such a thing can happen, however remote such a change may be.

There are people who think that once Mao is out of the way there will be a radical change in the leadership. I do not believe that I am that optimistic. I do not believe such a change will come quickly after Mao's death and departure from the scene. . . .

Sen. Church: Well, assuming then that you are right in your expectation that no great change in outlook occurs following the death of Mao Tse-tung, can you envision a time when China will ever admit that she has sinned? . . . Is this a kind of thing that ever really occurs in international affairs except upon the end of a war which has totally subdued a government and substituted an entirely new and different regime under the sponsorship of the victors?

Dr. Rowe: I would say there are two things that are equally unlikely to happen. One is that the Chinese Communists will admit that they were aggressors in the Korean war, which is what we say they are, and the other is what they want us to do, and that is for us to admit that we were the aggressors. I do not think either of these things is going to happen very soon.

Sen. Church: I do not either.

Dr. Rowe: And, therefore, what we have, as far as this U.N. is concerned, and what we have in so many other areas of Sino-American relations, is impasse. We have it, we are stuck with it.

Now, impasse is not nice. It is not easy, but it is better than a whole [lot] of other things. . . .

Sen. Church: Now, you stated earlier that the Chinese regime in Peking is not capable of representing the Chinese people. Do you mean that we should continue to oppose Chinese membership in the United Nations as long as there is a government in Peking of which we strongly disapprove?

Dr. Rowe: Well, which we do not believe represents the Chinese people. I should say this is one ground which has to do with this question of recognition by one country of another, and it is a valid consideration. Whether it should be of primary weight or not is another matter. [pp. 517–520]

The Chairman: Well, the purpose of it [the United Nations], it seems to me, is not to be a gentlemen's club. It was to try to bring about conditions where, if we found a nation not acting like a gentleman, we could use influence upon it to make it more agreeable, more decent, less warlike, and less inclined to cause trouble. Now, that was the main purpose of it.

Dr. Rowe: I never thought that was the main purpose of it.

The Chairman: You didn't? What do you think is its main purpose?

Dr. Rowe: The main purpose of the United Nations is to create an association, which it did create by the Charter, originating in 1945, of the people who could agree on certain standards of international conduct, vaguely defined as they were, and who would undertake to accept what were called in the Charter the obligations of the Charter that are clearly stated in it.

Now, it is not a matter of opinion as to whether the Chinese Communists would or would not accept the obligations of the Charter. This is not a matter of my opinion, of anybody else's opinion. It is a matter of fact, because the Chinese Communists state flatly they would not.

Now, if you want to have the United Nations as it is, that is one thing, and try to make it better than it is, and try to improve it from what you have got. But, if you want what the Chinese Communists want, you are talking an entirely different thing. You are not talking the United Nations at all because they say, as an indispensable prerequisite to admission, the whole Charter has got to be revised, and they are going to tell us later how they will revise it.

The Chairman: I know that is what they say. But they have not had an opportunity to turn it down. We do not know what they would do if they were offered an opportunity to join.

Every witness who has recommended that our opposition be withdrawn has also, at the same time, said he did not think the Red Chinese would accept it — they would not accept admission. But, nevertheless, they all still recommended that our opposition be withdrawn.

Dr. Rowe: Well, sir, that is where I have to differ with these people.

The Chairman: That is what I assumed is psychological warfare. They did not expect them to accept it in the near future. . . . Nearly all of them called attention to the same differences you have with regard to Taiwan and the accusation of the Red Chinese of aggression. This verges upon an aspect of what you call psychological warfare, whether or not you can take any moves that might have an effect upon a changing of their attitude. You do not think there is any hope of changing it?

Dr. Rowe: No, Senator. My view of the effective action, desirable effective action, to influence them in the direction of a change is this effective action should be taken from a fundamental point of view of hostility and opposition, and not of accommodation.

If you want them to change, the more you accommodate, the less they will change. . . .

The Chairman: You could be right. What precedents do you have in mind which would support that?

Dr. Rowe: Well, I tried to cite them before, involving the thoroughgoing changes that took place in Japan and Italy after World War II. I am not sure that these changes are going to come in the case of China because there is not going to be a war.

The Chairman: Weren't those conditions under extreme hostility?

Dr. Rowe: Of defeat, utter defeat.

The Chairman: [Do] I understand you to mean . . . that the only way we could get along with China is to completely defeat her militarily?

Dr. Rowe: I do not know whether we are going to have a military defeat of China or not. But I would say that if they were militarily defeated, and the Communist regime was uprooted and destroyed, that then there would be a possibility of the kind of change taking place which might make it possible for them to accommodate with us and for us to accommodate with them. . . .

The Chairman: The aim of these hearings, as I conceived it, was that of education, to discuss China. I would hope the way could be found to avoid a war with China, as I would like to avoid a war with anybody. . . . I do not know what we gain by it. We have had two or three wars in recent years, and they have not been very profitable. [pp. 539–542]

Testimony of Robert A. Scalapino and Hans J. Morgenthau

Sen. Lausche: Do you still recommend that Taiwan be declared a separate and new state?

Dr. Scalapino: I would strongly urge that we recognize the fact that Taiwan is a separate state with de facto control over 13 million people roughly, and that it exists quite apart from the mainland of China.

Sen. Lausche: How do you reconcile that conclusion with the argument that Chiang Kai-shek and Mao Tse-tung both declare vigorously that Taiwan and China are one unit, one soul, one people?

Dr. Scalapino: Well, Senator, I don't think that our policy should ever be dominated by what either Mao or Chiang think or say. Our policy with respect to Taiwan should be one based not only upon our interests but, broadly speaking, upon the interests of the people of Taiwan. It is my own belief that if the people of Taiwan could be questioned about this, they themselves would opt in overwhelming measure for an independent status. [p. 579]

Sen. Church: Now, you suggested . . . that you believe in self-determination as a sound principle for American foreign policy, not only as this may apply to the people of Vietnam or the people of Germany, but also [as] it may apply to the people on Taiwan.

Now, since Chiang Kai-shek moved onto Taiwan with his army and established himself in power there, has there been any kind of election or referendum involving the people of Taiwan that could be regarded as a self-determination?

Dr. Scalapino: Not in my opinion. Let me make it clear that there certainly have been elections in Taiwan, and it is also true, and should be pointed out that there are certain native Taiwanese who today hold elective office as mayors, as Members of the National Assembly and in other capacities. Nor would I say for a moment that the excesses, the political excesses, of the first years following the end of World War II have been perpetuated.

But in essence, as everyone knows, this is still a one-party state, and one strongly dominated by mainland refugees.

It should also be pointed out, in fairness, that there have been enormous economic strides in Taiwan, and that these are a people today who live well, measured against Asian standards. But an answer to the question which you ask, I think, boils down to this: The people of Taiwan are culturally distinct in certain important respects from the people of mainland China. Many of them are second or third generation, and they have had a long period of Japanese rule. They are a people who live at an infinitely higher level than the people on the mainland. If they were given their choice in totally free, fair elections, I strongly suspect that they would opt for independence.

Over time, of course, the island will become "Taiwanized" in political terms by a melding of mainland refugees and local people.

Sen. Church: Well, even then, though both the present government on Taiwan, Chiang Kai-shek's regime, and the present government on mainland China oppose self-determination for the people of Taiwan, do you think that we ought to advocate it as an element of American policy?

Dr. Scalapino: I certainly think as a long-range principle it is within our interests and within our morality to do so. It is one of those happy situations where our moral values and our political interests coincide.

Sen. Church: How do you feel about that proposition, Professor Morgenthau?

Dr. Morgenthau: Let me say, first of all, with regard to the general proposition that I do not believe that you can improve our relations with China by the exchange of professors, doctors, newspapermen, and what-not, as long as the military situation around the periphery of China remains what it is. For the real issue between ourselves and China is not the issue of social relations or of the amenities of international social life, but it is a fundamental issue of national interest and power.

Remember that the Seventh Fleet is protecting a counterrevolutionary regime on Taiwan from the Chinese government in Peiping, having interfered since 1950, what you might call in perpetuity, in the Chinese civil war. This is the basic fact which the Chinese government has time and again emphasized in the negotiations in Warsaw and elsewhere as the main stumbling block in our relations with China. I find it almost grotesquely paradoxical to want to maintain this position, on the one hand, and, on the other, to try to improve our relations with China by sending some newspapermen, professors, and medical men to the mainland.

Sen. Church: Are you saying, Professor Morgenthau, that you believe that we ought not to maintain or honor our commitment to defend Taiwan against mainland China?

Dr. Morgenthau: I am not saying that at all. What I am saying is that we ought to make up our mind as to what we want. If we want good relations with China, we cannot maintain the military status quo, and nothing we do on the superficial level of exchange of persons and so forth will make the slightest difference in the situation. On the other hand, if we are convinced that it serves our vital national interest to leave the Seventh Fleet in the Straits of Taiwan and to surround the periphery of China with a number of isolated military strongholds, then we must forego our aspiration of improving our relations with China, and we must face not only the possibility but the likelihood of a war with China. This is the essence of the point I want to make. . . .

Dr. Scalapino: I would note first, that there was another long-range problem concerning an area related to China that was solved without war, and that was the problem of Outer Mongolia. That was territory irridenta for the Chinese for a very long time. I would not anticipate any early solution of the problem of Taiwan that would satisfy Peking. But I am not convinced that because you live with an unsettled problem that you therefore live at precisely one level of tension or friction forever. There are some problems that will not be resolved to the satisfaction of Peking. There are others that will probably not be resolved to our satisfaction.

We will take certain firm positions; the Chinese may take others. Yet if one can mount the type of pressures on a global basis which I have discussed, we can avoid the extremities. I am not convinced, in short, that our alternatives are either war or surrender. [pp. 586–587]

10 THE WAR IN VIETNAM AND CHINESE-AMERICAN RELATIONS

Testimony of A. Doak Barnett

Mr. Barnett: [Prepared Statement] In regard to Vietnam particularly, there is considerable evidence, I believe, that while Peking hopes to avoid any major conflict with the United States it fears that American escalation will create situations demanding escalation on the Chinese side, which could lead to major conflict.

In recent months, in fact, Peking has repeatedly warned its own people of the dangers of American attacks and major war, and there appears to be a genuine apprehension that this may take place. No one can say with certainty what actions might provoke an increased Chinese response. Since Peking appears to view North Vietnam, like North Korea, as a vital buffer area, it is likely that if the Chinese concluded there was a major threat to the existence of the North Vietnamese regime, the result could be large-scale, direct Chinese intervention. There is no guarantee, however, that even less drastic forms of American escalation — such as bombing of North Vietnam's major cities — might not impel the Chinese to escalate their involvement in smaller ways which might lead to much higher risks of direct American-Chinese clashes that are not desired by either side.

In view of this uncertainty, it is essential that the United States exercise great restraint in the use of its power, especially in North Vietnam, and demonstrate by deeds as well as words that we are determined to avoid provoking any direct American-Chinese conflict. [p. 13]

Sen. Gore: From your knowledge of the Chinese, from your views, your studies, do you think that the size of an American expeditionary force in Vietnam could be a provocation to the Chinese?

Mr. Barnett: I think I would doubt that. I think the size of our forces in South Vietnam, in my opinion, would not be a provocation. I would add, however, that I have — and this is getting on to a different subject, which is Vietnam and perhaps I shouldn't — but I have some real causes of uneasiness about the consequences in Vietnam of too large an American presence, even though I realize the military argues in favor of it. . . .

Sen. Gore: You don't think then that an increase of the military commitment there, say to 600,000 troops, would in and of itself be a provocation that would constitute a further danger of confrontation with China?

Mr. Barnett: Six hundred thousand is a high number. I hadn't heard that one, and perhaps I should qualify my answer, at least to this extent: If the increase in our number of troops was combined, somehow, with the developments of events and forces that raised serious questions in the minds of the Chinese Communists as to what we were going to do with these troops, as to whether we were going to move against North Vietnam with those troops, then I could conceive of this being something that would confirm, might tend to confirm, Chinese apprehensions about U.S. objectives, despite what we have said about our objectives.

I think, though, that we could take a posture in which we kept trying to make it completely clear that our objectives were in South Vietnam, and that if we could convince the Chinese of this, we would continue to convince them that just having a large number of troops in South Vietnam would not in and of itself be a provocation that would lead them to any great escalation of what they are doing. [p. 36]

The Chairman: . . . Does it serve the Chinese purposes for us to have very large military activity in Vietnam, using up vast sums and quantities of materials, spending vast billions of dollars and suffering rather large casualties? Would you say this serves the Chinese purpose or not?

Mr. Barnett: Well, you know, you can argue this either way. You can argue, certainly, it would be to their advantage if we got out, and it would be to their advantage if we get bogged down, and I am not sure you can have it both ways. . . .

The Chairman: Let me put it this way. Is our gradual escalation in costs, manpower, and money more likely to cause them to be pleased than our maintaining strong fortified bases relatively easy to defend and relatively less costly? The latter course would give the impression we are going to stay there permanently, and they would be faced with the probability that we will be there indefinitely until they are willing to talk about some kind of settlement?

Mr. Barnett: I would say obviously they would not like either of these solutions.

The Chairman: Which would they like less?

Mr. Barnett: It is very difficult to say. . . .

The Chairman: Do you think the Chinese then would not be interested in removing us from military bases by negotiation? You do not think it matters to the Chinese whether we maintain military bases on her borders or close to her borders or not?

Mr. Barnett: I do not think they would like it, but I do not know that they would be terribly — I mean I do not know that they would be prepared to make any particular concessions to get us out of them, any more than they are willing to make concessions to achieve one of the other solutions. I find it very hard to see a big difference in their attitudes toward these two alternatives. [pp. 65–66]

The Chairman: I understood you earlier to say you did not attribute the origin of this warfare in South Vietnam to the Chinese; do you?

Mr. Barnett: I think the origins are independent of the Chinese, but the Chinese have become intimately involved in the situation.

I would say this, Mr. Fulbright, that if the Chinese did decide to shift their general strategy and posture in international affairs, six months from now, or three months from now, and began urging a different kind of a policy, a different type of strategy, began urging "Bandung" principles and a quiet type of coexistence, I think this would have an impact.

The Chinese do not control the North Vietnamese and Vietcong, but they have a real influence on them, and if the Chinese influence shifted, it would have a real influence on them.

The Chairman: Do you think our intrusion there with hundreds of thousands of men is likely to induce them to make such a shift?

Mr. Barnett: This is a terribly difficult thing to try to estimate. I think I am inclined to believe that failures of their belligerency, combined with a sense of different options — which is why I am in favor of a posture on our part that is much more receptive to different kinds of initiatives from the Chinese — I think the combination of these two elements presents the greatest possibility of exerting external influence on the Chinese to shift policy in a direction that is desirable from our point of view.

The Chairman: You will recall how excited this country became when it realized Russians had missiles in Cuba. Isn't it quite likely the Chinese react the same way when they see 250,000 Americans in Vietnam?

Mr. Barnett: Yes. But if the Chinese were to decide that the way to get the Americans out of Vietnam would be to have the insurrection — particularly in its form of extreme violence — calm down, so that the United States would be willing to agree to some kind of a solution, in which we might be willing to disengage, this might have a real influence moving the situation in Vietnam in a new direction. . . .

The Chairman: I cannot get away from the idea that our very presence so close to them on the mainland is, perhaps, the most provocative of all the elements that have induced this belligerence and bellicosity in the way they talk. Do you think that contributes to it?

Mr. Barnett: I think it is a contributory factor.

The Chairman: Well, an important one.

Mr. Barnett: Yes. But I do not explain their — I think that if we began to back off from our present policy in a way that tended to confirm the success of the Vietcong's and of the Chinese current general approach to this type of problem, this would not exert an influence inducing the Chinese to consider other optional strategies and policies.

I think if we took that action it might well confirm them in the course that they are now embarked on. . . .

Mr. Barnett: If one can look to the future, one can see, if one can be optimistic, a slow evolution toward a situation where a number of powers may be involved in, and exert various types of influence in, southeast Asia. China would certainly be one of them, and I think we can be one of them. I think Japan in time may well exert a significant influence, particularly economically. Although I do not think the Indians are now exerting very much influence outside their borders, in a longer perspective, it is very conceivable to me that they might. . . . These multiple influences would, it seems to me, be desirable. I would like to see an area that has a reasonable amount of stability, where the individual nations have a reasonable amount of confidence in their ability to preserve their independence, in their capacity to deal with a number of different powers without great inhibitions. It seems to me that this kind of complicated balance, with a minimum military element, would be what I would see as desirable in the long run. [pp. 80–86]

Testimony of John K. Fairbank

Dr. Fairbank: [Prepared Statement] Vietnam today gives us a more severe crisis of moral conscience partly because during most of our history we felt morally superior to the imperialist powers of the nineteenth century. Why must our land of the free now send its boys to kill and be killed in a civil war so far away? I would not claim that the history of power politics in East Asia automatically gives us the justification, but I do believe it helps explain how we got in. The problem of power relations has to be faced. Perhaps power has to be used in smaller wars if we are to avoid bigger wars. . . .

The main fact about our containment of the Chinese revolutionary influence in South Vietnam is that it is only in part military. In larger part, it is a competition in how to help in nation-building. . . .

Some argue, feeling culturally closer to Europe, that Vietnam is beyond our proper realm of concern. I don't agree. The Western powers have played major roles in southeast Asia for 400 years even if we have not. The West has made its contribution while also precipitating the nationalist revolutions. . . . We cannot now condemn and disown the old British Empire, for instance, just because we let the British fight dirty colonial wars while we got the profits. We were and are involved in East Asian power politics at least as much as in those of Europe, cultural differences notwithstanding. [pp. 105–106]

Sen. Morse: Assuming that it is inherent in our policy in South Vietnam to support and maintain a separate government in South Vietnam, do you think that that policy which was obviously not envisioned by the Geneva accords creates problems for us, not only with us with North Vietnam, but creates problems with us with China?

Dr. Fairbank: Oh, yes; we are in this because of Communist China, and we are in a competition. I personally believe that it has to be not just military. It has to be strongly constructive. . . .

Now, we face in this country [Vietnam] the Chinese Communist model, which is an alternative one, which derives from their culture, which is a more authoritarian culture, and which has Communist attributes of trying to modernize with regimentation, and to do it on your own resources. We are supporting a model of modernization with international aid, not so much on your own resources. You could argue back and forth as to which of these models is more attractive, because the Western model that we are pushing is one where Western domination may be felt, may be apparent in certain lines, Western technology is so superior, Coca-Cola and Madison Avenue come in. The alternative Chinese model has its difficulties, however, which I think make it less desirable. . . .

Sen. Morse: Do you think if we continue to escalate the war and inflict more and more damage on North Vietnam and bomb strategic military sites as close to the Chinese border as thirty miles, that we are increasing the risk of a possible future war with Red China?

Dr. Fairbank: Oh, yes. I think if we escalate, we are increasing the risk; there is no question about it. [pp. 112–114]

The Chairman: . . . You were mentioning an alternative to our creating a society in our image. My alternative would be that there be a neutralization, and that instead of America seeking to protect its own, whatever you want to call this, neocolonialism that this be done under nonnational auspices, for example, under the international organizations, either under the U.N., the International Bank, the International Development Association or the Asian Bank, which we have just recently created.

This would disabuse the Chinese and others of the idea of a new colonial era, an imperial era, of the Americans. We now happen to have the power that England had in her day, and others have had in their day. . . .

I would think, of all the things I can think of that would be persuasive to the Chinese to come to some kind of agreement on neutralization would be the assurance that the United States would not maintain itself permanently in this area militarily. Does that make any sense at all?

Dr. Fairbank: Some. (Laughter.)

The Chairman: . . . I am complimented that it makes any at all, because the administration stated categorically it made no sense at all. I am making progress, at least. (Laughter.) . . .

Dr. Fairbank: [The] Chinese Comunists' view of the world is a very embattled one. They have been revolutionaries all their lives, those leaders, of course. They believe in their revolution. It worked in China, they think it ought to work in South Vietnam, and if it does not work now it will work later. . . .

So the Chinese Communists are going to be pushing in their own way whatever we do.

Now, to get them into this happy future situation that you were describing you have to use some force as well as some diplomacy.

The Chairman: That is right.

Dr. Fairbank: And this force at the present time is in the form we are using it, for better or worse, in South Vietnam, that is, to make their system not work, to make the Maoist model of takeover ineffective and stalemated.

At that point there is no reason why the Chinese might not be motivated, if you are working on it diplomatically and offering them other alternatives, to come out into some kind of an international world and agree to some kind of international arrangement. Now, to get to that point is going to take a long time because they are not going to give up easily on the present tack.

The Chairman: Yes.

Dr. Fairbank: So I foresee that we have got to keep on fighting. That is the answer. [pp. 138–140]

Sen. McCarthy: Professor Fairbank, you said we needed a stiff position in order to get the other side to negotiate. Do you feel that the position we are maintaining now is stiff enough or do you think that it ought to be made firmer, or perhaps some relaxation might establish a better balance of stiffness as between our position and the position of the enemy?

Dr. Fairbank: I would like to phrase that not that we develop a strong position in order to get negotiations, but rather that we try both at once. In other words, I do not think that we can expect to go through a procedure in which there is first fighting, then a cease-fire, then negotiations, then a settlement.

It seems to me we have got to get into a situation where the negotiating and the fighting are both going along together in a struggle, because the Chinese understand a struggle. Their whole philosophy as Marxist Communists in China now is struggle. And it is very different from the Confucian idea, incidentally. This is one of the new things on the Chinese scene, a discontinuity with the past. . . . And so it seems to me that our great need at this time is to have more on the side of negotiations to balance what we are doing on the side of fighting, and to keep the two going. [p. 160]

Testimony of Benjamin I. Schwartz
and John M. H. Lindbeck

Sen. Church: Do you think, Professor Schwartz, that we are in any way performing the role that Peking has assigned to us by our military intervention in Vietnam?

Dr. Schwartz: Well, this is the difficult question, and I don't want to duck it. I think a great deal of Peking's view of the Vietnamese situation is based on the assumption that we are performing that role, and I think Vietnam is unique in the world in that it probably offers most parallels to the Chinese situation. . . .

But I do think that some of the assumptions of the other side based on the Chinese analogy may be wrong. . . .

Our [One?] assumption is that in a protracted war, public opinion in the United States will tend to favor withdrawal. This may well be a serious miscalculation. . . . While Mao Tse-tung has put forth the image of our fingers being chopped off one by one throughout the world, in other words, of the dispersion of our power as a result of national liberation wars, this presupposes that national liberation wars are going to take place everywhere in the next few years, which may not be a correct assumption. We may actually be able to fold our whole hand around Vietnam rather than having our fingers dispersed. . . .

Another miscalculation . . . may well be Giap's [North Vietnamese Defense Minister] doctrine that since . . . we are foreigners in Vietnam all genuine nationalist sentiment will polarize in the direction of the NLF [National Liberation Front]. I think probably the United States is genuinely unpopular in many circles in South Vietnam, but one thing that has rather surprised me is that there hasn't been a stampede in the direction of the NLF on the part of all non-Communist forces. In other words, I have a sense that the NLF does not quite enjoy the image in South Vietnam that the Communist Party was able to achieve for itself in China at the end of the war. . . .

Sen. Church: . . . But it is fair to say, is it not, that the Chinese interest in prolonging the war in Vietnam today stems from a judgment that has been made in Peking that the war is serving Chinese objectives?

Dr. Schwartz: Well, I would also add that they regard the war as a test case of their strategy, and in this their opinion resembles that in some quarters in our own government.

Sen. Church: Here in this country?

Dr. Schwartz: Yes. [pp. 207–208]

Sen. Pell: And the final question and perhaps the most important, is what is your own view, gentlemen, as to the outcome of the present course of events, if we continue pursuing our present policy in Vietnam, and the North Vietnamese have the temerity to continue opposing us, and we eventually have exhausted their manpower? Do you think the Chinese will fill that manpower vacuum or will they tend to let the North Vietnamese lose by default?

Dr. *Schwartz:* Well, I think there would be a great danger of confrontation with China in that case. It is not only that Vietnam is to them a test case of world revolution, but in the case of the crumbling of North Vietnam that would put them very much in the state of mind that they had when we were approaching the Yalu, an immediate danger on their borders, so that certainly it would be quite erroneous to rule out the possibility, in that event, of a confrontation with China. . . .

Dr. *Lindbeck:* I am horrified by the thought that the manpower available to Hanoi and the Vietcong might reach the low point where they had to call on others. This would suggest, of course, a tremendous destruction of life which might perhaps lead to the destruction of society and of our Nation. [pp. 220–221]

Testimony of Morton H. Halperin and Samuel B. Griffith

Dr. *Halperin:* [Prepared Statement] The Chinese leadership recognizes that the introduction of large numbers of American troops into Vietnam has drastically changed the situation from the favorable outlook of a year or so ago. They have been forced to concede that even when on the brink of victory a revolutionary movement can be turned back by America's military power. While the Chinese talk, as they did at the time of the Korean war, of the fact that the United States may be overextended, they do not doubt that we have the military capability to suppress the revolution in Vietnam for as long as we have the will to do so. The Chinese also accept that the United States has made Vietnam into a test case of whether or not it can successfully suppress wars of national liberation which follow the Chinese pattern. Thus the Chinese believe it is important to avoid a defeat in Vietnam.

By esoteric but clearly understood signals in their public statements, the Chinese have indicated to the Vietcong their belief that victory can come only after a protracted struggle. Drawing on their own experience, the Chinese now see the Vietnam struggle to be at a stage analogous to the Japanese invasion of China. They have urged on the Vietcong the need to adopt a strategy of survival until the American invaders tire of the war and withdraw from the country. Both by its actions and its words, Peking has told Hanoi that the Vietcong must be almost entirely self-sufficient in generating the supplies and equipment needed for their survival and their military operations. Nevertheless, Peking has told the Chinese masses that they have a duty to sacrifice for the people of Vietnam, and China appears to have provided substantial amounts of economic and military assistance to the Vietcong forces.

Thus, Peking now expects a long drawn-out war. The Chinese leaders would be very disappointed if Hanoi accepted a negotiated settlement which would imply an effort by the Vietcong to come to power by other means and might increase Soviet influence in southeast Asia. Peking, however, no longer expects a quick victory and even what may look to us like an American victory in Vietnam would look to the Chinese only as a temporary lull in revolutionary activity in preparations for the next stage of the revolution. The Chinese commitment to support for wars of national liberation is far too deep-seated to be erased by a temporary setback in a single country. [pp. 283–284]

Sen. Carlson: General Griffith, we had some experience with Chinese troops during the Korean war. They came up to the borders. Is China in a better position today to engage the United States in a war in Vietnam than it was when it was in Korea?

Gen. Griffith: Well, I think, Senator, you have got to take a look at the map there and study the terrain and study the situation. We have to remember that China, when they engaged us in the Korean war, had back of her the Soviet Union, she was basing on Manchuria, her frontline troops were 200 miles away. There were various corridors through which she could come; the Yalu is frozen in the winter. She did not need the bridges even if we had partially destroyed them. She could get stuff over there.

What we are talking about in Vietnam now is a situation where, from the nearest Chinese areas which bound Vietnam on the north, and these are underdeveloped areas, the terrain is extremely difficult, transportation routes are primitive. There is only one railway. They are now trying to parallel that, I understand. The road net is very poor.

They have got to come about 600, 700, 800 miles, Chinese formations, to even get in contact with American formations now.

I think the situation, both in terms of terrain, in terms of propinquity, in terms of immediate support, in terms of the base areas and so on, are entirely different, and in terms of what we can do to interdict these movements also.

Sen. Carlson: Is it your thought that, despite the logistics problems the Red Chinese have, they are helping or not helping the North Vietnamese, the Vietcong, in this war?

Gen. Griffith: Definitely, yes, sir; they are helping them, I should think, with advisers, technicians. They may be manning the antiaircraft guns around Haiphong and Hanoi. They probably sent doctors, medicines, they send everything from greaseguns to automatic rifles, ammunition, grenades, explosives, I am sure they are doing all this. But as with the Soviet advisers in the Korean war, we never — we cannot catch them at it.

Sen. Carlson: Of course, one of the problems we are facing in that great area is to find out where the responsibilities for this war lie. We hear much about it. We try to settle with Peking. We try to settle with Hanoi. We try to settle with the Vietcong, and really we haven't got it down to any one place yet. It seems to be scattered all over the area; is that right?

Gen. Griffith: Well, it takes two people to make a marriage, and the Chinese are very happy to see us mired down in southeast Asia. If I were Mao Tse-tung I would just be up there drinking tea and smoking cigarettes and feeling quite content with the situation. It is not costing them anything.

Sen. Carlson: I would wholly agree with that. I think it is a correct statement. Under those circumstances, is it your thought that we may be there for a long time?

Gen. Griffith: We are going to be there for a long time; yes, sir. [pp. 305–306]

Sen. Pell: Asking General Griffith this question, why is it that we do not accept time as a dimension of warfare and are not more willing to lose fewer men and spend a longer time doing it than always seeking to achieve a quicker victory; is that at all illogical?

Gen. Griffith: Senator, we have been a nation in a hurry ever since 1776. The Chinese have existed since about 500 B.C. and, perhaps, they have a better concept, or, should we say, a more sophisticated concept of what time means than we do.

I agree with you, Senator, that the Chinese, I think, are willing to sit out this situation in Vietnam until hell freezes over — it is a drain on us, we are losing men, we are losing resources. They hopefully think that our image abroad is being stained; our position and our power is being eroded, even if just gradually; and so I think, yes, we would like to have everything done tomorrow. But the Chinese will say, "We will let it get done next year."

Sen. Pell: I wonder, too, if we were willing to accept time as a fourth dimension along the lines of General Gavin's theories, and accepted the fact of a reasonably sized expeditionary force staying in South Vietnam for an indefinite period of time, we would not suddenly find time is on our side. Our presence in Indochina then would be just as embarrassing to the Chinese as their presence in Mexico would be to us. Would you agree with me?

Gen. Griffith: I would certainly agree the longer we are in southeast Asia, the more embarrassing the situation would be to the Chinese.

Sen. Pell: Wouldn't our objective be not to escalate it, but simply to let them know we are prepared to stay indefinitely?

Gen. Griffith: Well, if you recall the interview that Mao Tse-tung gave Edgar Snow about three or four years ago, Mao used the phrase, "Of course, the Americans are in Vietnam, but someday they will get tired and go someplace else," and he is apparently willing to sit in Peking and wait until we get tired and go someplace else. [p. 314]

Testimony of Donald S. Zagoria and Harold C. Hinton

Dr. Zagoria: [Prepared Statement] Peking and Hanoi, I want to stress, have both overlapping and conflicting interests in South Vietnam. They share an interest in eliminating American power and influence from South Vietnam, but Peking has a much greater interest in a protracted war. For Peking, the war in South Vietnam which, to be sure, it did not itself start, nevertheless provides a test case for its "liberation war" strategy. More important, it provides an opportunity to humiliate, divert, and to weaken the United States without any cost to itself.

This is why Peking, although concerned about the possibility of an American attack on China, is nevertheless not eager for a negotiated settlement in Vietnam. Hanoi, on the other hand, has a clearly more limited interest, namely, the unification of Vietnam under Communist hegemony, a goal that might — under certain conditions — be achieved through negotiations rather than through protracted war against a determined and superior enemy.

These different perspectives have resulted in differences in emphasis on the possibility of negotiations and the preconditions for them — differences that have gone largely unnoted in most of the American press. Peking has repeatedly been at pains to warn against U.S. deceit and, far more vehemently than Hanoi, has denounced all proposals to end the war in Vietnam short of U.S. disengagement. Moreover, Hanoi's conditions for negotiations have, in general, been more ambiguous and flexible than Peking's.

The crucial and, as far as U.S. policy is concerned, complicating factor is that Hanoi's leadership is itself divided. Hanoi has its own version of hawks and doves. . . .

In this situation there are some things the United States can and, in my opinion, should do. First, it seems to me imperative that we recognize — even if the Chinese Communists do not — that Communist successes in South Vietnam are not easily duplicable. . . .

Second, it appears that our best hope in Vietnam is to strengthen those groups in Moscow and Hanoi who have a more flexible approach to negotiations against the bitter-enders supported by Peking. These moderates can be strengthened by two complementary lines of American policy. First, our words and our actions could substantiate their realistic assessment that the United States cannot be forced out of South Vietnam and that a military victory for the Vietcong is in fact impossible. Second, our words and our actions could assure them that the United States is not insisting on unconditional surrender. On the first count, we have already made significant progress. A year or two ago Peking, Hanoi, and even Moscow seemed to believe that the United States would tire of the war and withdraw. It is now apparent that the moderate groups of the Communist world have revised their estimates. In my view, more effort must now be expended on the second line of approach. [pp. 373–375]

Sen. Pell: I think the basic question that bothers us is how accurately we are reading Chinese intentions. We misread Chinese intentions at the time of Korea. . . . I was interested in the opinion of each of you as to what will happen when the Vietcong are faced with the fact that they are going to be defeated or overwhelmed. The available North Vietnamese manpower is pretty well used up. Will, at that time, Peking let them be defeated or will she fill the gap with her own manpower? What is the view of each of you on that?

Dr. Zagoria: Well, sir, I think that for the Chinese to introduce their own manpower into South Vietnam would go against the very essence of Maoist strategy, which is essentially that these wars have to be fought by indigenous nationalist Communist revolutionaries, led by an indigenous Communist Party.

So, I attach a very low probability to the massive introduction of Chinese ground forces into South Vietnam. For that reason, and also for an additional reason, namely, that I don't think the Vietnamese Communists are very anxious to have the Chinese in there because they fear that maybe the Chinese won't go home. . . .

Dr. Hinton: I agree with what Professor Zagoria said. . . .

Sen. Pell: What is the present extent of the Chinese involvement in the fighting? What percentage of the arms are being furnished by them?

Dr. Hinton: I couldn't give you a percentage. I have the distinct impression that much of the heavier infantry equipment that the Vietcong and the North Vietnamese troops in South Vietnam are using comes from China.

In other words, there are substantial military deliveries. In addition to that, the Chinese have undoubtedly sent several thousands of their own technicians, military and civilian, to North Vietnam, and are providing training and advice and this sort of thing on Chinese soil to the North Vietnamese. They have also conducted an essentially defensive military buildup, so far as we can judge it, on Chinese soil and certain civil defense preparations. . . .

Dr. *Zagoria:* I would rather doubt . . . that there are sizable numbers of actual Chinese military personnel in North Vietnam, and I know of no evidence that they are anywhere else. . . . [pp. 409–410]

Testimony of Walter H. Judd

Dr. *Judd:* [Prepared Statement] So the key question for us is how best to keep Communist China contained until it fades or changes. What should we do to implement that basic policy in the period just ahead, and in the most crucial area of immediate contest — Vietnam?

1. We must recognize and state frankly that we are at war, however much it was unsought and unprovoked by us. . . .
2. We must develop a national will to wage this war with greater vigor and skill by all the measures — economic and social as well as military — that are required of us by the enemy's new and different tactics. . . .
3. We must develop a greater unity in support of the total war effort and the heroic sacrifices being made in Vietnam by our own brave men and by valiant Vietnamese and other allies. . . .
4. We must remember that the objective of a war is political, namely, to change the will of the adversary, killing as few people as possible. How are we likely to change the will of this adversary in Hanoi? By constantly repeated assurances that we will not make him suffer, no matter what he does? The administration has stated repeatedly that we have "no desire for the overthrow of Hanoi or Peking." Is it any wonder that Ho Chi Minh has felt no need to negotiate? By going all out in South Vietnam, perhaps he can win the struggle for Asia by humiliation of the United States. If he does not succeed, then he can go back to the 17th parallel with no penalty to himself and his regime. . . .

Why haven't we done these things? Because an almost hysterical fear has been built up that, among other things, it might lead to war with Red China, and "we must not get into a land war with Red China's masses."

Well, all things are possible; and there is no course without risk. But let us weigh realistically the small likelihood of such intervention against the absolutely certain dangers involved in going on as we are.

1. Red China would be inviting and justifying our destruction of her nuclear facilities — her greatest trump in this world power struggle. There is nothing in South Vietnam that is a fraction as valuable to Red China as those nuclear facilities.
2. How would Red China supply masses of troops in South Vietnam? A Communist army, just like Napoleon's, moves on its stomach. The

Communists are having all they can do to supply the Vietminh and Viet-cong forces already in South Vietnam.

3. Red China cannot forget for a moment the presence on her flank of powerful air and military forces on Taiwan. Most of mainland China's lines of communications run north and south and are within easy reach of the airbases we have helped the Chinese build on that island for the very purpose they are now serving — a powerful deterrent to Red China's entering the war and getting itself too far extended to the south.

Some 700,000 to a million Red Chinese are tied down opposite Tai-wan, on guard against possible action from that base. Red China also has to keep large numbers of troops on the long border with India, on the longer border with the Soviet Union, on the borders of Korea, and hun-dreds of thousands of soldiers are required to maintain order in Tibet, Mongolia, and at home.

4. If Red China were to get involved in southeast Asia, she would have to concentrate on it to a degree that would almost certainly make her lose her bitter struggle with the Soviet Union for control of the world Communist movement. That struggle is enormously more important to Red China than anything in Vietnam. Red China talks war — but hasn't done one reckless thing. The Soviet Union talks peace — but puts missiles into Cuba aimed at the United States, and it is supplying the sinews of war to North Vietnam.

Despite powerful considerations like the above, many in our country seem almost paralyzed by two words, "confrontation" and "escalation." They assert, without evidence to support it, that a firm confrontation with Communist aggression will lead to escalation into nuclear war — "and we must not have nuclear war."

Just to say that, of course, makes more likely the nuclear war we want to avoid. It encourages the Communists to believe we will surrender rather than have nuclear war, and that therefore at the right moment they can cow us into submission by the threat of it. It may well be that the out-come of this world struggle will be determined by which side appears to be less afraid of nuclear war. [pp. 447–450]

Testimony of David N. Rowe

Sen. Church: . . . Are you generally satisfied with the way we are con-ducting the war in Vietnam or are you dissatisfied?

Dr. Rowe: . . . I think there are probably a lot of things that can be done from a military point of view without bringing the Chinese Com-munists into the war that we are refraining from doing, and I am talking about such things as closing the harbor of Haiphong, of bombing the oil

tanks at Haiphong harbor, of bombing the docks that control the irriga-
tion of the major crop producing centers in North Vietnam. None of
these things would cause large losses of life. They would be very, very
heavy blows at war-making, and would materially increase our military
effectiveness vis-à-vis the enemy.

When I think of the fliers who go and shoot up trucks on the road
carrying the stuff that has come in through the port, that is, fueled with
stuff that come in through the port, and then you burn twelve trucks on
the road, the most difficult way you can do it, to me there is something
completely inexplicable in this. I cannot understand such a military
strategy. I am not talking about an adventurism that says, "No, you
can't fight the Vietcong without fighting North Vietnam, and you can't
fight North Vietnam without fighting Communist China, and you can't
fight them without fighting the Russians."

All this takes it to an extreme which makes it absurd. But I think that
the military inhibitions that we have inflicted upon ourselves in relation to
this war are self-defeating, and when I say defeating, I mean just that. I
do not think it can be done this way. [pp. 522–523]

Testimony of Robert A. Scalapino

The Chairman: One statement you make . . . that is quite striking, is
that Peking will not help us develop a new China policy because basically
she likes our old one, and does not want us to change.

As has already been implied, she believes that our present policy isolates
us more than it does her, and makes the United States a perfect scape-
goat, both before her own people and before others, and prevents, or at
least mitigates, the types of pressures developing upon China from
the outside that might be created from within.

I wonder if you would develop that a bit? It seems to me this statement
is not quite consistent with your later statement on approval of our policy
in southeast Asia, for example. . . .

Dr. Scalapino: The reason why, in broad terms, I support our position
in Vietnam, is that I think the Maoist challenge there must be met, although I do not for a moment believe that this can be met solely by
military means or merely by a Vietnam policy alone.

I believe very strongly that we have to have an enormously variated
policy that ultimately allows the Chinese, whether of this generation or of
the next, to see the advantages in moderation, and, equally, to see the
risks in extremism. That to me is critical to any workable American policy.

The Chairman: Implicit in what you have said is that the war in Vietnam was instigated and is largely inspired by Mao. Do you believe
that? . . .

Dr. Scalapino: I think that China anticipated a quick and easy victory in Vietnam, because she did probably miscalculate American intentions with respect to Vietnam. I think, on the other hand, that China has approved of our overall policy of seeking to isolate her because it is clearly this policy which has separated us from so many of our Allies and the neutrals. It is our policy of attempted isolation of which China approves.

With respect to the causes of the Vietnam war, I, of course, would not for a moment say that this war was triggered by Mao personally or by the Chinese Communists. But I think it is reasonably clear that the Vietnamese Communists are pursuing Maoist principles in the way in which this war has unfolded, and that is the point that I would want to emphasize. . . .

Sen. Church: I understood you to say also in this paper that China's objective is to involve us in a series of national liberation wars. How do you reconcile that with the answer you have just given?

Dr. Scalapino: Correct. I think this is a risk. Chinese policy is committed to this goal, and if, for example, the United States were to operate in its total military, political, and economic policies in such a fashion as to become simultaneously involved in a series of such wars, this would very much serve the Chinese interests. At the moment we are involved in one critical contest. This does not serve the Chinese interests.

Sen. Church: I take it that you would feel that our involvement in a series of such wars would, therefore, not serve the American interests?

Dr. Scalapino: Yes. It is also my position — and this applies to our foreign policy in general — that until we tackle the basic questions of socioeconomic change and development as well as questions of military deterrence, we are engaged in considerable risks. Foreign policy should never be an either/or question, either aid for change or resistance to aggression. It is a question of an integrated policy that involves political, economic, social, and military aspects. It also seems clear to me that we face a long-range problem, one which will not be solved quickly or easily. [pp. 575–577]

EPILOGUE

In retrospect, it was ironic that just as the Senate hearings focused attention on China's isolation, Communist China was launching a vigorous thought-reform movement, which developed into the "great proletarian cultural revolution." Few, if any, witnesses had foreseen the turmoil and violence that were to shake Chinese political and intellectual life throughout the rest of the year and even beyond. The spectacle of the Chinese Communists pillorying one another, a situation in which doctrinaire purists seemed to ally themselves with children against intellectuals, bureaucrats, and technicians, caused China's prestige to suffer in the whole of Asia and Africa. As the Chinese leadership was mired in a power struggle, there seemed little likelihood that the nation would be able to intervene forcefully in the war in Vietnam. American involvement there deepened, and less and less restraint was seen in the bombing of the areas of Hanoi and Haiphong and close to the Chinese border. In view of the fluid situation in China, no new American initiative toward redefining relations with that country was taken. The government in Washington instead concentrated on seeking areas of agreement with the Soviet Union and "building bridges" to Eastern Europe. As Sino-Soviet relations further deteriorated as a result of the Red Guard's attack on "revisionism," it was assumed in Washington that the Soviet government would welcome a degree of cooperation with the United States.

And yet the Chinese continued to undertake nuclear tests and try to develop thermonuclear warheads. Their progress was much more rapid and effective than had been expected, and revealed that the cultural revolution had not affected the work of nuclear scientists and the determination of the leaders to enhance the country's offensive military capabilities. After China's sixth nuclear test, carried out in June 1967, the Joint Congressional Committee on Atomic Energy predicted that China would be capable of launching a missile attack on the United States by the early 1970's.[1]

American policy toward Communist China since the spring of 1966 has had to take all these developments into account. Militarily, the Johnson administration has repeatedly assured the public that it does not seek a widening of the war in Vietnam by provoking China. At the same time, the United States has sought to make it clear that it would oppose any Chinese attempt to employ nuclear blackmail against its neighbors.

[1] *New York Times*, August 3, 1967.

203

In September 1967, Secretary of Defense Robert S. McNamara suggested that the nation establish an antiballistic missile system against possible Chinese attack.[2] Concerning the upheaval in China, Secretary of State Dean Rusk summed up official thinking when he stated, "We try to follow the situation as closely as we can. . . . I cannot pretend that we know how it is likely to come out. It is a most important historical development in the present period." He confessed ignorance of the actual situation in China but asserted, "I am not much embarrassed by ignorance on this point. Liu Shao-chi, Mao Tse-tung, Lin Piao, Chou En-lai probably don't know what is going to happen there."[3]

Military preparedness and political ignorance, however, have not reduced the significance of the China hearings. Quite independent of China's "cultural revolution" and nuclear experiments, there has been evidence of greater flexibility in America's attitude toward China. Although none of the specific steps advocated during the hearings by the exponents of the policy of "containment without isolation" has been taken, the idea itself has gained a degree of official endorsement. Vice-President Hubert Humphrey gave his blessings at the time of the hearings to the policy of "containment without necessarily isolation." Although Secretary of State Dean Rusk rejected the witnesses' various proposals for American initiative as impractical, he indicated that the United States had already taken steps to "break through this isolation" of Communist China. As he told reporters on March 25, 1966, "perhaps this situation will change. . . . [In] the long run, I cannot help but believe that all peoples and governments will recognize that somehow peoples and governments must find a way to live at peace with each other."[4] Though the United States did not explicitly endorse Chinese Communist representation in the United Nations, it voted for an Italian proposal for establishing a committee to explore the question of Chinese representation and to recommend "an equitable and practical solution." (The proposal was defeated by a vote of 34 in favor and 62 opposed.) In December 1966, the State Department invited ten academicians to organize an advisory panel on China. Five of them had been witnesses at the March hearings: Professors Barnett, Fairbank, Eckstein, Taylor, and Scalapino. All but Professor Taylor had urged the policy of greater flexibility toward China. Finally, in his State of the Union message in January 1967, President Lyndon B. Johnson expressed his hope for a "reconciliation between the people of mainland China and the world community." The United States, he declared, had "no intention of trying to deny her legitimate needs for security and friendly relations with neighboring countries."

"Americans," remarked Governor George Romney of Michigan in August 1967, "seem to be more and more willing to have their govern-

[2] *New York Times*, September 19, 1967.
[3] *New York Times*, September 9, 1967.
[4] *New York Times*, March 26, 1966.